Sanskrit Across Cultures

Sanskrit Across Cultures

Edited by
Shashiprabha Kumar

Special Centre for Sanskrit Studies
Jawaharlal Nehru University
New Delhi

in association with

D. K. Printworld (P) Ltd.
New Delhi

Cataloging in Publication Data — DK
[Courtesy: D.K. Agencies (P) Ltd. <docinfo@dkagencies.com>]

Sanskrit across cultures / edited by Shashiprabha Kumar.

xvii, 261 p. 23 cm.

Lectures delivered at the Sanskrit Week, 2006 organised by the Special Centre for Sanskrit Studies, Jawaharlal Nehru University.

Includes bibliographical references.

Includes index.

ISBN 812460424X

1. Sanskrit language — Social aspects. 2. Sanskrit language — History. 3. Language and culture. I. Kumar, Shashiprabha. II. Jawaharlal Nehru University. Special Centre for Sanskrit Studies.

DDC 491.202 22

ISBN 81-246-0424-X

First published in India in 2007

Published by:
Special Centre for Sanskrit Studies
Jawaharlal Nehru University
New Delhi - 110 067.

in association with

D.K. Printworld (P) Ltd.
Regd. Office: 'Sri Kunj', F-52, Bali Nagar
New Delhi-110 015
Phones: (011) 2545-3975; 2546-6019; *Fax*: (011) 2546-5926
E-mail: dkprintworld@vsnl.net
Website: www.dkprintworld.com

Printed by: D.K. Printworld (P) Ltd., New Delhi

Foreword

I consider it a great privilege to write this Foreword to welcome the new anthology on *Sanskrit Across Cultures*, which incorporates the lectures organized by the Special Centre for Sanskrit Studies of Jawaharlal Nehru University on the broad theme, "Sanskrit and World Languages." This anthology is a veritable symposium of far reaching multicultural and worldwide significance.

It was the Sanskrit language as the solar centre, which lit up the constellation of Indo-European languages and inaugurated a renaissance era of Comparative Philology and a comparative study of Indo-European languages. *Sanskrit Across Cultures*, edited by Dr Shashiprabha Kumar is a heartwarming attempt to revisit that renaissance in the study of comparative linguistics and to survey, update and take stock of the researches initially inspired and inaugurated by Sir William Jones whose intuitive and original contribution to Indology riveted on the common roots of Sanskrit and other Indo-European languages. After his arrival in India, Sir William Jones who was a barrister of the Middle Temple, a medieval Inn of Court in England of which I am privileged to be an Honorary Master and Bencher, struck gold when he found patent and palpable evidence of the common roots of Sanskrit and other Indo-European languages during his study of Sanskrit. He was a veritable genius in the field of linguistic sciences. During my long tour of diplomatic duty as India's High Commissioner in the United Kingdom, I had the honour to plant a commemorative William Jones Tree in the heart of Legal London.

Sir William Jones encapsulated his conclusions in eloquent words, which I have often cited with pride and gratitude. He said, "The Sanskrit language, whatever be its antiquity, is of a wonderful structure; more perfect than the Greek, more copious than the Latin, and more exquisitely refined than either, yet bearing to both of them a stronger affinity, both in the roots of verbs and in the forms of grammar, than could possibly have been produced by accident; so strong indeed, that no philologer could examine all the three without believing them to have sprung from some common source, which, perhaps, no longer exists." That common source might perhaps have been vouchsafed to humanity in the form of Vedic Sanskrit and its other ancient folk and classical variants. It is in that context that this anthology beckons all scholars to trace the common roots and branches of Sanskrit and its cognate languages. The book celebrates linguistic kinship and gives us an interesting indicative atlas of human origins and migrations which constitute the rainbow reality of global diversities in human speech as also the intimate thread of unity which wove them together.

A language is the edifice of culture. It is a temple in which the soul of those who speak is enshrined. Sanskrit and other European and Indian languages which are rooted in or related to Sanskrit are the treasuries of human civilization, containing the manifold manifestations of human pedigrees of Civilization in its varied and variegated manifestations. The great philosopher Emerson's cryptic remark is worth recalling. He said, "Language is the archives of history . . . it is fossil poetry." In that remark he linked the primordial antiquity of human expression and human civilization. Both in the Indian and the

Greek traditions, *Vac* and *Logos* are sacred and are treated as gifts of God. It is probably in that sense that it was received by revelation that we refer to Sanskrit, the oldest language known to humanity as *Deva-Vāṇī*. It is but natural that we in India who pride ourselves on our Sanskrit heritage and the way it fertilized human speech, that we should reflect on Sanskrit Across Cultures, particularly in the countries inhabited by the family of Indo-European languages and the countries which have had close cultural relations with India. Indeed that would lead to a better understanding of Sanskrit as a language, as a culture and as a catalyst. Sanskrit is by common consent, and verily indisputably the memory of the human race and its cultural history. It is the amber in which a million golden nuggets of thought have been embedded, refined, preserved and disseminated across cultures.

There can be no serious study of world civilization and the cultures of different countries of the world without the study of their languages. Nor can those languages and their structures and origins be understood without understanding Sanskrit in India and Across Cultures. That is why the study of Sanskrit is central to the study of world civilization and the multicultural world in which we live. This anthology initiates the process of survey, exploration and analysis. In the journey of languages and cultures, more specially the voyage of Sanskrit in different parts of the world, I consider this anthology a modest but significant and sagacious beginning with a mighty potential. I warmly congratulate the contributing authors and the editor Dr Shashiprabha Kumar.

L.M. Singhvi

Contents

Acknowledgement

SINCERE acknowledgements are due to the U.G.C. for sanction of funds under Tenth Plan, for the Research and Publication Programme of the Special Centre for Sanskrit Studies, JNU.

I am extremely grateful to the Vice-Chancellor, Rector and other administrative staff of JNU for their steady support and constant co-operation in all academic endeavours at the Centre.

The esteemed members of the Editorial Advisory Board have not only guided us but have also steered us clear through all academic difficulties and problems with their invaluable suggestions. Professor Satyavrat Shastri and Professor Kapil Kapoor in particular have put me under a debt of gratitude by their encouragement. Therefore, I am deeply indebted to them.

I must express my heartfelt gratitude to the distinguished speakers at the Sanskrit Week 2006, and other eminent scholars who made their written papers available for the timely publication of the book in hand.

I owe more than the words can convey to Dr L.M. Singhvi who has always been a source of inspiration for inter-cultural studies of this type. He has very kindly written a foreword to this volume and has further obliged me with his words of wisdom.

I thankfully acknowledge the co-operation extended in this publication by Dr C. Upender Rao, Chairperson, Special

Centre for Sanskrit Studies, JNU, New Delhi. My colleagues at the Special Centre for Sanskrit Studies have helped me during the course of publication of this volume in the best way they could; therefore, I thank all of them.

Shri Susheel K. Mittal of D.K. Printworld must be credited for bringing out a fine quality of production of the volume.

Shashiprabha Kumar

Key to Transliteration

VOWELS

अ *a*	आ *ā*	इ *i*	ई *ī*	उ *u*	ऊ *ū*
(but)	(palm)	(it)	(beet)	(put)	(pool)
ऋ *ṛ*	ए *e*	ऐ *ai*	ओ *o*	औ *au*	
(rhythm)	(play)	(air)	(toe)	(loud)	

CONSONANTS

Guttural	क *ka*	ख* *kha*	ग *ga*	घ *gha*	ङ *ṅa*
	(skate)	(blockhead)	(gate)	(ghost)	(sing)
Palatal	च *ca*	छ* *cha*	ज *ja*	झ *jha*	ञ *ña*
	(chunk)	(catch him)	(john)	(hedgehog)	(bunch)
Cerebral	ट *ṭa*	ठ* *ṭha*	ड *ḍa*	ढ* *ḍha*	ण* *ṇa*
	(start)	(anthill)	(dart)	(godhead)	(under)
Dental	त *ta*	थ *tha*	द *da*	ध* *dha*	न *na*
	(path)	(thunder)	(that)	(breathe)	(numb)
Labial	प *pa*	फ* *pha*	ब *ba*	भ *bha*	म *ma*
	(spin)	(philosophy)	(bin)	(abhor)	(much)
Semi-	य *ya*	र *ra*	ल *la*	व *va*	
vowels	(young)	(drama)	(luck)	(vile)	
Sibilants	श *śa*	ष *ṣa*	स *sa*	ह *ha*	
	(shove)	(bushel)	(so)	(hum)	
Others	क्ष *kṣa*	त्र *tra*	ज्ञ *jña*	ळ* ḷ	ॠ* *ṝ*
	(*kṣatriya*)	(*triśūla*)	(*jñānī*)	(*play*)	

अं (ं)*ṁ anusvāra* (nasalisation of preceding vowel) like *saṁskṛti*

अः *visarga* = *ḥ* (aspiration of preceding vowel) like (*prātaḥ*)

ऽ *Avagraha* consonant #'consonant (like:- *ime 'vasthitā*)

Anusvāra at the end of a line is presented by m (म्) and not ṁ

HINDI LETTERS (extras)

ँ = ñ	ं = ṅ	ड़ = *ṛa*	ढ़ = *ṛha*
(*candrabindu*)	(*anusvāra*)		

* No exact English equivalents for these letters.

Introduction

Shashiprabha Kumar

THE Special Centre for Sanskrit Studies, JNU has been celebrating Sanskrit Week since 2002 and organizing a series of lectures under the programme. In the year 2005, it was decided that a specific theme be chosen for the purpose, so that the lectures could be published later on and provide reading material to the students of the Centre.

Since an M.Phil. course titled "Sanskrit Across Cultures" was offered by me in the Monsoon Semester, 2006, hence it was decided to organize a series of lectures on "Sanskrit and World Languages" under the Sanskrit Week Programme, 2006. But after the lectures were over and the written papers were received, it was felt that the speakers had not dealt with the theme from a linguistic angle only; they had rather discussed it from a wider cross-cultural perspective. Therefore, it was deemed fit to title the volume in its present form.

The volume in hand is basically a collection of articles presented by the eminent speakers in the above programme. There are, of course, two articles which have been borrowed from already published books or journals. "Sanskrit in Indonesia" by J. Gonda is one of those articles borrowed from a volume of the same name published by International Academy of Indian Culture, New Delhi. Another article, "Sanskrit and Arabic" was originally published in *Gaganāñcal,* a Hindi magazine of Indian Council for Cultural Relations, New Delhi. It has been got translated in English and incorporated here, for it was deemed that this would add to the thematic value of the book. The third article added in the volume later on is "Sanskrit and Persian" which has been contributed by a senior reader in Sanskrit who is currently pursuing a second PhD on this very topic. Last, but not the least, an exhaustive paper by a Greek scholar entitled "Greek Logos and Vedic Vāc : Creative Power" is included in this volume since this highlights a very significant aspect which was left uncovered in the volume.

II

The first article in this volume is written by *Prof. Saroj Kumar Choudhuri*. The learned author has brought out valuable information on Sanskrit Grammar recorded in Chinese works and contributions of Sanskrit to Chinese linguistics, particularly in the area of phonetics, which is the main thrust of his paper.

Dr Shashibala in her article on "Sanskrit and Japan" has highlighted the vast quantities of Buddhist manuscripts written in Sanskrit which are available in Japan. She has shown that a rich literary treasure of Sanskrit literature consisting of *dhāraṇī*s, *tantra*s, *sūtra*s and other texts has been kept in Japan for nearly 1400 years. She has exhibited through calligraphic details that Sanskrit manuscripts in Japan were written in Gupta script, Śāradā script and Siddham script.

The next article "Sanskrit and Russian" has been penned by *Prof. Hem Chandra Pande* and *Anubha Shukla* wherein similarities and regularities in the phonetic system, grammar and vocabulary of these two languages have been discussed. Further, phonetic correspondences of Sanskrit and Russian as well as common vocabulary of the two languages have been shown.

Prof. Satya Vrat Shastri, in his paper entitled "Sanskritic Vocabulary of South-East Asia," which is small in size but rich in content, has highlighted the wide prevalence of Sanskrit in the vast stretches of South-East Asia. Citing numerous examples from and showing their equivalents in Malay, Thai, Lao, Cambodian and Indonesian vocabulary, the learned author has concluded that the absorption and assimilation of Sanskrit must have been a gradual process spanning several centuries of acculturation.

Prof. Lokesh Chandra in his comprehensive paper entitled "Sanskrit in the Renaissance of European Languages" has propounded that Sanskrit was the discovery of the primal soul of Europe, the discovery of her deeps. With the study of Sanskrit, dictionaries of European languages were taken up on historical principles. He concludes by saying that the Modern Civilization again needs the aroma of Sanskrit.

Dr M.K. Byrski, in his article titled "A Preliminary Search for the Common 'Deoxyribonucleic Acid' of Indo-European Civilizations," has argued that although there is a prevalent opinion among the comparative linguists that Slavonic languages cannot be simply compared with Sanskrit, yet we should consider the fact that there most probably existed a Proto-Indo-European language. Accordingly he proposes to conduct two types of comparisons: *rūpavāda* and *arthavāda* — and demonstrates how this type of analysis helps immensely in better understanding not only the many terms but also the accounts of a special feeling of kinsmanship between Indians and Slavs.

The next paper "Sanskrit and German" is written by Prof. *G.C. Tripathi* who is well-versed in both the languages. Elaborating on the specific features of German language, he has dwelt upon the similarities between German and Sanskrit, namely *samāsas*, consonants, vowels, genders, cases, numbers, tenses, verbs, prefixes and suffixes.

Prof. Makarand Paranjape in his article "Sanskrit-English Relations: Some Reflections" has outlined three phases of the Sanskrit-English encounter in terms of the two cultural systems they represent — the three phases being those of competition, contact and service respectively. He has observed that in order to serve the larger cause of global culture, Sanskrit and English need to work together, the former yielding some of its wisdom and ideas to the latter, which can then spread far and wide, for the benefit of all humanity.

"Sanskrit in Indonesia" — this article is reproduced from the volume authored by *J. Gonda*. The renowned scholar has expounded that when two languages come into contact the ways in which they exert influence on each other, are proportionate to the degree of linguistic pressure. According to him, it might be an attractive task to compare, from this point of view, all the borrowings from Sanskrit to various languages as also the "reverse" loans from other languages to Sanskrit. Dr Gonda has particularly dwelt upon these mutual borrowings between Sanskrit and Indonesian languages.

The next article "Sanskrit and Arabic Similarities" has been authored by *Dr Khalid Bin Yusuf Khan* wherein it has been argued that although the languages of the world have been classified on several counts and it has been usually held that Sanskrit and Arabic belong to two different families, yet it is worthwhile to examine the similarities between these two languages.

"Sanskrit and Persian" — this essay is written by *Dr Lalita Kuppuswamy*. The authoress has tried to elaborate how translations from one language to another have played an important role in preservation as well as dissemination of knowledge. The issue has been discussed with special reference to the Sanskrit classic text *Yoga-Vāsiṣṭha* which was translated into Persian by several scholars.

Prof. Nicholaos Kazanas in his paper "Greek Logos and Vedic Vāc : Creative Power" has propounded that the *śabda-Brahman* of the (mainly but not exclusively later) Vedic tradition corresponds to what has come to be known in the West as Logos Doctrine. After examining various references in detail, the learned author concludes that the Vāc doctrine is not merely an academic affair; it has much greater certitude, comprehension and width in its connotations than evangelist *logos* which denotes "reason, wisdom" rather than "speech" as it was in the Greek philosophical tradition.

The volume is being offered to the academic fraternity with an earnest hope that this will succeed in furthering future studies in the area.

1

Sanskrit in China

Saroj Kumar Chaudhuri

1. Introduction

IN China, the Central Asian and Indian monks painstakingly projected Sanskrit as the divine language, but their Chinese disciples just branded it as a language of the barbarians.[1] It was doomed from the very beginning, because in about a thousand years of Sino-Indian Buddhist contacts, nobody took the trouble to prepare a grammar of the language for the Chinese. The famous Chinese pilgrim I-Ching laments that Sanskrit grammar was thoroughly neglected in China, although it held the key to understanding the language.[2] The textbook that was used widely in China and Japan is just a four-page work, prepared with the sole object of reading *mantras* written in Siddham letters, the form of Brāhmī script used in China. The first part of this paper will make a brief review of some of the information on Sanskrit grammar recorded in Chinese works and this textbook. The second part will deal with contributions of Sanskrit to Chinese linguistics, rather phonetics to be precise, which is the main topic of this paper.

2. Grammar and Translation

2.1 HIUEN TSANG

Hiuen Tsang (CE 602-64) did not write much about Sanskrit in his travelogue. The monks Hui-li and Yen-tsung, however, give some information on Sanskrit grammar in their biography of Hiuen-tsang *Ta-tz'u-en-ssu-san-tsang-fa-shih-chuan*. The information can be summed up as follows.[3]

The *chuan* (inflection) can be divided into two groups, *tiṅanta* and *subanta*. The *tiṅanta* group (verb) is divided into *parasmai(pada)* and *ātmane(pada)*, and each has nine inflections, making eighteen in all. The nine inflections are made up of three forms of "a thing," three forms of "others," and three forms of "self." The three forms are singular, dual, and plural. (Here, "a thing," "others," and "self" mean third person, second person, and first person respectively.) The nine inflections are made up of three persons and three numbers. In the case of *parasmai(pada)*, they are /*bhavati*/, /*bhavataḥ*/, /*bhavanti*/ for third person; /*bhavasi*/, /*bhavathaḥ*/, /*bhavatha*/ for second person; and /*bhavāmi*/, /*bhavāvaḥ*/, /*bhavāmaḥ*/ for first person. The three examples are for singular, dual, and plural respectively. The *ātmane(pada)* forms are obtained by adding /*vi*/, /*ya*/, and /*te*/ to these nine forms. The *subanta* noun group has three genders, *nan-sheng* (masculine), *nü-sheng* (feminine), and *fei-nan-fei-nü-sheng* (neuter). It has eight inflections, *t'i* (nominative), *so-tso-yeh* (accusative), *tso-chü* or *neng-tso* (instrumental), *so-wei* (dative), *so-yin* (ablative), *so-shu* (genitive), *so-i* (locative), and *hu-chao* (vocative). Each inflection has three forms *shuo-i* (singular), *shuo-erh* (dual), and *shuo-to* (plural). So there are twenty-four inflected forms in all. Table 1 shows the inflected forms of /*puruṣa*/ (man) given in this work.

Table 1: Twenty-four inflections of puruṣa

Nominative	*puruṣaḥ*	*puruṣau*	*puruṣāḥ*
Accusative	*puruṣam*	*puruṣau*	*puruṣān*
Instrumental	*puruṣeṇa*	*puruṣābhyām*	*puruṣaiḥ*
Dative	*puruṣāya*	*puruṣābhyām*	*puruṣebhyaḥ*
Ablative	*puruṣāt*	*puruṣābhyām*	*puruṣebhyaḥ*
Genitive	*puruṣasya*	*puruṣayoḥ*	*puruṣāṇām*
Locative	*puruṣe*	*puruṣayoḥ*	*puruṣesu*
Vocative	*he puruṣa*	*he puruṣau*	*he puruṣāḥ*

2.2. I-CHING

I-Ching (CE 635-713) also gives us a brief account of Sanskrit in his travelogue *Nan-hai-chi-kuei-nei-fa-chuan,* written around CE 691-92. In it I-Ching says that there are forty-nine letters which combine with each other and which are arranged in eighteen sections. Every noun has seven cases, and each case has three numerical categories, i.e. singular, dual and plural. One man is called /*puruṣaḥ*/, two men: /*puruṣau*/, and three men: /*puruṣāḥ*/. Besides the seven cases, the vocative case constitutes an eighth case. The nouns are called *subanta*. There is a note saying that they have twenty-four forms. There are ten /*la*/ sounds which indicate the three tenses. The verbs have three forms, first, second, and third persons. In all there are eighteen verb forms called *tiṅanta*. I-Ching does not explain these terms.[4]

2.3. FA-TSANG

Fa-tsang (CE 643-712), a monk of Sogdian descent, has given some information on Sanskrit grammar in his *Hua-yen-ching-t'an-hsüan-chi,* a commentary on the *Buddhāvataṁsaka-sūtra*. He refers to the six *samāsa*s and the eight declensions. The six *samāsa* are *i-chu-shih* (*tatpuruṣa*), *ch'i-yeh-shih* (*karmadhārāya*), *yu-*

ts'ai-shih (*bahuvrīhi*), *hsiang-wei-shih* (*dvaṁdva*), *lin-chin-shih* (*avyayībhāva*), and *tai-shu-shih* (*dvigu*).

About declension, he says that one must know the eight types of declensions in order to understand the books of the West. He gives the following example of */puruṣa/* (man) in Chinese transcription of the eight declensions:

puruṣaḥ	:	The case of direct indication. (Nominative)
puruṣam	:	The case indicating something to which something has happened. (Accusative)
puruṣeṇa	:	The case indicating the instrument with which something is done. (Instrumental)
puruṣāya	:	The case indicating for whom something is done. (Dative)
puruṣāt	:	The case indicating a causal relation. (Ablative)
puruṣasya	:	The case indicating possession. (Genitive)
puruṣe	:	The case indicating staying with. (Locative)
he puruṣa	:	The case for calling somebody.

Fa-tsang also says that there are masculine, feminine, and neuter genders. The examples cited above are those of the masculine. Each of the cases mentioned above has three forms, *sheng* (singular), *sheng-shen* (dual), and *to-sheng-shen* (plural). Thus there are twenty-four declensions. There are twenty-four declensions each for the feminine and neuter genders also. In all, there are seventy-two declensions.[5]

2.4. UNDERSTANDING THE GRAMMATICAL TERMS

The grammatical terms used in the above works create more problems than solving them. Let us take the case of, say, plural. Hiuen-tsang's biography gives it as *shuo-to*, literally meaning "explain-many." Fa-tsang gives it as *to-sheng-shen*, literally meaning "many-voice-body." The word *yu-ts'ai-shih* used by Fa-tsang for *bahuvrīhi samāsa* literally means "possessing-wealth-explanation." Considering the resources available in those days, it is doubtful if any contemporary Chinese could have formed any idea of the true meanings of the terms even with the help of a teacher.

2.5. WRONG TRANSLATION OF SŪTRAS

The victim of the neglect of Sanskrit grammar in China was the translation of *sūtras*. It ruled out the possibility of any Chinese acquiring a good knowledge of written Sanskrit sitting in China. Similarly, very few Central Asian and Indian monks acquired any reasonable degree of knowledge of written Chinese. But a good knowledge in the two written languages is indispensable for accurate translation. The first-ever biography of the Central Asian and Indian monks in *Ch'u-san-ts'ang-chi-chi* written between CE 510-18 repeatedly laments wrong translations. In one place in the biography of Kumārajīva it says: "A look at the translations done till that (Kumārajīva's) time shows that there are lots of mistakes in meanings. This is because the earlier translators lost the meanings of expressions and did not match them with the Western books."[6]

2.6. *HSI-T'AN-TZU-CHI*, THE SIDDHAM PRIMER

Around CE 800, a Chinese monk Chih-kuang (CE ? - 806) wrote *Hsi-t'an-tzu-chi* (An Account of Siddham Letters), a four-page work, under the guidance of a south Indian monk named Prajñābodhi.[7] It became the standard textbook of Sanskrit in China and the Far-East, or at least that's what they believed popularly. As the title shows, it deals only with the Siddham letters, the form of Brāhmī script used in the Far-East, and their combinations, like compound letters and vocalic combinations. The pronunciations are given in Chinese transcript. It says nothing about grammar. Tāntric Buddhism with primary emphasis on *mantra*s was very popular at that time. This book was prepared for training the Tāntric monks to pronounce the *mantra*s correctly.

2.7. CHINA AS A SOURCE OF INFORMATION ON SANSKRIT

Some people are interested in data and dates. For instance, when was the *varṇamālā* conceived? For them, China holds some answers. The Chinese, following the native tradition of historiography, wrote down the information they received on Sanskrit along with the date. This has left very valuable dated evidence for the posterity. For instance, the oldest specimen of *varṇamālā* (in Chinese transcription) appears in the *Mahāparinirvāṇa-sūtra* translated by Fa-Hien in CE 418. Another instance is the letter /*ṛ*/ pronounced something like /*ri*/ in some areas of India and /*ru*/ in others. The textbook *Hsi-t'an-tsu-chih* mentioned above discusses this phenomenon in Group 3 letters of Section 18. Again, the word *deva* (god) is pronounced as *deba* in some linguistic areas. It is recorded in *Ch'u-san-tsang-chi-chi* written between CE 510-18.[8]

3. Sanskrit and Chinese Phonetics

Although Sanskrit failed as a language in China, the story is quite different when it comes to Sanskrit phonetics. Acceptance of Sanskrit phonetics is a unique phenomenon in Chinese intellectual history that did not repeat until the modern times. It is a secular area, and the Chinese response to it was dictated by sheer necessity. The Chinese were badly in need of the phonetic ideas of Sanskrit, especially those embedded in the *varṇamālā*. It will not be an exaggeration to say that Chinese phonetic ideas are based to a large extent on Sanskrit phonetics.

3.1. INTELLECTUAL BACKGROUND

The Chinese rulers were governing the country with the help of scholar-officials, recruited through civil service examinations, at the time when Buddhist monks were introducing Sanskrit to the Chinese via translation of Buddhist scriptures. As these civil servants were the most powerful group in the society, there were many aspirants for these jobs. As anybody could appear in the examinations, educational institutions sprang up all over China to coach the aspirants. Although very few succeeded, the positive side is that this created a vast pool of literary class. There is evidence to show that the activities of Buddhist monks from the western regions attracted the attention of Chinese intellectuals around CE 100. The poem titled "Hsi-ching-fu" (Ode to the Western Capital) written around this date by a Chinese poet named Chang Heng (CE 78-130) says that even the virtuous *śramaṇa* (Buddhist monk) would be captivated by the beauties of Ch'ang-an (the western capital).[9] It will not be wrong to assume that a few of these intellectuals became curious to know about these missionaries. After meeting the missionaries, these intellectuals must have been amazed to find that anybody from any region or time period would read a Chinese character in just one way once it was written down in Siddham, the script of the monks. The amazement was because the Chinese had no means to write the readings of their characters. Moreover, the readings differed from region to region and also with the passing of time.

3.2. PROLIFERATION OF CHINESE CHARACTERS AND ASSOCIATED PROBLEMS

The Chinese wrote their language with the help of ideographs that conveyed meanings and not readings. The number of characters proliferated because a character was conceived for every idea and object. The number of characters soon became so great that it was physically impossible to remember them. The gravity of the situation can be guessed easily from *Shou-wen-chieh-tzu,* the oldest extant dictionary of Chinese characters, compiled around CE 100. It contains more than nine thousand characters. The situation was aggravated by the fact that the sounds of the characters changed with locality and with the passing of time. A victim of such changes in the readings of characters was Chinese poetry. Rhyming was a basic component in Chinese poems. So when the readings changed, as can be seen in the example given in the next section, the rhyming syllables in a poem did not rhyme in many cases. In fact, their ancient poems that were at the core of literary activities during the period often did not rhyme. Academic study and appreciation of such poems became a big problem for the literati. This is one of the important factors that forced the Chinese intellectuals to strive hard to evolve a method for recording the readings of Chinese characters that would not change.

3.3. THE *TU-JO* SYSTEM OF READING THE CHINESE CHARACTERS

The results of the initial attempts fructified in the form of using a known character to express the sound of a difficult one. The use of this method, called *tu-jo,* can be found in the dictionary *Shou-wen-chieh-tzu* mentioned above. For instance, the reading of the character *jih* (sun) is given here by the character *shih* (fruit).[10] The readings differ today, but at that point of time they were the same, although there is no way at present to determine precisely what the sound was. This is also a good example to show that the readings of characters changed with the passing of time. The *tu-jo* method is indeed very cumbersome since one must know the reading of a character beforehand.

3.4. COMPOSITION OF CHINESE SYLLABLE

An idea of the composition of Chinese syllables is needed now to understand the next stage of development. Each Chinese character consists of a monosyllabic sound that can be represented by *S* = *IMVE/T*, where *S* = syllable, *I* = initial consonant, *M* = medial vowel, *V* = main vowel, *E* = end consonant, and *T* = tone. The group *MVE* is called the final or rhyme, and as against this, *I* is called the initial. For instance, in the character /*kuan*/ (official), /*k*/ is *I*, the initial; /*u*/ is *M*, the medial vowel; /*a*/ is *V*, the main vowel; and /*n*/ is *E*, the end consonant. There are characters where, of the *IME*, one or two or all the three are missing. In short, a character must have the sound *V*, and the others may or may not be there.

3.5. THE *FAN-CH'IEH* SPELLING SYSTEM

The Chinese soon found that the *tu-jo* system of knowing the reading of a character with the help of another was impractical. Their attempts to solve the problem produced what is known as the *fan-ch'ieh* system of spelling. In the *fan-ch'ieh* system, two characters are used to express the sound of a character. The first character represents the initial (*I*), and the second character represents the final or rhyme (*MVE*). For example, the reading of the character /*tung*/ (east) is given with the two characters /*te*/ (virtue) and /*hung*/ (red) with the character *fan* or *ch'ieh* added below as a technical term to tell the reader that the initial /*t-*/ should be taken from /*te*/ and the final or rhyme /*-ung*/ should be taken from /*hung*/, and the character concerned should be read as /*tung*/. This system also suffers the same limitation that one should know the reading of a character beforehand. Moreover, it cannot take care of the changes in readings with locality and time. Yet it became the accepted and standard means of spelling the characters.

The oldest referencc to the origin of the *fan-ch'ieh* system appears in *Yen-shih chia-hsün* by Yen Chih-t'ui (CE 531-91). It says that Sun Yen, who lived towards the end of the Han period (latter half of the second century), was the only man who knew the system. It was practised extensively during the Wei period (CE 220-65), but people could not understand its principle.[11] What is interesting here is that in CE 291 an Indian monk Mokṣala (Chi. Wu-lo-ch'a) introduced forty-two Siddham letters in Chinese transcription in his translation titled *Fang-kuang-po-jo-ching*. The letters start with /*a*/, /*ra*/, /*pa*/, /*ca*/, /*na*/, /*la*/, /*da*/, /*ba*/. . . . In short, this set consists of one vowel letter /*a*/, one compound letter /*sva*/ and forty consonant letters.[12] It would not have been very difficult for a scholar with interest in linguistics to notice the fact that the sounds of the consonant letters consisted of an initial consonant plus the vowel /*a*/. About a century separates Sun Yen, mentioned above, from Mokṣala, but he may have extracted similar information from some missionaries of his time.

3.6. INTRODUCTION OF SANSKRIT PHONETICS

Sanskrit came to China along with its phonetic script and information at this critical point of time. The first Chinese to discover the script and phonetics of Sanskrit and write about them was Hsieh Ling-yün (CE 385-433), a leading poet of his time. An Indian monk Dharmakṣema (Chi. Wu-ch'en) had translated the *Mahāparinirvāṇa-sūtra*, a very important Buddhist text, between 414-26. As its chapterization did not suit the Chinese, the local Buddhist brotherhood requested Hsieh Ling-yün and two others to rearrange it in Chinese fashion.

While doing so, he came across the *varṇamālā* (in Chinese transcription) along with some relevant phonetic information. He was so impressed by the phonetic script of *varṇamālā* and the related information that he studied them seriously with the help of Indian and India-retuned Chinese monks. Hsieh Ling-yün had a valid reason for doing so. As a poet, it is certain that he was also facing the problem of reading the characters. This is because, as stated above, rhyming was a basic feature in Chinese poems, and when reading changed with time and place, quite often the rhyming syllables no longer rhymed. So Hsieh Ling-yün had a natural curiosity for phonetic script, since here the readings never changed. He wrote down the information he got on the *varṇamālā* and its phonetics for his fellow Chinese intellectuals.

He says that Sanskrit has fifty letters divided into two groups, sixteen vowels and thirty-four consonants. Of the consonants, */ka/*, */kha/*, */ga/*, */gha/*, */ṅa/* are tongue-root sounds, */ca/*, */cha/*, */ja/*, */jha/*, */ña/* are within-the-tongue sounds, */ṭa/*, */ṭha/*, */ḍa/*, */ḍha/*, */ṇa/* are sounds produced close to the tip of the tongue, */ta/*, */tha/*, */da/*, */dha/*, */na/* are tongue-tip sounds (they are also called tongue-top sounds), */pa/*, */pha/*, */ba/*, */bha*, */ma/* are called within-the-lips sounds, and */ya/*, */ra/*, */la/*, */va/*, */śa/*, */ṣa/*, */sa/*, */ha/*, */llaṃl* are behind-the-lips sounds which reach up to the tip of the tongue.[13]

In sounds, there are half-sounds. When the sounds of letters are joined together, they are called full. The sounds are half-letters. When half-sound letters are joined together they form full-letters. In sounds, the half-sounds form the basis. In letters, half-letters naturally form the basis. Unlike the usual practice, letters are derived from sound. Sound is the basis here. Sounds are not derived from letters.[14] By half-letters Hsieh Ling-yün may have meant the vocalic signs and consonantal ligatures, and by full-letters he may have meant the compound consonants and the combination of vocalic signs with the consonants. It is difficult to come to a definite conclusion from this meagre information. He knew that the letters carried phonetic values and that a number of them joined together to form a word.

Hsieh Ling-yün knew that the consonants came in two groups, the plosive group made up of twenty-five letters and the non-plosive group consisting of nine letters. He mentions "five letters" in his writing. It refers to the twenty-five plosive consonants, which come in five groups of velars, etc. and each group consisting of five letters. His definition of the groups differs somewhat from that used in traditional Indian grammar. In Sanskrit, both the unvoiced and voiced letters have unaspirated and aspirated forms. Hsieh Ling-yün uses the terms *ch'ing* meaning "light" and *chung* meaning "heavy," which stand for unaspirated and aspirated forms respectively in Chinese phonetics, only with the fourth and the third letters, i.e. the voiced letters.[15] This suggests that Chinese of his time had an unaspirated-aspirated distinction in unvoiced sounds but not in voiced sounds. The Chinese, therefore, had no problem with the unvoiced letters. The problem was with the voiced letters. So, while revising *Mahāparinirvāṇa-sūtra,* Hsieh Ling-yün added the note to caution the readers about the unaspirated-aspirated distinction in the voiced letters. He also touched upon the mechanism involved in the production of plosive and non-plosive sounds, exhaling in the case of plosive sounds and inhaling in the case of non-plosive sounds.

3.7. SPECULATION ON THE ORIGIN OF THE *FAN-CH'IEH* SYSTEM

The *fan-ch'ieh* system of denoting the sound of a character became very refined and well established by the sixth century.

Yü-p'ien, a dictionary compiled in CE 543 gives the *fan-ch'ieh* readings of all the characters recorded in the dictionary. All the subsequent dictionaries give the readings of characters in *fan-ch'ieh*. Speculating on the origin of *fan-ch'ieh*, a Southern Sung period (1127-1279) scholar Shen Kua writes in his *Meng-hsi pi-t'an* that the science of *fan-ch'ieh* came from the western regions. In reading a character, people during the Han period (206 BCE–CE 220) used to cite another character with the same reading and say that the character was read like the character thus cited. They did not use the *fan-ch'ieh* system.[16] Other Sung (SUNG) period works like *T'ung-chih* of Cheng Ch'iao (CE 1104-60) also ascribe a Western origin to *fan-ch'ieh*. In short, many Chinese scholars considered Siddham as a major contributory factor in the development of the *fah-ch'ieh* system of writing the sound of a character.

3.8. CONSONANT CLASSES

One of Siddham phonetic concepts that the Chinese adopted is the classification of consonants on the basis of their places of origin. The Chinese scholars adopted this phonetic classification of consonants, but there was no standardization in China. The identity of consonants varied from author to author. Taking the dentals */ta/*, */tha/*, */da/*, */dha/*, */na/* as an instance, Hsieh Ling-yün described them as tongue tip or tongue top sounds, whereas Chih-kuang defined them as guttural sounds.[17]

In China, there was a traditional form of classifying sounds called *wu-yin* or the five sounds used in music. The musical scale was divided into the five steps known as *kung*, *shang*, *chüeh*, *chih*, and *yü*, starting with the lowest and ending in the highest. These terms were also used in phonetic writings. After the Sanskrit terms were introduced, the Chinese phoneticians switched over to the Sanskrit concept in their writings, with some modification. The Chinese established seven consonant classes to cater to the needs of their language. The terms used by the Chinese for these classes differ somewhat from those of Siddham, although the concept remains the same. The English equivalents of the Chinese terms are given below, along with their literal meanings, in order to avoid any misunderstanding. First, there are five major classes. They are *ya-sheng* meaning "molar sounds" or velars, *ch'ih-sheng* meaning "tooth sounds" or dentals, *she-sheng* meaning "tongue sounds" or linguals, *hou-sheng* meaning "throat sounds" or gutturals, and *ch'un-sheng* meaning "lip sounds" or labials. In addition to the above five, there are two minor sound classes, consisting of one consonant each, viz. *pan-ch'ih-sheng* meaning semi-dental and *pan-she-sheng* meaning semi-lingual.

A speculation on the link between Siddham and the evolution of the concept of seven consonant classes in Chinese can be found in a passage in the preface of *Ch'i-yin-lüeh*, a work of Cheng Ch'iao (CE 1104-62) on rhyme tables. It states as follows:[18]

> The literati of the Han period knew how to analyse characters (graphically) according to the (dictionary called) *Shuo-wen*, but they did not know that each word consisted of a mother (*mu*) and a child (*tzu*). The mother starts the word and the child follows. . . . The classification of sounds in seven categories originated in Western countries and from there was introduced into China. . . . Chinese monks adopted this system and gave it a definite form.

3.9. SOUND TYPES

Chinese sounds come in four basic types. The sounds can be unaspirated, aspirated, unvoiced, and voiced. It appears that the terms *ch'ing* (light), *chung, ch'ing* (pure),[19] and *cho* respectively were coined for them. These terms appear quite frequently in the writings of the Six Dynasties period (220-581), although their usage was not standardized.

These terms also appear with the Siddham letters given in the Buddhist texts. In the case of earlier texts, these terms are additions made at some later date. A study of the Siddham letters in the Buddhist texts reveals that the term *chung* is used quite often with voiced aspirated consonants. As against this, the term *ch'ing* (light) is used with unaspirated consonants, but to a lesser extent.

The usage of these two terms, however, lacks consistency in Chinese texts. Shen Kua has mentioned the terms *ch'ing* (pure), *tz'u-ch'ing, cho,* and *pu-ch'ing-pu-cho* in his work *Meng-his-pi-t'an*. He has given examples from which the terms can be reconstructed as unvoiced unaspirated, unvoiced aspirated, voiced, and nasal respectively. In the rhyme dictionary *Yün-ching,* the terms *ch'ing* (pure), *tz'u-ch'ing, cho,* and *ch'ing-cho* have been used to mean the unvoiced unaspirated, unvoiced aspirated, voiced and nasal sounds respectively.

3.10. FOUR TONES

Tones are a basic feature in Chinese. There are four tones officially recognized in Chinese. They are *p'ing-sheng* (even tone), *shang-sheng* (rising tone), *ch'ü-sheng* (departing tone), and *ju-sheng* (entering tone). The Siddham phonetic ideas introduced into China in the wake of Buddhism perhaps played a major role in the identification of the phenomenon. *Meng-hsi pi-t'an,* mentioned earlier, states that the science of phonetics started with the identification of four tones by Shen Yüeh (CE 441-513). The science slowly became thorough with the introduction of Siddham from India into China.[20] Shen Yüeh indeed took a leading part in advocating the theory of four tones. He wrote a work entitled *Ssu-sheng p'u* dealing with the four tones in which he says that the existence of four tones was established by Chou Yung (died around CE 488). *Nan-ch'i shu*, the *History of Southern Ch'i Dynasty*, compiled by Hsiao Tzu-hsien (CE 489-537) says that Chou Yung excelled in the science of phonetics. He was also well versed in Buddhist theology.[21]

A modern Chinese cultural historian, Ch'en Yin-k'o, has proposed a hypothesis on identification of the four tones. Historically, all words ending in */-p/*, */-t/*, and */-k/* have just one tone, the entering tone. As against this, the words with nasal endings like */-m/*, */-n/*, and */-ng/*, and with vocalic endings like */-a/*, */-i/*, and */-au/*, and so on, belong to the other three tones. Ch'en Yin-k'o says that, of the four tones, the entering tone could be easily identified because words of this tone ended in */-p/*, */-t/*, and */-k/*. The other three tones were distinguished on the basis of Sanskrit. Traditionally three *svara* or pitch accents, *udātta*, *anudātta*, and *svarita*, were involved in the recitation of the Vedas, and the Buddhists incorporated this feature in reciting the *sūtra*s. This way of reciting migrated to China along with Buddhism and monks used it in reciting the *sūtra*s. The three remaining tones were identified on the basis of these three *svara*.[22]

3.11. CHARACTER BUNDLE *NIU*

Following the establishment of the four tones, the concept of *niu* was evolved to bundle, i.e. group the characters rationally. The characters thus bundled have the same initial and the same final. They belong to the same unvoiced, voiced, unaspirated or aspirated category. Three typical examples of character bundles are given in Table 2.[23] The tonal order here is even, rising, departing, and entering.

Table 2: Character bundles and their Siddham correspondences

kam		*kam*	*kam*	*kap*
gan		*gen*	*gan*	*gat*
dong		*dong*	*dong*	*dok*
pa	*pha*	*ba*	*bha*	*ma*
ta	*tha*	*da*	*dha*	*na*
ka	*kha*	*ga*	*gha*	*ṅa*

In the above examples, the first three characters in each set have the same sound and the last one differs, ending in */-p/*, */-t/*, and */-k/* instead of */-m/*, */-n/*, and */-ng/* respectively. The apparent discrepancy can be explained easily from the arrangement of the Siddham letters. In Sanskrit, */p-m/*, */t-n/*, */k-ṅ/* are considered to be consonants of the same class because they originate from the same point of articulation. This correspondence was accepted, and retained ever since in Chinese.

4. **Rhyme Dictionaries**

4.1. RHYME DICTIONARIES

There are three broad stages in the development of lexicography in China. In the first stage dictionaries giving just the meanings of characters were prepared. *Shuo-wen chieh-tzu* belongs to this category. *Yü-p'ien*, compiled in CE 543, initiated the second stage by adding readings to the characters. The readings were given in *fan-ch'ieh* spelling, and this became the standard practice in all the subsequent dictionaries. The third stage started with the compilation of the rhyme dictionary *Ch'ieh-yün* in CE 601. This was a specialized dictionary where all the characters were arranged under rhyme headings. This dictionary is lost, but *Ta-sung ch'ung-hsiu kuang-yün*, popularly known as *Kuang-yün*, published in CE 1007 is extant. *Kuang-yün* has 206 rhymes.

4.2. COMPOSITION OF *KUANG-YÜN*

4.2.1. *Rhymes*

Kuang-yün, which exists in complete form, provides a good view of the composition of rhyme dictionaries. In *Kuang-yün*, the rhymes are arranged under the four tones. The first two volumes of the dictionary are devoted to rhymes belonging to the even tone. The third volume lists the rising tone rhymes, and the fourth volume gives the departing or falling tone rhymes. The fifth and final volume covers the entering tone rhymes.

Each tone starts with a table of contents showing all the rhymes given there. The first two volumes give 57 rhymes belonging to the even tone. The third volume contains 55 rhymes sharing the rising tone. The fourth has 60 rhymes constituting the departing or falling tone, and the fifth consists of 34 rhymes belonging to the falling tone. All these rhymes added together make 206 rhymes in all.

A scrutiny of the order in which the 206 rhymes are distributed among the four tones reveals the cardinal role the concept of character bundles (*niu*) played in compiling the rhyme dictionaries. The rhymes can be divided into two types, one type ending in a vowel and the other type ending in a consonant. If the vowel-ending rhymes are skipped and the order in which the remaining consonant-ending rhymes appear in the dictionary is investigated, the role of the character bundle concept becomes very obvious. The first four rhymes listed under the four tones are: even tone /*-ung*/, rising tone /*-ung*/, departing tone /*-ung*/, and entering tone /*-uk*/. As has been discussed earlier, a character bundle consists of four characters of four tones with the same initial and the same final. The same final in this case also means that the end consonants belong to the same sound category. The end consonants in the four rhymes given above belong to the velar category. These four rhymes are, in effect, nothing but a character bundle minus the initials.

The first four rhymes seen above have /*-ng*/ and /*-k*/ as the end consonants. They are followed by other rhymes ending in /*-ng*/ and /*-k*/. After this, the rhymes ending in /*-n*/ and /*-t*/ appear, followed by the rhymes ending in /*-m*/ and /*-p*/. In short, the consonant ending rhymes in *Kuang-yün* appear in the order /*-ng*/~/*-k*/, /*-n*/~/*-t*/, and /*-m*/~/*-p*/. This is also the order in which the consonants appear in the Siddham *varṇamālā*, albeit with the positions of the oral and nasal consonants reversed.

4.2.2. *Small-rhymes*

It is stated above that the characters are arranged under 206 rhyme headings in *Kuang-yün*. There are 26,194 characters listed in *Kuang-yün*. Consequently, each rhyme, on average, consists of more than one hundred characters. These characters are arranged in the rhyme scheme according to a system called *hsiao-yün* or "small-rhyme." Small-rhyme groups together the characters with identical pronunciation, i.e. identical IMVE/T of a rhyme. Thus, a small-rhyme gives the actual pronunciation of characters listed under it. Now, within a rhyme the MVE/T is common. So, a small-rhyme differs from another if the initial consonant differs. *Kuang-yün* lists 3,874 small-rhymes in all.

5. **Rhyme Tables**

5.1. SOUND TABLES — SHOU-WEN'S WORK

The rhyme dictionaries motivated the Chinese scholars to put the rhymes in the form of tables. Such tables were prepared to serve the purpose of a ready reckoner for knowing the readings of characters. The rhyme tables, along with one devoted to the initial consonants, covered the entire sound system of the Chinese language. So they are popularly known as the Chinese sound tables. The rhyme tables are a direct offshoot of the rhyme dictionaries.

One of the earliest works that can be directly associated with the sound tables is that of Shou-wen, a monk who is believed to have lived towards the end of the T'ang period (CE 618-907). Only three pages of his work, popularly known as *Shou-wen ts'an-chüan*, have been found. There are references to other sound tables like the one entitled *Hung-yün* prepared around this time by Buddhist monks, but they are now lost.[24]

The monk Shou-wen first gives the consonants, thirty in all, dividing them into five categories, labials, linguals, velars, dentals, and gutturals. There are four labial sounds, with the probable values */p/*, */p'/*, */b'/*, and */m/*. The linguals are divided into two groups. One has the probable values */t/*, */t'/*, */d'/*, and */n/*, and the other /$t^{/}$/, /$t^{/}$'/, /$d^{/}$'/, and /$n^{/}$/. The velars are given by six characters. One stands for */l/* which latter-day phoneticians established as a separate category, viz. semi-lingual. The probable values of the other five are */k* , */k'*, */g'/*, and */ng/*. One character is in excess here. The dentals are also divided into two groups, one with the three probable sounds: */ts/*, */ts'/*, and */dz'/*, and the other with four probable sounds, either */ṭs/*, */ṭs'/*, */ḍz'/*, */ṣ/* or /$ts^{/}$/, /$ts^{/}$'/, /$dz^{/}$'/, / $s^{/}$ /. There are six guttural sounds divided into two groups, three unvoiced sounds: /*s*/, /ʑ/, and /χ/, and three voiced sounds: /γ/, / ʼ /, and / ? /. Shou-wen divides the rhymes into four *teng* or divisions, and gives their examples under the four tone headings, viz. even tone, rising tone, departing tone, and entering tone.[25]

This framework of Shou-wen developed into the latter-day sound tables. The sound tables that have survived in complete form and come down to us were prepared during the Sung (CE 960-1279) and subsequent periods. One such work, the *Yün-ching*, will be discussed here.

5.2. *YÜN-CHING*

The sound tables of the *Yün-ching* basically deal with the sound values of characters for the period from around the sixth century to the tenth century. The author of the *Yün-ching* is not known. There are forty-four sound tables in *Yün-ching*. These forty-four tables accommodate the entire sound system of the Chinese language. The first table listing the initial consonants appears in the introductory section. The remaining forty-three tables are devoted to the rhymes and constitute the main text of the work. All the rhyme tables have an identical set-up.

5.2.1. *Table of Initial Consonants*

Appendix 1 shows the table of consonants given in the introductory section of *Yün-ching*. It has 36 consonants. The phonetic values given below are based basically on the values proposed by Bernhard Karlgren.[26] The table is divided into six groups. The first group carries the heading *ch'un-yin* or labials. Then there are four sub-headings, *ch'ing*, *tz'u-ch'ing*, *cho*, and *ch'ing-cho*, meaning unvoiced unaspirated, unvoiced aspirated, voiced, and nasal respectively. It will be seen that the unvoiced sound has two forms, unaspirated and aspirated, whereas the voiced sound has only one form. It is generally assumed that it represents the voiced aspirated sound. The labial sounds */p/*, */p'/*, */b'/*, and */m/*. The second group carries the heading *she-yin* or linguals. The four sub-headings are the same as those mentioned above. The sounds are the dental consonants */ṫ/*,*/ṫ'/*,*/ḋ'/*, and */ṅ'/*. The third group carries the heading *ya-yin* or velars. The same four sub-headings are given here, representing the consonants */k/*, */k'/*, */g'/*, and */ng/*. For lack of space, Appendix I shows these three groups only.

5.2.2. *Rhyme Tables — Their composition*

5.2.2.1. *Initial Consonants*

Yün-ching contains forty-three rhyme tables in all. Each rhyme table carries on the top the initial consonants given in the above section. The consonants are given by their phonetic headings, viz. labial, lingual, velar, dental, guttural, and lingual/dental, along with their unvoiced, voiced, unaspirated, aspirated, and nasal sub-headings. Appendix II shows the Rhyme Table 1 of *Yün-ching*. Only the portion related to the above three groups, viz. labial, lingual and velar is shown here.

5.2.2.2. *Tones*

As shown in Rhyme Table 1, the rhyme tables are divided into four broad rows, each row assigned to a tone, even, rising, departing, and entering. In arranging rhymes in the four tones, the end consonant E of the final MVE constitutes an important criterion. Some Chinese characters do not have end consonants, for instance, the character *ta* (big). The rhyme tables accommodating such characters have only three tones, even, rising, and departing. There are no entering tone row entries in these tables. The end consonant comes in three categories, velar /*-ng*/ and /*-k*/, lingual /*-n*/ and /*-t*/, and labial /*-m*/ and /*-p*/. In these pairs, the first is nasal and the second is oral. Rhymes accommodating these characters have entries in all the four tones. Here, the even, rising, and departing tones have nasal endings, and the entering tone has oral endings.

5.2.2.3. ***Small Rhymes***

It has been stated above that there are 3,874 small-rhymes in *Kuang-yün*, which are distributed among the 206 rhymes. The rhyme tables of *Yün-ching* are based almost entirely on these small rhymes. Since the *Yün-ching* tables contain about 3,790 characters, almost all the small rhymes of *Kuang-yün* are given here. However, there are some entries in *Yün-ching* that are not present in *Kuang-yün*. This is perhaps due to the changes that took place in the language during the period between *Kuang-yün* and *Yün-ching*.

5.2.2.4. ***Reading the Rhyme Table***

The tables of *Yün-ching* are designed in the form of a grid. The point where the vertical axis meets the horizontal axis gives the actual reading at that point. For instance, in the case of the first entry from right in the top row of the Rhyme Table 1, the vertical column says that the initial consonant is a labial voiced sound. So its phonetic value is /*b'-*/. The horizontal row gives the rhyme as /*-ung*/. So the reading of this character is *b'ung*. Similarly, in the case of the last character in the first column from the right, the initial consonant is labial unvoiced. So it is /*p*/. Similarly, the rhyme is /*uk*/. So, its reading is *puk*.

6. **Current Status of Sanskrit Phonetics**

One may be interested to know about the current status of the Chinese adaptation of Sanskrit phonetics discussed above. It is very much alive and in use today. For instance, the Chinese have devised a phonetic script for the initial consonants and the rhymes discussed above about one hundred years back. As will be seen in Appendix III, the first year primary school students start their education with this script. It is also used in dictionaries of Chinese characters to give the phonetic readings of the characters.

7. Concluding Remarks

The Sanskrit language failed to take root in China despite around one thousand years of translation activities. One of the reasons is that nobody dared to write the grammar of the language for the Chinese. Attempts to write on grammar ended up in coining of grammatical terms that were totally unintelligible to the Chinese. The Chinese, on the other hand, accepted Sanskrit phonetics because it provided them with the crucial know-how to evolve a system to express the sounds of the characters phonetically. The Chinese literati needed such a system badly for assigning a standard reading to the characters. They required this for, among other things, appreciating their poems that constituted one of the major intellectual activities of all ages.

Appendix I
Initial Consonants of *Yün-ching*

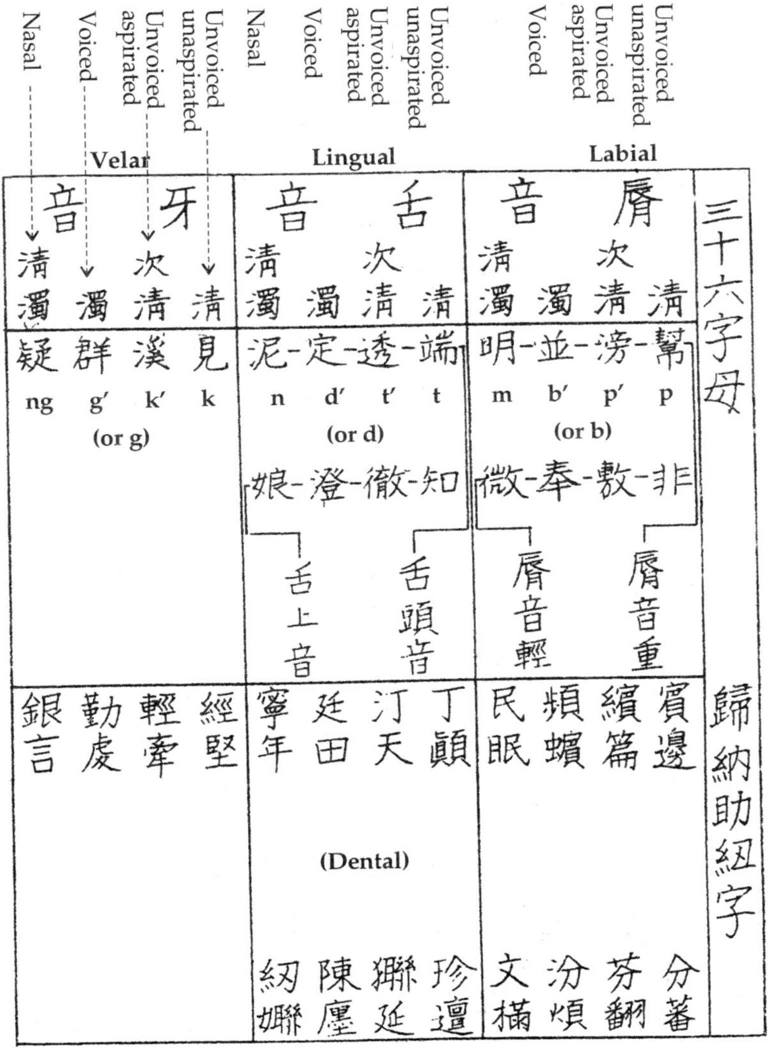

Appendix II
Rhyme Table 1 of *Yün-ching*

Nasal	Voiced	Unvoiced aspirated	Unvoiced unaspirated	Nasal	Voiced	Unvoiced aspirated	Unvoiced unaspirated	Nasal	Voiced	Unvoiced aspirated	Unvoiced unaspirated	
Velar 牙音				Lingual 舌音				Labial 脣音				内轉第一開
清濁	濁	次清	清	清濁	濁	次清	清	清濁	濁	次清	清	
𡸣		空	公		同	通	東	蒙	蓬			
豣	窮	穹	弓		蟲	忡	中	瞢	馮	豐	風	
		孔		癑	動	桶	董	蠓	菶		琫	
					(Dental)							
		控	貢	齈	洞	痛	凍	夢	槰			
		焪			仲		中	幪	鳳	賵	諷	
		哭	穀		獨	禿	豰	木	暴	扑	卜	
砡	𩦠	麴	菊	朒	逐	蓄	竹	目	伏	蝮	福	
ng	g′ (or g)	k′	k	n	d′ (or d)	t′	t	m	b′ (or b)	p′	p	

Appendix III
Current Status of Chinese Adaptation of Some Sanskrit Phonetics

Primary school textbook

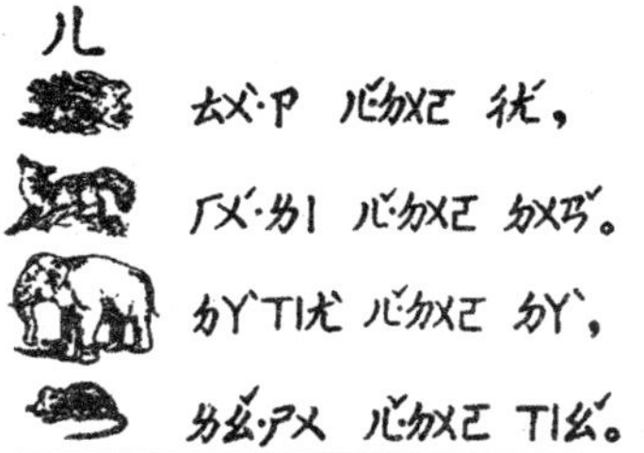

ㄅㄆㄇㄈ	ㄉㄊㄋㄌ
ㄍㄎㄏ	ㄐㄑㄒ
ㄓㄔㄕㄖ	ㄗㄘㄙ
ㄚㄛㄜㄝ	ㄞㄟㄠㄡ
ㄢㄣㄤㄥ	ㄦㄧㄨㄩ

Phonetic script devised for initial consonants and rhymes

/p//ph/

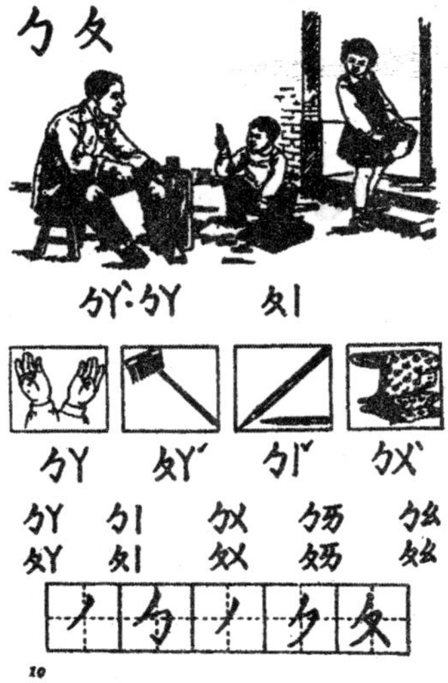

References

1. Seng-yu, *Ch'u-san-tsang-chi-chi*, Taishō Shinshū Daizōkyō, V. 55, pp. 95B18, 99M26.

2. I. Tsing, *A Record of the Buddhist Religion as Practised in India and the Malay Archipelago*, tr. J. Takakusu, Delhi: Munshiram Manoharlal, 1966, p. 168.

3. Hui Li and Yen Ts'ung, *Ta-tz'u-en-ssu-san-tsang-fa-shih-chuan*, Takada, Shū, tr., *Daijionji Sanzōhōshiden*, Kokuyaku Issaikyō, Wakan Senjutsubu, Shidenbu 11, Daitō Shuppansha, Tokyo, pp. 90-96 (The Sanskrit forms of the examples are those found in this work.); Beal, Samuel, tr., *The Life of Hiuen Tsiang by the Shaman Hwui Li*, Westport, Connecticut, Hyperion Press Inc., 1973, pp. 122-24.

4. I. Tsing, pp. 173-74.

5. Fa-tsang, *Hua-yen-ching-t'an-hsuan-chi*, Sakamoto, Sachio, tr.,

Kegongyō Tangenki, V. 1, Kokuyaku Issaikyō, Wakan Senjutsubu, Kyōsobu 6, pp. 273-77; Van Gulik, R.H., *Siddham*, Sarasvati Vihara Series, V.36, Nagpur, International Academy of Indian Culture, pp. 19-20.

6. *Ch'u-san-tsang-chi-chi*, p. 101M18-19.
7. Chih-kuang, *Hsi-t'an-tzu-chi*, Taishō Shinshū Daizōkyō, V. 54, pp. 1186-90.
8. Fa-Hien, *Ta-pan-ni-yüan-ching*, Taishō Shinshū Daizōkyō, V. 12, pp. 887B29-888B20; Annen, p. 461; *Ch'u-san-tsang-chi-chi*, p. 100T5.
9. Ch'en, Kenneth K.S., *Buddhism in China, A Historical Survey*, Princeton: Princeton University Press, 1973, p. 42.
10. Konishi, Jinichi, *Bunkyō Hifuronkō*, V. 1, Kyoto, Daihachishū Shuppan Co. Ltd., 1948, p. 184.
11. Yen Chih-t'ui, *Yen-shih chia-hsün*; Utsunomiya, Kiyoshi, tr., *Ganshi Kakun*, Chūgoku Koten Bungaku Taikei, V. 9, Tokyo, Heibonsha, 1977, pp. 580B-581T.
12. Mokṣala, *Fang-kuang po-jo-ching*, Taishō Shinshū Daizōkyō, V. 8, p. 26.
13. Annen, *Shittanzō*, Taishō Shinshū Daizōkyō, V. 84, pp. 409M-410T.
14. Annen, p. 432M.

    This statement means that in Siddham, letters are derived from sound, and in Chinese, sounds are derived from characters.
15. Annen, p. 409B.
16. Shen Kua, *Meng-hsi pi-t'an*, Umehara, Kaoru, tr., *Mukei Hitsudan*, V. 2, Tokyo, Heibonsha, 1989, p. 107.
17. Annen, *shittanzō*, p. 409B; *Hsi-t'an-tzu-chi*, p. 1188T.
18. Van Gullik, pp. 43-44.
19. A problem in Chinese is the homonyms. Here, *ch'ing* (light) usually meaning unaspirated, and *ch'ing* (pure) usually meaning unvoiced are homonyms. They are easily differentiated when the characters are given. Here, "light" and "pure," the literal meanings of the characters, is added to differentiate them.
20. Shen Kua, p. 89; Van Gulik, p. 42.
21. Konishi, p. 421.

22. Konishi, pp. 459, 422-23; Yasuda, Jiro, "The Changing Aristocratic Society of the Southern Dynasties and Regional Society: Particularly the Hsiang-yang Region," *Acta Asiatica*, Tokyo, Toho Gakkai, V. 60, 1991, p. 50.
23. Konishi, p. 150.
24. Tōdō, Akiyasu, *Chūgokugo Oninron*, Kōseikan, Tokyo, 1980, p. 132.
25. Misawa, Junjirō, *Inkyō no Kenkyū*, Inkyō Kenkyūkai, Kobe, 1960, pp. 190-92.
26. Karlgren, Bernhard, *Compendium of Phonetics in Ancient and Archaic Chinese*, Stockholm, The Museum of Far Eastern Antiquities, Bulletin 22, 1954, pp. 230, 218-19.

Chinese characters of the Chinese expressions used in the text

[A] Annen 安然 **[B]** *b'ung* 蓬 *Bunkyō Hifuronkō* 文鏡秘府論考 **[C]** Ch'ang-an 長安 Chang Heng 張衡 Cheng Ch'iao 鄭樵 Ch'en Yin-k'o 陳寅恪 *ch'ieh* 切 *Ch'ieh-yün* 切韻 *chih* 徵 Chih-kuang 智廣 *ch'ih-sheng* 歯聲 *ch'ing* 輕 (light) *ch'ing* 清 (pure) *ch'ing* 輕 (light) *ch'ing-cho* 清濁 *ch'i-yeh-shih* 持業釋 *Ch'i-yin-lüeh* 七音略 *cho* 濁 Chou Yung 周顒 *chuan* 轉 *chüeh* 角 *chung* 重 Chih-kuang 智廣 *Chūgokugo Oninron* 中国語音韻論 Chūgoku Koten Bungaku Taikei 中国古典文学大系 *ch'un-sheng* 脣聲 *ch'un-yin* 脣音 *Ch'u-san-ts'ang-chi-chi* 出三藏記集 *ch'ü-sheng* 去聲 **[D]** Daihachishū Shuppan Co. Ltd. 第八洲出版 *Daijionji Sanzōhōshiden* 大慈恩寺三藏法師傳 Daitō Shuppansha 大東出版社 **[F]** Fa-Hien 法顯 *fan* 反 *fan-ch'ieh* 反切 *Fang-kuang-po-jo-ching* 放光般若經 Fa-tsang 法藏 Fa-Hien 法顯, *Fang-kuang po-jo-ching* 放光般若經 Fa-tsang 法藏 *fei-nan-fei-nü-sheng* 非男非女聲 **[G]** *Ganshi Kakun* 顔氏家訓 **[H]** Heibonsha 平凡 *hou-sheng* 喉聲 *hsiang-wei-shih* 相違釋 Hsiao Tzu-hsien 蕭子顯 *hsiao-yün* 小韻 Hsi-ching-fu 西京賦 Hsieh Ling-yün 謝霊運 *Hsi-t'an-tzu-chi* 悉曇字記 Hiuen-tsang玄奘 *Hua-yen-ching-t'an-hsüan-chi* *hu-chao* *Hui-li* *hung* *Hung-yün* **[I]** I-ching 義淨 *i-chu-shih* 依主釋 *Inkyō no Kenkū* 韻鏡の研究 Inkyō Kenkūkai 韻鏡の研究会 **[J]** *jih* 日 *ju-*

sheng 入聲 **[K]** *Kegongyō Tangenki* 華嚴經探玄記 Kokuyaku Issaikyō 國譯一切經 Konishi, Jinichi 小西甚一 Kōseikan 光生館 Kyōsobu 經疏部 *kuan* 官 *Kuang-yün* 廣韻 *kung* 宮 **[L]** *lin-chin-shih* 隣近釋 **[M]** *Meng-hsi pi-t'an* 夢渓筆談 Misawa, Junjirō 三沢諄治郎 Mokṣala 無羅叉 *mu* 母 *Mukei Hitsudan* 夢渓筆談 **[N]** *Nan-ch'i shu* 南斉書 *Nan-hai-chi-kuei-nei-fa-chuan* 南海寄歸内法傳 *nan-sheng* 男聲 *neng-tso* 能作 *niu* 紐 *nü-sheng* 女聲 **[P]** *pan-ch'ih-sheng* 半歯聲 *pan-she-sheng* 半舌聲 *p'ing-sheng* 平聲 *pu-ch'ing-pu-cho* 不清不濁 **[S]** Sakamoto, Sachio 坂本幸男 Seng-yu 僧祐 Shen Kua 沈括 *shang* 商 *shang-sheng* 上聲 *sheng-shen* 聲身 *sheng* 聲 Shen Kua 沈括 *she-sheng* 舌聲 *shih* 實 Shidenbu 史傳部 *Shittanzō* 悉曇藏 Shou-wen 守温 *Shou-wen* 説文 *Shou-wen-chieh-tzu* 説文解字 *Shou-wen ts'an-chüan* 守温殘巻 *shuo-erh* 説二 *shuo-i* 説一 *shuo-to* 説多 *so-i* 所依 *so-shu* 所属 *so-tso-yeh* 所作業 *so-wei* 所爲 *so-yin* 所因 *Ssu-sheng p'u* 四聲譜 Sun Yen 孫炎 **[T]** *ta* 大 Taishō Shinshū Daizōkyō 大正新修大藏經 *tai-shu-shih* 帯数釋 Takada, Shū 高田修 *Ta-pan-ni-yüan-ching* 大般泥疑經 *Ta-sung ch'ung-hsiu kuang-yün* 大宋重修廣韻 *Ta-tz'u-en-ssu-san-tsang-fa-shih-chuan* 大慈恩寺三藏法師傳 *te* 徳 *teng* 等 *t'i* 體 Tōdō, Akiyasu 藤堂明保 *to-sheng-shen* 多聲身 *tso-chü* 作具 *tu-jo* 讀若 *tung* 東 *T'ung-chih* 通志 *tzu* 子 *tz'u-ch'ing* 次清 **[U]** Umehara, Kaoru 梅原郁 Utsunomiya, Kiyoshi 宇都宮清吉 **[W]** Wakan Senjutsubu 和漢選述部 Wu-ch'en 無讖 Wu-lo-ch'a 無羅叉 *wu-yin* 五音 **[Y]** *ya-sheng* 牙聲 Yen Chih-t'ui 顔之推 *Yen-shih chia-hsün* 顔氏家訓 Yen-ts'ung 彦琮 *yü* 羽 *Yün-ching* 韻鏡 *Yü-p'ien* 玉篇 *yu-ts'ai-shih* 有財釋

Table 2: Character bundles and their Siddham correspondences

含	*kam*	頷	*kam*	憾	*kam*	合	*kap*
元	*gan*	阮	*gen*	願	*gan*	月	*gat*
同	*dong*	動	*dong*	洞	*dong*	独	*dok*

2

Sanskrit in Japan

Shashibala

SANSKRIT manuscripts crossed the boundaries of India along with transmission of Buddhist philosophy, art and thought, and reached Japan via Central Asia and China. Thousands of Sanskrit texts were translated into Khotanese, Tokharian, Uigur and Sogdian in Central Asia, on their way to China and Japan. They travelled with scholars, pilgrims, adventurers and the politically ambitious, and prospered there often by virtue of state patronage. Sanskrit was carried not merely as a medium of communication but as a divine language in which were written sacred words of the Buddha, the words that could lead them towards enlightenment and upliftment.

With destruction of monastic libraries, most of the Sanskrit literature perished leaving behind a large number of fragments which are discovered by the great explorers from Germany, Russia, British India, Sweden and Japan. These excavations have uncovered vast quantities of manuscripts in Sanskrit in fragmentary condition. Only those manuscripts and texts have survived in complete form which were taken to Nepal and Tibet or other parts of Asia. Their translations into Tibetan, Chinese and Mongolian, etc. fill the gap, but to some extent only.

Slating Gupta script, fifth-sixth century, ink on paper Udanavarga, Dunhuang, China (Zwalf No. 35)

North-western Gupta script, seventh century, ink on birch bark, Vinayavastu of Mūlasarvāstivādins from a *stūpa* at Gilgit (now) Pakistan (Zwalf No. 46)

Among the ancient Sanskrit manuscripts strewn in the monasteries nestling among high mountains and waterless deserts, the earliest known Sanskrit manuscripts go back to the first century CE, found from Afghanistan, in a sad condition. Following them are the fragments of a Sanskrit manuscript of a drama: *Sāriputraprakaraṇa*, from the Kuṣāṇa period, that is

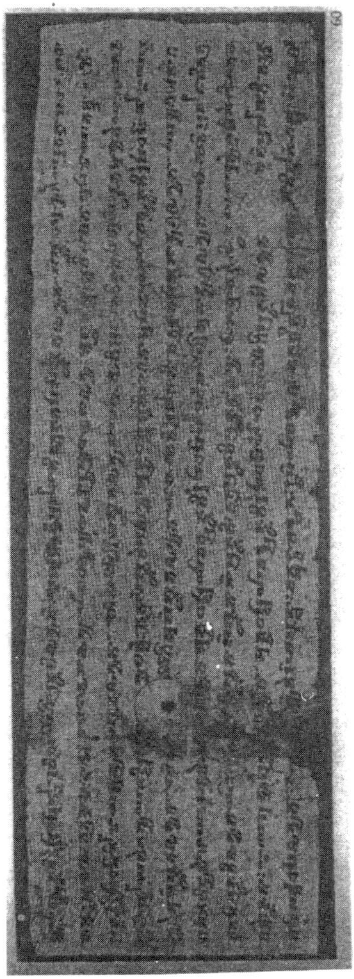

Upright Gupta script, seventh-eighth century, ink on paper, *Aṣṭa-Sāhasrikā-Prajñā-Pāramitā-Sūtra* from as *stūpa* at Khadalik, Xinjiang (Zwalf No. 60)

second century CE, discovered from Qyzil in the Turfan area of Central Asia.

Two Indian scripts that were used to write Buddhist scriptures and edicts of Aśoka are Brāhmī and Kharoṣṭhi. Kharoṣṭhi was used in north-western India and in the neighbouring area of Central Asia roughly between fifth century BCE to third century CE. Aśokan edicts discovered from two places in the NW in modern Pakistan are written in Kharoṣṭhi. But Brāhmī came into common use in the NW India after the third or fourth century CE displacing Kharoṣṭhi.

In Japan, the emperors in search of transcendental values, embraced the tradition of *sūtra*s written in Sanskrit as a core for national unity and integrity. Today a rich literary treasure of Sanskrit literature consisting of *dhāraṇī*s, *tantra*s, *sūtra*s and other texts has been kept in Japan for nearly 1400 years. Entry of Sanskrit Buddhist scriptures into Japan was their indentification with the central axis of human advance because Buddhism opened up unfathomed spheres of thought as soon as it reached Japan officially in CE 552.

Philosophical speculations opened up new avenues and horizons. The idea of *bahujana-hitāya bahujana-sukhāya* overwhelmed the minds to such an extent that the great Japanese Prince Shōtoku Taishi decided to carve out the first constitution of Japan, known as Seventeen Article Constitution based on the Buddhist ideology. He himself wrote commentaries and lectured on *Saddharmapuṇḍarīka-sūtra*, *Śrīmālā-devī-siṁhanāda-sūtra* and *Vimalakīrti-nirdeśa-sūtra*. They can be heard in the daily recitation of the Japanese up to the day. It was the first time when Sanskrit manuscripts entered Japan. With the coming of a new political system the country began to emerge out of a clan to a state system.

The second milestone in the history of Japan as a state stands during the reign of King Shōmu who used Sanskrit *sūtras* as a core to create a unified country and himself became a supreme monarch. During mid-eighth century he dispatched Sanskrit *sūtras* to all the provinces and ordered for their recitation on fixed days and time. And thus the whole of Japan began to unite. The system of education saw a phase of democratization in the ninth century with creation of Sanskrit based alphabets invented by the monk scholar Kōbōdaishi.

The language of Mahāyāna-*sūtras* and the northern Hīnayāna Buddhist *sūtras* was Sanskrit and they were written

A Sanskrit inscription on an octagonal pillar, created in CE 1104 in the Lo-yang district, China, discovered by Raghu Vira. The last line reads: *mahāmudre svāhā*.

in northern Brāhmī characters. Brāhmī gave the basis to a number of scripts to be devised in Asia. The scripts developed on the basis of north Indian style of Brāhmī are different from those developed from its south Indian style. The scripts in South-east Asian countries like Sri Lanka, Myanmar, Thailand, Cambodia, etc. are derived from southern Indian scripts so they follow rounded form of Brāhmī. Brāhmī characters in north India began to become a little different from those used in the south. And the difference became more marked as time passed. The northern characters became very angular while those in the south became noticeably rounded.

The oldest printed item from China dated CE 757 is Sanskrit *mantra*s written for Goddess Pratisarā, in ornamental Rañjana script, concentrically around the figure. World's oldest printed book dated 11 May 868 is *Vajracchedikā-sūtra* on transcendental wisdom, written on paper, which is now kept at the British Museum.

Manuscripts in Gupta Script

UṢṆĪŚAVIJAYĀ-DHĀRAṆĪ AND PRAJÑĀPĀRAMITĀ-HṚDAYA-SŪTRA

The Sanskrit manuscripts found in Japan are much older than those found in India. *Uṣṇīśavijayā-dhāraṇī* and *Prajñāpāramitā-hṛdaya-sūtra,* written on palm leaves were taken to Japan from China in 609 which most probably belonged to Monk Yashi and before him they were in the possession of Ācārya Bodhidharma who had gone from India to China in CE 520. Certainly the manuscripts cannot be dated later than the first half of the sixth century being evidently written by an Indian scribe. In spite of their transmission from India to China and from there to Japan and preserved there over the past fourteen centuries, they are legible although having suffered partly on the margins and partly due to fading of ink. They are primarily valuable for their palaeographic antiquity. The material and the techniques used and the style of writing resemble those which were used in India later also.

Prince Shōtoku Taishi drew up the first Japanese constitution in Seventeen Articles wherein the *triratna*: Buddha, Dharma and Saṅgha were a fundamental factor. The new order was consecrated by the *Uṣṇīśavijayā-dhāraṇī* whose Sanskrit manuscript in Gupta script is preserved at the Hōryuji monastery. Hōryuji means the temple for the flourishing of Dharma — dharma-vardhana-vihāra.

The manuscript of *Prajñāpāramitā-hṛdaya* was copied by Jiun Sonja in the eighteenth century, the last of the Sanskritists of Japan in the traditional style. He lived from CE 1718 to 1803. A saint of great learning and noble virtues, he stands unique in the history of Mantrayāna as the doyen of traditional Sanskrit

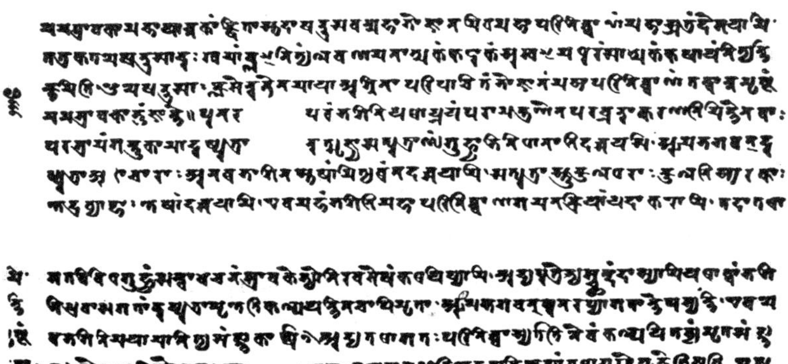

45

A page from a Sanskrit manuscript preserved at the Reihokan Museum, Koyasan, eighth century

studies in Japan, and in recognition thereof he was given the honorific title "Sonja" which means *ārya* or *arhat*. Nobody else in Japan was given this honour.

Manuscripts in Śāradā Script

Seven palm-leaf manuscripts in the Tōji, Kairyoji, Seiryoji, Kokiji, Gyokusenji, Shitennōji and Tennōji monasteries in the Kansai district are identified as a part of *Abhidharmakośa* of Sarvāstivāda by some of the Japanese scholars but Prof. Matsuda Kazunobu believes them to be folios of *Lokaprajñapti*, a part of *Prajñapti-śāstra* of Sadpāda of Sarvāstivāda. *Prajñapti-śāstra* is found in Chinese and Tibetan versions also. *Lokaprajñapti* is a part of *Prajñapti-śāstra* of Maudgalyāyana, the other two parts are *Karaṇaprajñapti* and *Karmaprajñapti*. It is an important point to be noted that the Chinese translation dated back to eleventh century while the Japanese manuscripts are dated ninth century.

1. The folio kept at the Tōji monastery speaks on five *skandhas*, aggregates.
2. The one that is in Kairyoji deals with the twenty-two *indriyas*.
3. The subject matter of the folio kept at Seiryoji is on *anusaya*.
4. The manuscript from Kokiji monastery talks about "end of *kalpa* and *sapta sūryodaya*."
5. The manuscript from the Gyokusenji temple gives a description of mount Sumeru.
6. The manuscript kept at the Shitennōji monastery contains 170 folios. The manuscript kept at the Chionji monastery has 172 folios.

7. The subject matter of these (Gyokusenji and Shitennoji) manuscripts is teaching the effects of one's deeds. If someone follows *paritāpa dharma,* evil actions, then he goes to hell called *niraya* but those who follow *aparitāpa dharma,* they are bound to go to heavenly abodes called *sugati.* The lesson is taught through stories.

The folios preserved at the Gyokusenji temple are similar in content to Gilgit manuscript identified as *dharma skandha.*

Sanskrit manuscripts in the possession of the Faculty of Letters, University of Kyoto: *Aparimitāyur-dhāraṇī, Abhidharmakośa-vyākhyā, Abhidharmottarottara-tantra, Aṣṭasāhasrikā-prajñāpāramitā-sūtra* and others.

Hymn to Thousand-armed Mañjuśrī

A complete Tantra devoted to Mañjuśrī was translated by Amoghavajra in CE 740 (Nj. 1044, T 1177a, K 1272, STP. 16.6378) on imperial orders. The Master explained the Sanskrit text and Hye-ch'o wrote it down. On 19 February 742 Vajra took the Sanskrit manuscript to an Indian teacher, gave it to Monk Mokṣānanda Bhaga[vān] for being returned to Ratnabodhi of India and Sri Lanka.

Along with the main Tantra, there is a Sanskrit hymn of 108 epithets of *Sahasrapātra Mañjuśrī* called Sempatsu Monju in Japanese in *Taisho Tripiṭaka* (1177b, 20.776-77, Lokesh Chandra, *Dictionary of Buddhist Iconography* 2003:8.2240) in Siddham script. Its source stems from the T'ang dynasty. There is another hymn written in Siddham in Nagatani Hoshi's collection of Sanskrit *mantras* brought from China by Kōbō Daishi which is based on some other source.

The following epithets of Mañjuśrī approve his relation to state:

- *Mahāmaṇḍala-Śāsakaḥ*, ruler of the vast state
- *Rājyadadaḥ*, giver of the state
- *Cakravartī*, monarch
- *Jitāntakaḥ*, destroyer of the vanquisher

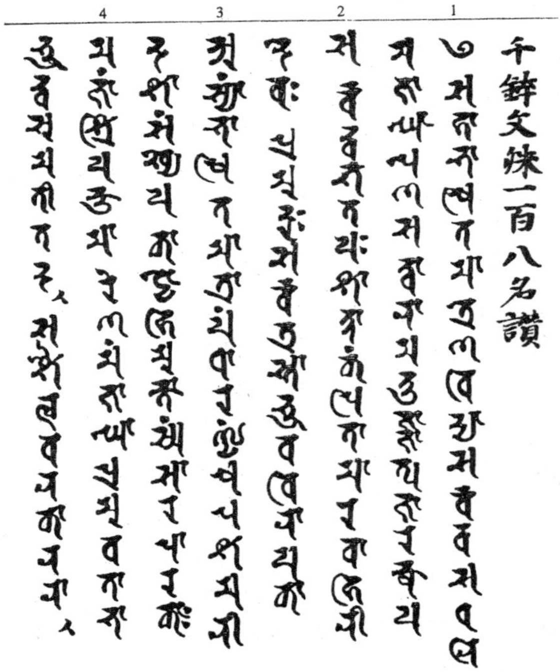

Devanāgarī transcription of the above text:

ॐ सहभाषितमात्रेण विद्या सर्वार्थ-साधनी ।मञ्जुघोषेण सत्वानामतुज्जत्पज रक्षा या ॥१॥
सर्वदुर्गतयः शान्ता कम्पिता मारवाहिनी। देवाः प्रमुमुदुः सर्वे त्रस्ता भुवः विनायकाः ॥२॥
अस्यां जपितमात्रायां धारण्यां शापशमन्याम् / दशासंख्येयकोटयो हि मुक्ता संसारपारकाः ॥३॥
मञ्जुश्रिया कुमारेण मञ्जुघोषप्रमुक्ताभा ।अभूद्वसुमती तदा सशैलवनकानना ॥४॥

Mañjuśrī is a symbol of *śastra* and *śāstra,* the weapons and the scriptures. He looks lovely and pleasing and holds a double-sword in his right hand and a manuscript of *Prajñāpāramitā* placed on a blue lotus in his left hand. The sword cuts across delusions and destroys all that stands against truth. Symbolically it represents righteousness, justice, equity, love and creativity. The book is a symbol of transcendental wisdom. His ride, a golden haired lion is a symbol of action and energy.

SAMANTABHADRACARYĀ-PRAṆIDHĀNA-RĀJA

Samantabhadracaryā-praṇidhāna-rāja is a prayer in melodious *doḍhaka* stanzas, which ranks among the most beautiful expressions of Buddhist piety and has been used for worship in all the countries of Mahāyāna Buddhism ever since fourth century CE. It is found at the end of *Gaṇḍavyūha* in Sanskrit manuscripts as well as in the Chinese and Tibetan translations. It is also found as an independent text and was translated into Chinese several times in the fourth and eighth centuries and into Tibetan in the ninth century. Its manuscripts are found in the collections of Sanskrit manuscripts at Paris and Cambridge. The Peking xylograph edition consists of 19 folios and gives the Sanskrit text in Lantsha and Tibetan characters. It was copied by Sage Jiun Sonja, a teacher of the Shingon sect, who was born in the 57th year of K'ang-hsi of Sheng-tsu of Ch'ing dynasty (CE 1718). He used to recite the text of *Samantabhadracaryā-praṇidhāna-rāja* and other texts daily. He was well versed both in exoteric and esoteric doctrines, particularly in the Vinaya teachings.

The pages of *Samantabhadracaryā-praṇidhāna-rāja* (shown on nextpage) are taken from the xylograph reproduced by the International Academy of Indian Culture, presented to Prof. Dr. Raghu Vira by the Akademia Nauk of the USSR. The same xylographic edition is referred to in "A Catalogue of Japanese

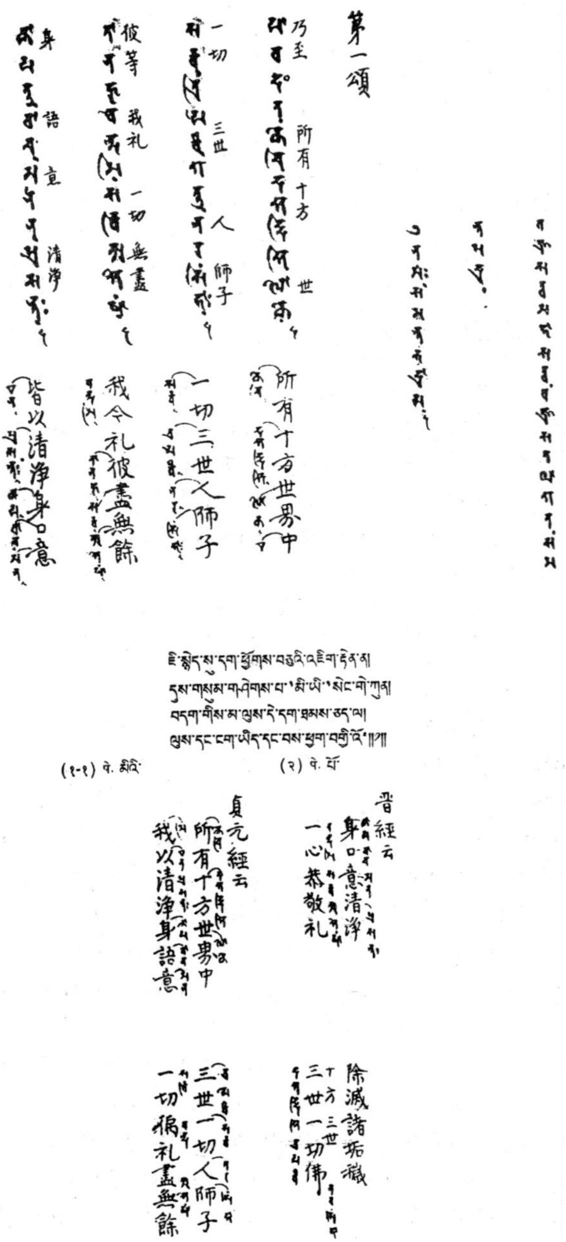
第一頌
所有十方世界中
一切三世人師子
我今禮彼盡無餘
皆以清淨身口意
ཇི་སྙེད་སུ་དག་ཕྱོགས་བཅུའི་འཇིག་རྟེན་ན།
དུས་གསུམ་གཤེགས་པ་མི་ཡི་སེང་གེ་ཀུན།
བདག་གིས་མ་ལུས་དེ་དག་ཐམས་ཅད་ལ།
ལུས་དང་ངག་ཡིད་དང་བས་ཕྱག་བགྱིའོ།
晉經云
身口意清淨
一心恭敬礼
除滅諸垢穢
十方三世一切佛
貞元經云
所有十方世界中
我以清淨身語意
三世一切人師子
一切徧礼盡無餘

and Chinese Books and Manuscripts" by Bunyiu Nanjio. Sanskrit text is given in Siddham characters with lateral Chinese word-meanings, followed by three translations in Chinese. The first is by Amoghavajra (CE 746-71) of the T'ang dynasty, the second is a translation by Buddhabhadra (CE 420) of the Eastern Tsin dynasty and the third is done by Prajña (CE 796-98) of the T'ang dynasty (Sushma Devi, *Samantabhadracaryā-praṇidhāna-rāja,* International Academy of Indian Culture, New Delhi, *Śatapiṭaka,* vol. 4). Sanskrit books translated into Chinese are the lost heritage of India. The Taishō edition of the *Tripiṭaka* comprises over 3360 works translated from Sanskrit.

The great sage Jiun Sonja was a man of great virtue. At the age of 14 he became thoroughly familiar with Siddham. He was a talented calligrapher. His calligraphy was highly regarded. His writings comprise a thousand fascicules (*kwans*). Some of them were published by the "Jiun Sonja One Hundred Fiftieth Death Anniversary Commemorative Society." International Academy of Indian Culture, New Delhi, published some of his works in two volumes.

A large number of hymns were taken to Japan from China for recitation on special occasions. Special musical notations were written to chant the *mantra*s. This special genre of music is termed Bombai or Shōmyō. To this day there are special colleges of Buddhist music at Kyoto and Kōyasan.

Siddham

Siddham, a variety of Brāhmī, and an elder sister of Nāgarī, owed its popularity in China and Japan especially to the rise of the Mantrayāna Buddhism. It was used for writing *dhāraṇī*s, *mantra*s and *bījākṣara*s (seed syllables). It became a living script of such intrinsic value as to deserve a place in the realm of fine arts and is indeed considered on a par with painting. It is

Portrait of the Indian scholar Śubhakarasiṁha from a ninth century scroll

"*Siddham*" written by a Japanese calligrapher

used for calligraphic and decorative purposes. A number of Chinese and Japanese monks devoted themselves to study the script and for more than a thousand years they guarded this treasure of Indian culture.

The Japanese write *mantras* in artistic Siddham Nāgarī script which was not purely a writing system but a visual medium of an intrinsic dimension. It is the Nāgarī script of eighth-ninth century which was introduced to Kōbō Daishi by the Kashmiri scholar Prajña. It has been designated by the Japanese as Shittan, a corruption of Sanskrit term Siddham. This form of Nāgarī has a calligraphic charm of its own, in expressive curves and subtle nuances of brush and ink. It is also written in sturdy and dynamic strokes of a wooden stylus.

Though Amoghavajra propagated the correct writing of the Indian script and evolved a unified system of transcribing Sanskrit sounds with Chinese characters yet the Tāntric teachers stressed that a *mantra* transcribed as accurately as possible could never be as efficacious as those written in the original script. So Śubhakarasiṁha, Vajrabodhi, Amoghavarja and other masters wrote a variety of Brāhmī script that seems to have been widely used in India. Thus the script became the

Writing Siddham with brush

Writing with a stylus

The great monk scholar Kōbō Daishi was the first who began the study of Sanskrit letters known as Siddham in Japan. They were used in northern India from sixth to twelfth century CE as the northern Brāhmī script. Most of the scriptural manuscripts carried to China during the *T'ang* dynasty (618-907) were written in Siddham characters.

"*ha*" written in Siddham artistically by a Japanese artist

style of writing favoured by the Chinese and the Japanese Buddhists for writing *mantra*s and *dhāraṇī*s which has remained in use till the present day.

The script was used in India around CE 1000 as has been written by the Arab scholar Al-Beruni:

> The most generally known alphabet is called Siddhamāṭrkā which by some is considered as originating from Kashmir. . . . But it is also used in Varanasi. . . . The same writing is used in Madhyadeśa. . . .

The term Siddham is also mentioned by I-Ching:

> They (Indians) begin their (Sanskrit) study with the His-t'ang-chang or Siddham writing tables. This book is also called *his-ti-ra-su-tu* (*siddhirastu*). . . . This means success and good luck.

Every time the teacher used to write a new paradigm on the writing board he would first write at the top *siddham* or *siddhirastu*. This passage gives the reason why the script was known as Siddham.

The word *siddham* became a common parlance, a designation for script, a colloquial equivalent of the literary word *lipi* and the Chinese pilgrims adopted this term *siddham* for the form of the Indian script that they found in use there in the seventh-ninth century. Since the boards used for teaching this script were called *siddham* writing boards this term was later used as the title of books containing elementary writing lessons (R.H. Van Gulik, *Siddham,* pp. 52-55).

In China and Japan the name Brāhmī actually refers to the Siddham script. Another northern-Brāhmī-derived script is Tibetan devised for writing translations of Indian texts around the seventh century CE. The Haṅgul writing system of Korea is thought to have been created under the influence of the Tibetan script.

Siddham Letters as Objects of Worship

*Bījākṣara*s, the symbolic syllables written in Shittan are objects of worship when they represent the essence of the divine beings, such as "अ" is written for Agni, "च" for Candra, "इ" for Indra and so on. Sūrya in Japan represents the time aspect of human life, and along with Candra it denotes eternity in cosmic order. The seed syllables are placed on lotus flowers to indicate their divine origin.

Many Japanese who do not know Sanskrit are familiar with the Indian Siddham letters. Thus Buddhist *sūtra*s inspired

As objects of worship "a" for Agni and "I" for Indra written in Siddham as seed syllables for the two deities

"gaḥ gaḥ" and "gaḥ" written in Siddham as seed syllables for dual Gaṇapati and Gaṇapati

the finest calligraphy and printing styles in Japan. No book was printed outside a temple. The Japanese manuscript is a commentary on the *Lotus Sūtra,* by Shōtoku Taishi (573-621). He was a symbol of the speical relationship between Buddhism and the state. The earliest surviving example of printed matter in Japan is *Hyamanto darani, One Million Pagoḍā Dhāraṇī,* produced between 764 and 770 by the order of Empress Shōtoku as thanksgiving for the defeat of a rebellion. Emperor Shōmu (701-56) strongly promoted copying the entire Buddhist *Tripiṭaka.* Thus *sūtra* copying became a major industry in Japan. Wooden tablets called *sotōba*s, i.e. *stūpa*s, written in Siddham letters are often found in cemeteries.

The Japanese alphabets Katakana and Hiragana are based on the Sanskrit sound sequence: *a, i, u, e, o, ka, ki, ku, ke, ko* . . . . The alphabets were devised by the great monk Kōbō Daishi who began to democratize education by founding a school for the children of the common people. Hiragana alphabets are the cursive form which was woven into the *Iroha* poem. *Iroha uta* contains 47 letters, each letter occurring only once. It was a literary marvel. It is a free translation of a Buddhist poem composed in ancient India:

Sanskrit alphabets according to Hiragana and Katakana sound sequence

sarve saṁskārāḥ anityāḥ utpadavyayadharmiṇaḥ ।
teṣām vyūpāsamaḥ sukham avadat mahāśramaṇaḥ ॥

The new syllabary was a revolutionary step in Japan's civilization. It is called *dhvani pañcāśikā*. To this day every Japanese begins his education with this *Iroha* poem. Sometimes dictionaries are arranged in this sequence.

Sanskrit is a common linguistic inheritance of India and Japan. In Japan *bandai* was used in place of 'yours truly' at the end of a letter. It is Sanskrit *vande*. The Japanese word *tsunumi* for drum is Sanskrit *dundubhi*.

Usage of Indian script as sacred has an uninterrupted history in Japan. The above illustration is 'अ' calligraphed by Kakuban (CE 1095-1143). The initial letter 'अ' is emerging from a pristine white eight-petalled lotus, situated on the adamantine place of the *vajra*. The sound symbol 'अ' is prime among all letters and the supreme immutable: *akṣarāṇām akāro 'smi* (*Gītā* 10.33).

Siddham letters written by a modern Japanese calligrapher

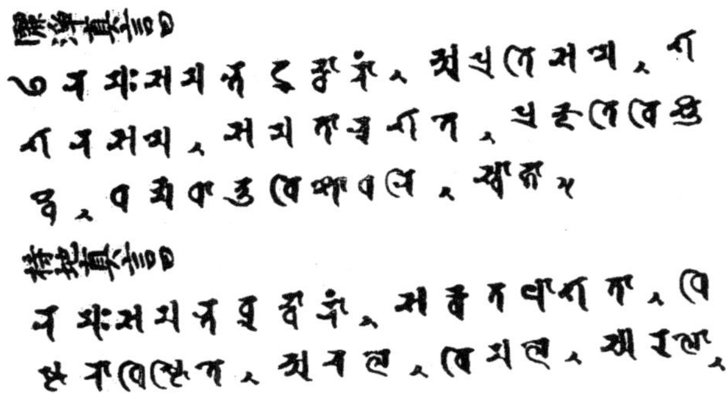

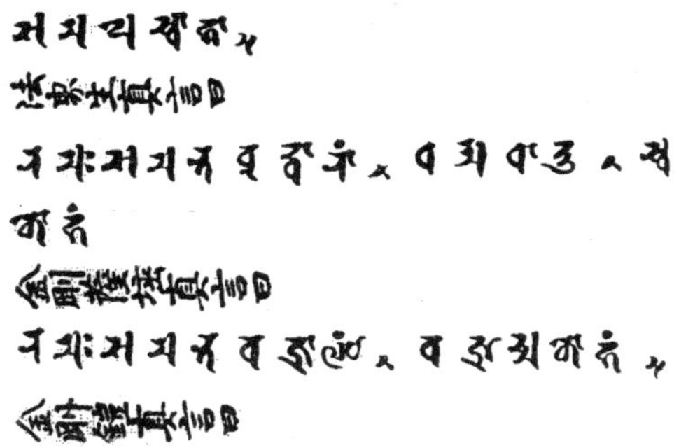

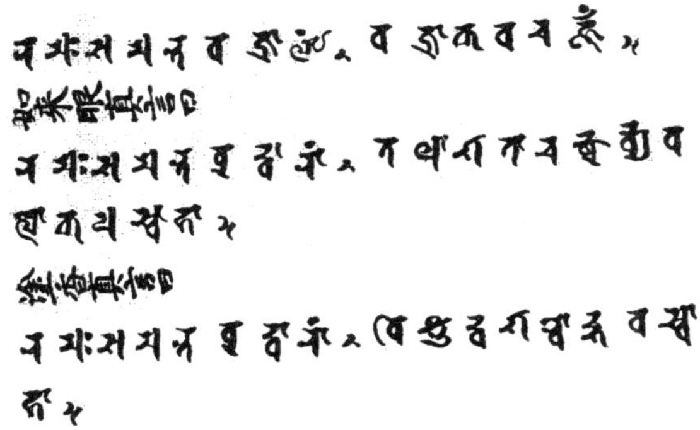

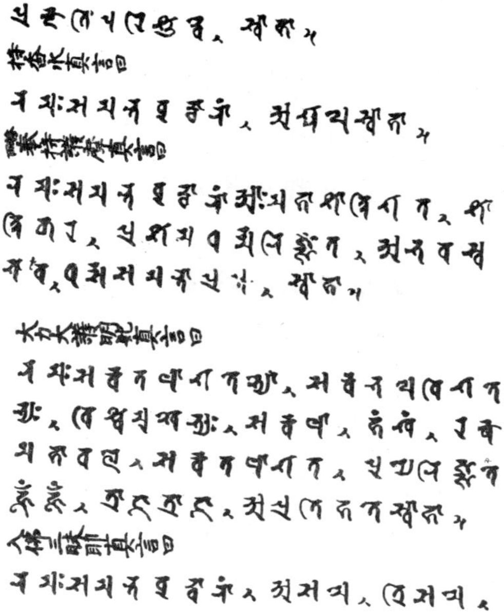

Mantras written by Kōbō Daishi

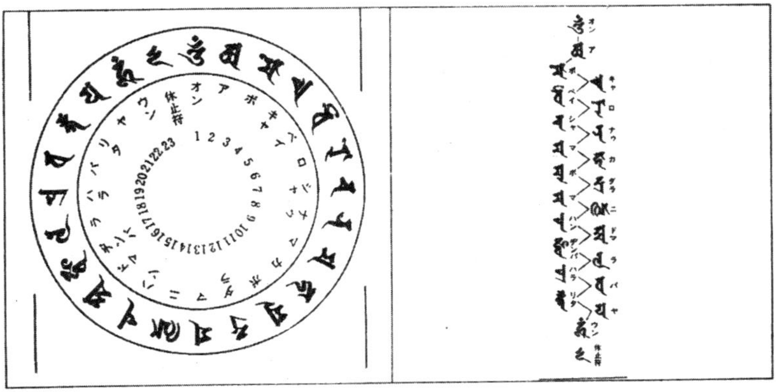

A dhāraṇī written artistically

Prof. Nagara is one of the most outstanding living masters of Siddham calligraphy. His brush bruises against the canvas, shaping itself in the reflexion of dynamism. Prof. Nagara tries to reach out to the Buddha in his calligraphy of force and strength. As a professor of design in an institute of technology his calligraphy is the sound mingling with the mind and merging with mists drifting in mountain vales.

Through the storming calligraphy the artist portrays the tempestuous mind of Lord Śiva, delimited by free and vigorous strokes. The holy waters of the river Gaṅgā meander across the dark and majestic Himalayas in a running brush in its indomitable *tāṇḍava.*

Vāyu is written in simple pure lines, rustling in the mind as cosmic breath. As wind blows unobstructed in the sky, so

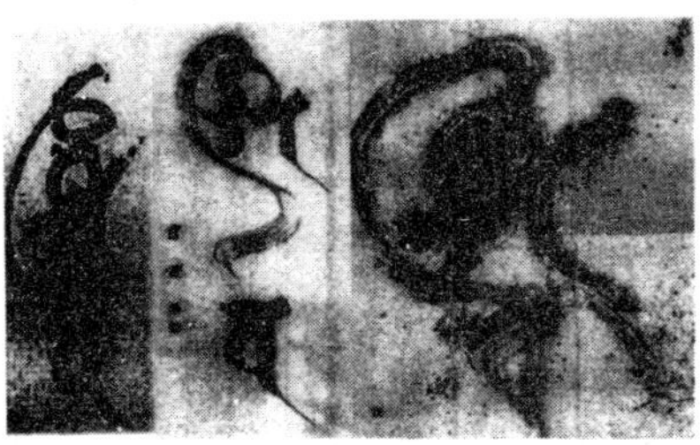

Śiva written in three different styles by Prof. Nagara

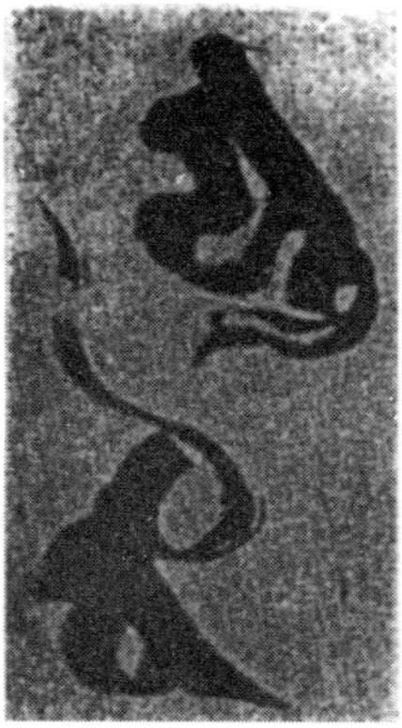 

do the supernatural power of the Buddha emancipate all beings. The energy of Vāyu in the space of Nothingness expresses the intensity to be free from all things.

Bhaiṣajya, the symbol of Bhaiṣajyaguru, the Buddha of healing, is written in monumental, absolutely final and sweeping in a downward movement. It has the boldness of a sword that defends the faith. It is the dance of hand on paper.

यन्मङ्गलं क्षितितले दिवि नागलोके रत्नत्रयं सुगतरत्नसुताभिधानम्।
क्षेत्रं जनैश्च शुभसंचयबीजपुष्टैस् तन्मङ्गलं भवतु शान्तिकरं तवाद्य॥ १९॥

Devanāgarī transcription of the following *maṅgala-gāthā* in Siddham script with Kana transcription, published in the Edo period.

Thus it may be concluded that languages do not stand in isolation. They bear an aura around them. Geographical features, ways of living and thinking of the people, their historical and cultural backgrounds, customs and beliefs influence the development of languages. Moreover they advance with advancement of civilizations; higher levels of thought, new discoveries and experiences constantly require coining of new terms that in turn enrich the languages.

"a, vi, ra, huṁ, khaṁ" wirtten in Siddham on palm leafs and tied near a river in Kōyasan in Japan

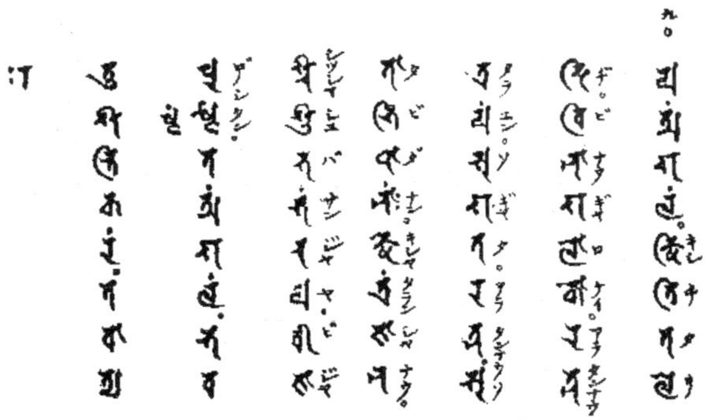

刻吉慶阿梨沙伽陀序
夫灌頂供養時大日經説奉
攝意音樂吉祥伽陀等廣多
美妙言疏釋此文其意謂此
讃釋[illegible]羅阿遮[illegible]經[illegible]起[illegible]經
所説此曲具在瑜伽大本中
此頌凡有三種一吉慶二吉
祥三遍吉祥[illegible]如次爲
應身故云下文且出一種[illegible]
皆是阿梨沙伽陀用此慶
慰弟子心仍有加持之用阿
闍梨當自説之次於下文且
出吉慶一種於此方所用已
粗周備耳而疏所載十一頌

3

Sanskrit and Russian

Hem Chandra Pande & Anubha Shukla

BOTH Sanskrit and Russian belong to the Indo-European family of languages. Sanskrit belongs to the Indo-Aryan branch of the Indo-Iranian group of languages, and Russian belongs to the Eastern Slav Branch of the Slavic group of languages. Sanskrit is being dealt with here as an ancient language and Russian as a modern language. That is, the examples of similarities between Sanskrit and Russian have been taken from the ancient and modern forms of these two languages, respectively. We have tried to analyse here the vocabulary of common Indo-European origin of these two languages. While analysing this vocabulary we have discussed their similarities in terms of the range of items covered by them and regularities of phonetic changes found in them.

In the nineteenth century attention of some Russian scholars was drawn to this subject. Amongst such scholars we may mention A. Ulferdig (1853) and A.S. Khomyakov (1855). They have separately written on this topic. Rahul Sankrityayana (1957) and Ramvilas Sharma (1961) have also dealt with this topic. Besides these studies, books on comparative philology and some works on Sanskrit by Western scholars have also mentioned about the similarities in the vocabulary of Sanskrit and Russian. The present article is an attempt to systematize the existing material on this topic.

As we know, the Indo-European languages are divided into *satəm* and *centum* [*kentum*] groups. One of the basic similarities between Sanskrit and Russian is that both the languages belong to the *satəm* group. The first consonant of the word *satəm* meaning "hundred" is preserved as *s* or *š* in some languages, while in other languages it has been changed to *k* or *h*. Here are some examples of *satəm* and *centum* languages:

satəm	Centum
Sanskrit *satəm*	Latin *centum* [*kentum*]
Avesta *satəm*	Greek *hekatón*
Old Slav *sŭto*	Gothic *hund*
Russian *sto*	German *Hundert*
Lithuanian *šim̃tas*	English *hundred*

This regularity of change in *s/ś* and *k/h* can be seen in several other words also, for example: Sanskrit *sūryaʰ*, Russian *solntse*, Greek *helios;* Sanskrit *daśam*, Russian *desyat'*, Greek *deka;* Sanskrit *aṣṭam*, Russian *vosem'*, Greek *okto*, Latin *octo*, Gothic *ahtau*.

It is clear from these examples that Sanskrit and Russian come under *satəm* group. Besides these languages Baltic languages — Lithuanian and Latvian — are also *satəm* languages.

Every rule has an exception. Here is an example of exception to this rule: Sanskrit *hr̥daya*, Russian *serdtse*, Latin *cordis*.

While discussing the relation of Sanskrit and Russian one notices some similarities and regularities in the phonetic system, grammar and vocabulary of these languages. We will first mention some similarities in the phonetic correspondences of the two languages.

Vowels of Sanskrit and Russian

(a) Sanskrit *a/ā*	Russian *e*
ad	*est'* "to eat"
catu^{h}	*cetyre* "four"
tama	*temnota* "darkness"
dvāra	*dver'* "door"
vastu	*vešč'* "thing"
saptan	*sem'* "seven"

(b) Sanskrit *a/ā*	Russian *o*
akṣa	*os'* "axis"
akṣī	*oko* "eye"
agni	*ogon'* "fire"
navan	*novyi* "new"
nāsā	*nos* "nose"

(c) Sanskrit *a/ā*	Russian *u*
ahi	*uzh* "grass-snake"
patha	*put'* "Path"
makṣi	*mukhā* "fly"
haṁsa	*gus'* "goose"

(d) Sanskrit *a/ā+nasal*	Russian *ya [j+a]*
daśan	*desyat'* "ten"
navan	*devyat'* "nine"

pañcan	*pyat'* "five"
māṁsa	*myaso* "meat"

(e) Sanskrit *u*	Russian *o*
udak	*voda* "water"
ubhau	*oba* "both"
duhitṛ	*doç* "daughter"
snuṣā	*snokha* "sister-in-law"

(f) Sanskrit *ū*	Russian *y*
dhūm	*dym* "smoke"
bhū	*byt'* "to be"
muṣ	*myš* "mouse"
sūnu	*syn* "son"

Consonants of Sanskrit and Russian

	Sanskrit aspirated	Russian unaspirated
(a)	Sanskrit *th*	Russian *t-*
	asthi	*kost'* "bone" (with insertion of *k* initially)
	path	*put'* "path"
	sthā	*stat'* "to become"
	sthāna	*stan* "settlement"
(b)	Sanskrit *dh*	Russian *d*
	dhū	*dut'* "to blow"
	dhūma	*dym* "smoke"
	budh	*budit'* "to wake up"
	madhu	*myod* "honey"
	vidhavā	*vdova* "widow"

(c)

Sanskrit *ph*	Russian *p*
phala	*plod* "fruit"
phalaka	*polka* "shelf"
phena	*pena* "foam"

(d)

Sanskrit *bh*	Russian *b*
ubhau	*oba* "both"
jambha	*zub* "tooth"
nabhas	*nebo* "sky"
bhrū	*brov'* "brow"
bhū	*byt'* "to be"

(e)

Sanskrit *ś/ṣ*	Russian *s*
iṣ	*iskat'* "to search"
daśan	*desyat'* "ten"
śarkarā	*sakhar* "sugar"
śveta	*svet* "light"

(f)

Sanskrit *h*	Russian *z*
lih	*lizat'* "to lick"
vah	*vezti* "to carry"
hima	*zima* "winter"
hiraṇya	*zoloto* "gold"

The common vocabulary of Sanskrit and Russian covers such themes as parts of body, family, home, space and time, animals, agriculture and plants, numerals, pronouns. Besides these, there are similarities in several verbs and adjectives also. Other Indo-European languages have also parallel equivalents. Examples of this common vocabulary are given below.

Sanskrit	Russian

Parts of body

akṣī	*oko* "eye"
udara	*utroba* "womb"

grīva *griva* "mane"

nāsā *nos* "nose"

Family

mātṛmat' "mother"

bhrātā *brat* "brother"

sūnu *syn* "son"

duhitṛ *doč'* "daughter"

devara *dever'* "brother-in-law"

vidhavā *vdova* "widow"

śvaśura *svyokor* "father-in-law

śvaṣrū *svekrov'* "mother-in-law"

snuṣā *snokha* "sister-in-law"

Home

dama *dom* "home"

dvāra *dver'* "door"

phalaka *polka* "shelf"

Space and time

dina den' "day"

nabhas *nebo* "sky"

nakta *noč'* "night"

Animals

avi *ovtsa* "sheep"

vṛka volk "wolf"

hariṇ *olen'* "deer"

Agriculture and Plants

dāru derevo "tree"

bhūrja *beryoza* "birch tree"

śākhā *sokha* "plough"

Numerals

dvā dva "two"

trayaḥ *tri* "three"

catu^{h} *ĉetyre* "four"

pañca *pyat'* "five"

Pronouns

aham *ya* "I"

tvam *ty* "you"

va^{h} *vy* "you"

Verbal Roots

jī *žit'* "to live"

jñā *znat'* "to know"

pac pec' "to cook"

pā *pit'* "to drink"

plav plavat' "to swim"

bhar brat' "to take"

tras tryastis' "to tremble"

vid vedat' "to know"

sthā stoyat' "to stand"

Adjectives

kṛṣṇa *krasnyi* "red"

tanu tonkii "thin"

dīrgha	*dolgii* "long"
pūrṇa	*polnyi* "full"
priya	*priyatnyi* "pleasant"
bṛhat	*bol'šoi* "big"
manda	*medlennyi* "slow"
śuṣka	*sukhoi* "dry"
harṣa	*khorošii* "good"

In both the languages there are some words whose similarity is hidden behind their meanings. In the following examples the relevant roots have been underlined:

Sanskrit	Russian
go "cow"	*govyadina* "beef"
tala "ground"	*utlyi* "fragile" (here *u-* is an extinct prefix meaning "not"
stana "breast"	*stan* "body"
śākhā "branch"	*sokhatyi olen'* "elk"

The above-mentioned similarities between Sanskrit and Russian show the closeness of these two languages as compared to some other distantly related Indo-European languages. The similarities are observed not only in vocabulary but also in the regularities of phonetic changes.

References

Burrow, T., *The Sanskrit Language,* Faber and Faber, 1965.

Gune, Pandurang Damodar, 1918/1958, *An Introduction to Comparative Philology,* Poona: Oriental Book House.

Khomyakov, A.S., 1855, "Comparison of Sanskrit words with Russian," *IIAN po otdeleniyu russkogo yazyka i slovesnosti,* St. Petersburg, vol. 4, issue 3, pp. 385-429.

सांकृत्यायन, राहुल, 1957; 'रूसी भाषा और भारत,' *मध्य एसिया का इतिहास*, भाग 2, पटनाः बिहार राष्ट्रभाषा परिषद्।

शर्मा, रामविलास, 1961, 'मूल शब्द–भंडार – संस्कृत और स्लाव,' *भाषा और समाज*; नई दिल्लीः पीपुल्स पब्लिशिंग हाउस (प्रा०) लिमिटेड।

त्रिपाठी, रामदेव, 1968–69, 'मूल आर्यभाषा, *परिषद् पत्रिका*, वर्ष 8, अंक 3–4 पृ० 17–51।

Ulferdig, A., 1853, "Comparison of Slav Language with Sanskrit," *IIAN po otdeleniyu russkogo yazyka i slovesnosti*, St. Petersburg, vol. 2, *Material for a dictionary*, Booklet 2, pp. 209-52, 273-323, 337-55, Booklet 3, pp. 401-89.

व्यास, भोलाशंकर, 1961, *संस्कृत का भाषाशास्त्रीय अध्ययन*, कलकत्ताः भारतीय ज्ञानपीठ।

n 1987, "An Outline of Sanskrit Grammar," *Sanskrit-Rushi Shabdakoshah*, compiled by V.A. Kochergina, Moscow: "Russkii yazyk" Publishing House.

4

Sanskritic Vocabulary of South-East Asia

Satya Vrat Shastri

EVEN a casual visitor to South-East Asia with a Sanskrit background is struck by the presence of Sanskrit words in the vocabularies of the languages there. It fills his heart with great satisfaction to notice the wide prevalence of Sanskrit in the vast stretches going by the name of South-East Asia with a variety of languages and dialects and sub-dialects, a standing testimony to the close cultural links between India and South-East Asia. The absorption of so much of Sanskrit must have been a gradual process spanning several centuries of acculturation.

It may well be argued that language is not the only link between countries and regions, there could be, indeed there are, other links as well, links of ethnicity, history, religion, mythology and so on but everything said and done, it is the linguistic link which is the most important for its being the most basic one pertaining as it does to expression, something through which a man gives vent to his thoughts, ideas and feelings. That Sanskrit could make such deep inroads into the languages of South-East Asia speaks volumes for its expressiveness which must have provided the need to the speakers of these languages over the ages to adopt words from it — in the case of some languages like Thai the adoption is an ongoing process — and integrate them with words of their own, a phenomenon we are witnessing in the case of English in India these days which has resulted in the adoption of enormous number of words from it by Indian languages which have come to be accepted as much original as the original Indian words. Their translations attempted in many cases have remained moribund with people merrily using English words even in their vernacular conversation for want of better equivalents, something that had happened in the case of Persian and Arabic words from which had percolated in large numbers in Indian languages in ages gone by for their better expressiveness. What is happening in the case of English or had happened earlier in the case of Arabic and Persian in India happened in South-East Asia as well. Words of Sanskrit that "migrated" from India are no longer Sanskrit words at present, they are local words now. They have been assimilated into the respective languages, given their phonological form in an overwhelming number of cases and assigned even their own meaning. This has resulted in the evolution of an interesting phenomenon of "connect" and "disconnect," the words do maintain some connection, however indistinct, with their originals to make their identification with them possible, yet they are not the same, having assumed a different form in accordance with the phonology of the language into which they have been assimilated.

Once integrated into the mainstream of the respective languages these foreign words give up their foreign tag and become part and parcel of the current coin in them. To the Sanskritists of India they may be Sanskrit words, if they are *tatsama*s, of the form resembling Sanskrit or words of Sanskrit origin if they are *tadbhava*s, derived from Sanskrit. To ordinary men and women who speak the language they are the words of their own language and not words come from any other source, words borrowed and assimilated. They are their words reflecting very much as they do their ethos. In this connection I am tempted to recount my own experience. It is some two decades; I was going to Kuala Lumpur from Bangkok by train. I had with me the name and address of a person I was to meet there. As the train was nearing Kuala Lumpur I took out the address book. It carried the address "Uttara Long," Kuala Lumpur. Unable to make sure as to what Uttara Long was; whether it was the name of a locality or a road or a street, I enquired of the conductor of the compartment. He looked at the address book and said "*uttara* is a Malaysian word which means north." His remark both amused and delighted me. Well, *uttara* is Malaysian. As is with *uttara*, so with other Sanskrit words. They are at present either Malaysian or Cambodian or Lao or Thai or Indonesian.

Now, when through an attempt like the present one, the people of South-East Asia will be made aware that what is their's is India's also, they cannot but be impressed with the thought of sharing what is common with each other. And that is precisely the aim of the present attempt. It is the link that will bind the peoples of the countries of South-East Asia with the people of India, the link that is vital in forging a common bond between them with enormous possibilities of bringing about better understanding which is the precursor of goodwill, harmony and friendship.

A close look at the words of Sanskrit origin of South-East Asia reveals that some of them are sometimes more expressive and better suited being less heavy and more direct than their counterparts in use in India. A couple of instances would bear it out. For the English word prejudice the Malay word is *pūrvaśaṅkā* (written as *pūrvaśaṅgkā*) which in any case is a trifle more catchy than the *pūrvāgraha* of Hindi. In the same category are the words *wārtāwān,* Sanskrit *vārtāvān* for journalist and *berita utama,* Sanskrit *vārtā uttama* or *uttama vārtā* for headlines in that language which are more expressive and to the point than *patrakāra* and *surkhiyāṅ* (Urdu word meaning those in red) in use in Hindi. Similary more simple and direct and certainly less heavy is the word *anekprasong,* Sanskrit *anekaprasaṅga,* of Thai for multi-purpose than its Indian counterpart *bahūddeśyīya.* Other words falling in the same category are *lokasattva* of Bahasa Indonesia for animals and *dhanāgāra,* pronounced as *thanākhān* (lit. meaning house of money) of Thai for bank or *dūralekha,* pronounced as *thoralekh* of Thai for telegram.

An observation that may be of interest here is that in a few languages — it is particularly relevant in the case of Thai — the Sanskrit quotient goes up with hierarchical order. There is more of Sanskrit among elites, the nobility than among the common folk. For son-in-law the Thai elites would use the word *jāmadā,* pronounced as *chāmadā,* a derivative of Sanskrit *jāmātā* while the common folk would prefer *lookhey.* Similarly the common word for marriage in Thai is *tāṅ ṅān* while among the elite it is either *vivāhamoṅkhon,* Sanskrit *vivāhamaṅgala* or *moṅkhon somrot,* Sanskrit *maṅgalasamarasa* or just *vivāha.* Added to this is the observation that the locals while adopting words from Sanskrit have not unoften imparted them an aesthetic look. To celebrate the fiftieth anniversary of the coronation of the present king the Thais used the word *kāñcanābhiṣek*(*a*) rather than the *suvarṇajayantī* of *abhiṣeka* which would have been used in India.

There is a whole lot of technicai terms, educational, economic and political, drawn from Sanskrit, particularly in Lao and Thai, a study of which could be revealing. They could provide a good material to a researcher in this field. For him a work like the present one could be of inestimable value. So will it be to one who wants to take up the socio-cultural study.

Sanskrit words in the languages of South-East Asia are found in four forms: One, in their original Sanskrit form, e.g. *vipāka,* Cambodian, consequence; *āgama,* Indonesian and Malay religion; *gaja,* Indonesian, elephant; *put(e)ra, put(e)ri,* Indonesian, son and daughter respectively; *yāpana,* Lao, life maintenance, *yāmika,* Lao, watchman; *nāga,* Lao, a noble man; *nandī,* Lao, happiness, rejoicing; *alpa,* Malay, careless, negligent; *dayā,* Malay, force, deceit, cunning; *aneka,* Malay many; *dāna,* Malay, charity, gift; *prārthanā,* Thai desire; *velā,* Thai, time; *naḍikā,* Thai hour; *vivāh(a),* Thai, marriage; two, with negligible change in sound like the loss of final vowel, the dentalization of palatal *ś* and cerebral *ṣ* and *ṇ,* the *o* form of *a* (a common feature even in eastern part of India), the *w* form of *v,* the insertion of *g* before a nasal, the deaspiration of aspirates like *bh* which is pronounced as *b* in Indonesian and Malay or *p* and *ph* in Lao and Thai respectively, the appearance of anaptycal vowel among conjunct consonants and so on, e.g. *bhāsā,* Thai and Lao; *bahāsā,* Cambodian, Malay and Indonesian; *bhāṣā,* language; Thai and Lao *nāyok, nāyaka,* chief, leader, *kāy,* Cambodian, Malay and Thai, *kāya,* body; *dharmaniyom, dharmaniyama,* Thai, custom; *sāsana,* Thai and Lao, religion; *wanitā,* Indonesian, *vanitā,* woman; three, with phonetic variation of Sanskrit words according to local pronunciation, e.g. *ākād,* Thai, *aṅgkās,* Malay and Indonesian, *ākāśa,* sky, space; *khana,* Cambodian, *kṣaṇa,* moment; *khana,* Thai, *gaṇa,* group (vide *khanabody,* dean of the faculty); *dontrī,* Thai, *tantrī,* music; *phan,* Lao and Thai, *bandha,* utensil; *cuaca,* Malay, *svaccha,* clear and so on; four (a) in combination with another word, a synonym, a combination seemingly superfluous, carrying the same meaning for which either of the two would have sufficed, e.g. *mit(d)sahāy,* Lao and Thai, *mitrasahāya,* friend; *cidtacet,* Lao, *cittacetas,* mind; *kāmalāg,* Lao, *kāmarāga,* sexual passion, *nained,* Lao, *nayananetra,* eye; *nītinai,* Lao *nītinaya,* by law, dejure; *phalaphon,* Lao, *phalaphala,* fruits, big and small; *vanudyān,* Lao, *vanaudyāna,* forest preserve; *supamoṅggon,* Lao, *śūbhamaṅgala,* good luck, welfare; *sukhakṣema,* Lao, happiness; *sunyākād,* Lao, *śūnyākāśa,* vacuum; *kulavaṅgsa,* Malay, *kulavaṁśa,* family; *kiyattiyot,* Thai *kīrtiyaśas,* fame, (b) in combination with a synonymous Sanskrit word, the combination yielding an altogether different meaning, *hedkān,* Lao, *hetukāraṇa,* proceedings, situation, event, (c) in combination with a local word, both of them meaning the same, e.g. *rāṅgkāy, rāṅg* = body, Thai *kāy* = *kāya,* Sanskrit *rāṅgkāy* = body, (d) in combination with a local word both having separate meanings (this category has larger number of words), e.g. *orang bisaya, orang,* Malay, *bisaya,* Sanskrit, *viṣaya,* a person from *śrīvijaya; pañcalima, pañca,* Sanskrit, *lima,* Malay, *pañcalima* = jugglery; *pelasari, pela, phala,* Sanskrit, *sari,* Javanese, *pelasari* = a plant with yellow scented flowers; *bāṅgrāk, bāng,* place, Thai, *rāk,* Sanskrit *rāga, bāngrāk* = a place for love; *namtān, nam,* Thai, water (extract or juice), *tāl* (pronounced as *tān*), Sanskrit *tāla, namtān* = sugar; *pholomāi, phala,* Sanskrit, *māi,* Thai, *pholomāi* = fruit; *tonmāi, ton,* Sanskrit *taru, māi,* Thai, *tonmāi* = tree; (e) in combination with a non-local word, *wargadunia,* Malay, *warga, varga,* Sanskrit, *duniā,* world, Arabic, *wargaduniā* = a stateless person; *mahāmiliā,* Malay, *mahā,* great, Sanskrit, *milia,* Arabic, *mahāmiliā* = Highness.

In many cases the Sanskrit words in South-East Asian languages have undergone change in meaning. Thus in Thai *prārthanā,* already noticed, means desire; *karuṇā* means please; *pramān* (*pramāṇa*) means approximately; *viniccaya,* Sanskrit *viniścaya* in Cambodian means judgement; *kasina āyu,* Sanskrit *kṣīṇa āyu,* in Lao means one who is eighteen year or over eighteen years old; *bitha,* Sanskrit *pīṭha,* in Lao means to hurt, to kill; *saṅketa* in Lao means agreement, condition; *cercā,* Sanskrit *carcā* in Malay means abuse; *saṅg kat,* Sanskrit *saṅgata* in Lao means similar, comparable; *saṅgked,* Sanskrit *saṅketa,* means abuse, revile; *nāḍī,* Sanskrit the same, in Malay means wrist; *peribhāsā,* Sanskrit *paribhāṣā,* in Malay means proverb, idiom; *remaja,* Sanskrit *ramya,* in Malay means adolescent, youth; *perwara,* Sanskrit *pravara,* in Malay means court-damsel; *laksamana,* Sanskrit *lakṣmaṇa,* in Malay means a naval admiral; *ajita,* Sanskrit the same, in Indonesian means undependable; *anartha,* Sanskrit the same, in Indonesian means poor, needy; *āsvāsa,* Sanskrit *āśvāsa,* in Indonesian means whiteness; *camara,* Sanskrit the same, in Indonesian means bull, male cow; *cāṇḍāla,* Sanskrit the same, in Indonesian means a person in exile; *sāmanta,* Sanskrit the same, in Indonesian means neighbour; *sārathi* Sanskrit the same, in Indonesian means, vehicle, carriage; *svāhā,* Sanskrit the same, in Indonesian means heaven; *pāpa,* Sanskrit the same, in Indonesian means, difficulty, bad luck; *pradātā,* Sanskrit the same, in Indonesian means judge, lawyer, server of justice; *prajā,* Sanskrit the same, in Indonesian means grandchild, *pratāpa,* Sanskrit the same, in Indonesian means discussion, negotiation; *sampāna,* Sanskrit *sopāna,* in Balinese (Indonesian) means high wall, barricade.

South-East Asia has been the bastion of Indian culture for centuries. It is no wonder then that there should be so much of presence of Sanskrit in its vocabularies. The present is only a sample survey of it.

5

Sanskrit in the Renaissance of European Languages

Lokesh Chandra

THE names of Asia and Europe were learnt by the Greeks from an Asian people. Assyrian monuments contrast between *asu* "(the land of) the rising sun" and *ereb* "(the land of) darkness or the setting sun." *Asu* became *Asia* and *ereb* came to be *Europe.* These names were passed on by the Phoenicians to the Greeks. In Homer, Europa is a young Phoenician princess whose beauty fires the love of Zeus. She is the personification of the continent of Europe. The earliest mention of Europe is in the Homeric "Hymn to Apollo." The distinction between Europe and Asia is found in Aeschylus in the fifth century BCE. The contrasts and contradictions of Asia and Europe have dominated the history of man. The intellectual domination of Asia by European civilization continues. The sun rises in the East, ideas arise in the West.

In 1801, Sir William Jones wrote in the first volume of the *Asiatick Researches*: "Though we cannot agree with the sage preceptor of that ambitious Prince (Alexander) that the Asiaticks are born to be slaves, yet the Athenian poet seems perfectly in the right when he represents Europe as a sovereign princess and Asia as her handmaid." This was the main thrust in the six substantial volumes of *The History of British India* by the renowned utilitarian philosopher and writer James Mill, which appeared in 1817. They made an astounding and continuing impression. Mill attacked the eternity of India. By his assessment, contemporary as well as ancient India, whether in science, religion, government, law, or political economy, was barbarous. Ever since the first publication of Mill's famous work, the perception of India has been under his shadow. A decade or later after it was published, Macaulay referred to the History in the House of Commons as "on the whole the greatest historical work which has appeared in our language since that of Gibbon," and afterwards in his famous Minute on Indian Education paid it the compliment of using some of his material.

For India, rays of hope were to shine from the transformation of conscience that Europe had been undergoing since the Renaissance. The forces liberated in the Renaissance took a specific bias, namely that of Humanism, the particular form assumed by human self-esteem. It indicates the endeavour of man to reconstitute himself as a free being, away from theological thrall, and he derived peculiar assistance in this effort from Greek and Roman literature, leaning rather to the side of man than of divinity. For a generation nursed in theological scholasticism, it was the fountain of renascent youth, beauty and freedom, the shape in which the Helen of art and poetry appeared to the ravished eyes of mediaeval Faustus.

As monarchical rule was overthrown in the United States and France, the citizenry discovered an emotional identification with the forms and images of the ancient republics. To them Greece and Rome were not dead civilizations, but the living birthplaces of freedom and democracy. Their affinity with the ancient world not only gave them a sense of heroism and glory, but it also furnished convenient precedents for the new governments in America and France, and to a certain extent the British constitutional monarchy. The ancient Athenian commonwealth and Roman republic became the symbols of liberty and the new order. The senior legislative houses in the United States, France and later in the Latin American republics, were named senates after the old Roman prototype.

The passion for Hellenism brought Europe to the threshold of Eternal India. After all, the Greeks had admired India as the source of all philosophy. Dusebios (fourth century BCE) reports that an Indian had discussed philosophy with Socrates at Athens. The philosopher Pythagoras, who swayed Greek intellectual life from the sixth century BCE onwards, transmitted Indian ideas. It was commonly held among the Greeks that India was the land of wisdom: for instance by the noted author Alexander Polyhistor (*ca.* 70 BCE), Apuleius (*ca.* CE 150) and Philostratos (early third century). The popular satirist Lucian (second century CE), in his "Runaways," lets the Goddess of Philosophy tell Jupiter that she first descended upon "the Indians, the mightiest nation upon earth." To cite Sedlar: "India served as an object upon which educated Greeks projected their own demoralization, namely their loss of confidence in contemporary Greek culture and institutions. Thus India became an idealized country, abundantly fruitful, while Indian philosophers came to possess a wisdom superior to that of the Greeks." The linguistic affinity between Sanskrit and their language had, however, eluded the Greeks.

The European quest for the origin of languages is recorded as early as Herodotus. In his History he notes that since the days of Psammetichus of Egypt men searched for the origin of language and the reason for their similarities and diversities.

In the Mediaeval Ages, Hebrew was taken as the starting point for the evolution of Greek and Latin, compare for instance, Richardson's *A Dissertation on Language*, published in 1777. The Hebraic hypothesis led to blind alleys.

Boxhorn was the first to postulate a theory of common origin of Indo-European languages. He did not publish any work. His ideas became known through his friend George Horn in the latter half of the seventeenth century. He postulated some sort of a common language which he called Scythian, as the mother of Greek, Latin, German and Persian from which "like dialects would start." No less a person than Leibniz added his authority to this theory of the "Scythian" origin of the peoples and the languages of Europe. In the first volume of the Memoirs of the Berlin Academy, Leibniz attacked the old Hebraic hypothesis. He put forward a theory which was very similar to that of Boxhorn and he clearly distinguished the Indo-European from the Semitic and the Finno-Ugrian groups. Now linguistics had rightly bid goodbye to its Mediaeval moorings. Studies reached the threshold of a new era. The ancient Greeks were over-whelmed by Persian might. The new term for the family was "Scythian." It was natural that Scythian or Persian dominate the scene. It is evident from a letter of William Jones to Prince Czartoryski dated 19 February 1779:

> Procopius, I think mentions the great intercourse both in war and peace between the Persians and the nations in the north of Europe and Asia whom the ancients knew by the general name of Scythians. Many learned investigators of antiquity are fully persuaded that a very old and almost primaeval language was in use among these northern nations from which not only the Celtic dialects but even the Greek and Latin are derived.

In 1786, on the horizons shone a new light, the light of Sanskrit. Sir William Jones started to learn Sanskrit in September 1785 and after a study of mere four months he was led to a realization which sparked off the discovery of comparative and historical philology. "The Sanskrit language, whatever be its antiquity, is of a wonderful structure; more perfect than the Greek, more copious than the Latin, and more exquisitely refined than either, yet bearing to both of them a stronger affinity, both in the roots of verbs and in the forms of grammar, than could possibly have been produced by accident; so strong indeed, that no philologer could examine them all three without believing them to have sprung from some common source, which, perhaps, no longer exists."

Jones added Sanskrit to the "Scythian" family of languages. The scientific age of historical linguistics had dawned. Europe was on the verge of discovering the origins of her own culture and its original meanings, that had eluded the Greek Euhemerus in the third century BCE, or the Roman statesman, scholar and orator Cicero in the first century BCE.

The observations of William Jones were in tune with the mood of the times. The European mind had been moving away from the Age of Reason, to a movement that is known in general as Romanticism. The idea that the Europeans migrated from a distant and unknown land soon fired the imagination of the Romantic mind. Friedrich Schlegel, a high priest of the Romantic movement, coined the word "Comparative Grammar." The English translation of the *Śākuntalā* of Kālidāsa was done into German in 1791 by Georg Forster, and it awakened the highest enthusiasm of literary men like Herder and Goethe. The European litterateurs were surprised that India too had excellent dramas. Dramas were no more the monopoly of the Greeks. To the Classical Graeco-Roman world was added the more ancient and pristine Classical world of India. The Romantic movement idealized the Classical world of Greece and Rome. The emotional espousal of Greek independence that was prevalent all over Europe and the U.S. was actively expressed in letters and the arts. Both classical countries — Greece and Italy — were under the yoke of foreign tyrants, and intellectuals and poets passionately championed their cause. Byron's *Isles of Greece,* Shelley's *Hellas* and *Prometheus Unbound,* Friedrich Holderlin's *Hyperion,* Victor Hugo's *Les Orientales,* and Vittorio Alfieri's tragedies, all upheld these liberation movements.

For the Romantic School, headed by the brothers Schlegel, Indian literature had a special attraction. Friedrich Schlegel, the father figure of the Romantic movement, expected from India nothing less than "the unfolding of the history of the primeval world which up till now is shrouded in darkeness."

The thorough investigator Franz Bopp (1791-1867) published in 1816 the results of his researches on the conjugation system of the Sanskrit language in comparison with those of Greek, Latin, Persian and German. The Indo-European family of languages was thus established. In fact, Bopp used the term "indo-europaisch." Europe had found a new identity with Sanskrit. European man had found his consciousness lapsed in space and time. Sanskrit was the discovery of the primal soul of Europe, the discovery of her deeps. To cite Pablo Neruda: "deracination of human beings leads to frustration in one way or another obstructing the light of the soul." Sanskrit has the majestic and mysterious syllables from the dawn of time, the deep-rooted vitality, inexhaustible history, and limitless growth. Winternitz says: "if we wish to learn to understand the beginnings of our own culture, if we wish to understand the oldest Indo-European culture, we must go to India, where the oldest literature of an Indo-European people is preserved."

As Sanskrit broke upon the scene, European languages found a new *raison d'être* for their efflorescence. European languages were trying to assert themselves for at least five centuries. For instance, Martin Luther (1483-1546) translated the Bible into German. His remarkable handling of the German language influenced and shaped the development of modern German. English prose owes in abundant measure to King James' Authorized Version of 1611.

These efforts of biblical translations did not take the European languages very far. With the study of Sanskrit, dictionaries of European languages were taken up on historical principles. These lexicographical monuments revealed their deep roots, their evolution over centuries, and their rich semantic spectra. The European languages gained a new self-confidence. Moreover, Greek and Latin were no longer the original or prime languages. Sanskrit was more ancient than both of them, more transparent, more logical, and could explain the formation of these Classical languages themselves. Now modern European languages could stand by the side of Greek and Latin, which like them, stood in the same relation to primordial Sanskrit.

The National Revival (about 1775-1850) of Czechoslovakia was a great social movement characterized above all by a national consciousness on the part of the people, and a drive for economic and cultural independence. Thanks to one of the reforms of Joseph II, the German language became the only official language of the country. At the same time he abolished feudalism in 1781. As a result former serfs could now move to the towns and their children could study. The Czech language started to gain momentum. Dobrovsky (1753-1829) wrote a definitive grammar of Czech. The existence of linguistic connection between Czech and the ancient and perfect Sanskrit was a great encouragement to the oppressed nation in its efforts to improve its language. Many others shared Dobrovsky's interest in India. The advocates of Czech pointed out that their language was closer to Sanskrit than German, hence was more ancient and deserved a place of honour. They cited the example : *stara matra dati medu* = Sanskrit *sthavirā mātā dadāti madhu* स्थविरा माता ददाति मधु "the old mother offers honey" (to the guest).

The Bulgarians struggled hard in the ninth century against the Three-Language Doctrine brought forward by the German clergy. According to this dogma church services could be held only in Hebrew, Greek and Latin. Brothers Cyril and Methodius created the Cyrillic alphabet to replace them by Old Bulgarian, so that in every Bulgarian church the people would hear their own tongue. Cyril defended the right of the Slavs to have their own script. Doesn't God send an equal amount of rain to all? And doesn't the sun shine for everybody. . . . How is it that you are not ashamed of recognizing only three languages, and of decreeing that all other nations and tribes should be deaf and blind? A people are naked without books. Once again in the nineteenth century, during the struggle of National Revival language became important. Leaders were proud that their language Bulgarian was closer to Sanskrit and hence older than any current non-Slavic European language. Old Bulgarian has *synu* for Sanskrit *sūnu* "son," and *dini* for Sanskrit *dina* "day." This fired the Bulgarians with a new enthusiasm for their language.

The Germanization of Lithuania started from the twelfth century as a result of the proclamation of a crusade against them by the Pope. The Lithuanians lost on the battlefield, lost their ancient faith and as a result their language declined. Czarist regime in the nineteenth century forbade the use of Lithuanian. Grandmas in remote villages narrated folk-tales to eager grandchildren in their Lithuanian language which was despised by the Slavized nobility and punished by the Czarist regime. The traditional folk-hymns called *daina* (from Sanskrit *dhyāna*) were abandoned by the courts, but they lived on in the villages, faithfully preserved by the poorest people of the country, guarded by the mother of the family, during the darkest period of Lithuanian history: the occupation by Tsarist Russia between 1795 and 1918. The grandmothers and mothers would tell their children and grandchildren: *dievas dave dantis, duos ir duonos* "God has given teeth. He will give food." The sentence meant: when God has given life, he will grant us freedom. Language and freedom were inseparable.

To this day Sanskrit is associated with Lithuanian as a symbol of national identity. We can go to a classroom at the Vilnius University of the Lithuanian Republic. The professor writes sentences on the black-board in Lithuanian and Sanskrit:

Lithuanian	Sanskrit	Meaning
kas to esi	*kas tvam asi*	Who are you?
kas tavo sunus	*kas tava sūnuḥ*	Who is your son?

Kas to esi is an eternal question before man in his quest for knowledge. The answer is as brief in Lithuanian as it is in Sanskrit : *tas tu esi=tat tvam asi.*

Sanskrit opened up new universes of how man has expressed ideas. Sanskrit had preserved a rich system of inflexions, both declension of nouns and conjugation of verbs.

It had transparent roots which showed the dynamics of vocabulary creativity. Sanskrit revealed the unique linguistic phenomenon of Indo-European languages wherein prefixes enriched human horizons of communication, for example, inspect, suspect, aspect, respect, conspectus — all from spect, specere "to see, look at." Language is formed. Man has created words through them ideas, thoughts, categories, and they in turn have brought into existence solid objects, the machines and so on. Language is a living organism. It gives man an ever-renewing life. Language led to science. Language was the epic of creativity.

Sanskrit led to two new principles in the methodology of research: (i) comparative study (ii) historic development. The newly evolved comparative-historical method was applied to the study of language and it resulted in the publication of the biggest *Sanskrit-German Dictionary* in seven large volumes by Böhtlingk and Roth in 1852. It created a new intellectual climate in which evolution of language was fully established as a part of human march onwards. This milieu influenced the natural sciences. Seven years after the appearance of the dictionary, came out Darwin's monumental work *Origin of Species* in 1859, which soundly established the theory of organic evolution, that was to determine the development of natural science.

Dictionaries of European languages on historical principles were undertaken on the model of the *Sanskrit-German-Dictionary*. In 1854 was published the first volume of Grimm's *German Dictionary*, whose completion took a century. Jacob Grimm and Wilhelm Grimm were the most distinguished brother-scholars of the German Romantic period, renowned as the collectors and editors of *Grimm's Fairy Tales* (1812-15). They worked assiduously at the great dictionary of the

German language, a task so large that it was impossible for the brothers to finish it themselves. Its last volume appeared in 1960.

"Ever since the Normans conquered England in 1066, the everyday tongue of the British Isles had suffered a long eclipse. Even in its native land, English was a second-class citizen, owning neither the status of Latin and Greek nor the aristocratic patina of French. Those who studied the origins of the language of Chaucer and Shakespeare were essentially amateurs, as there was little prestige to be gained by such work." In 1857 James Murray commenced *A New English Dictionary on Historical Principles* to show the extensive heritage of the English language. Its first section was printed in January 1884 by the Oxford University. It gave the historical development of every English word. It opened up a new wonder. Its editor, its moving spirit, James Murray, was knighted. It embodies and interprets to this day the culture of the English language from its earliest documentation to the present times. English now had a rich heritage and was as respectable as any of the Classical languages or elegant French or intellectual German. Continuous progress and sustained development arising out of historical-comparative studies afforded a new esteem to European languages. The *Oxford Dictionary* took the etymologies of English words far back to Sanskrit, e.g. the word thousand has the base *teu:* Sanskrit *tava*s "strong, energetic" (from the root *tu*) and *hundred.* It can be seen in Old Norse *thūs-hund*, Old Frankish *thus-chunde,* as the "great hundred." Thousand was power, strength. Time, Latin, *tempus* was Sanskrit *tapas* (with a nasal *m* inserted) which mean "heat." Day is the hot part of the cycle of 24 hours. The vast time scales in Sanskrit exploded the Biblical myth of 6000 years of creation. In Sanskrit the *Sṛṣṭi Saṁvat* or Era of Creation runs to two billion years. This made possible geological time, palaeontological time, and astronomical time with billions of years of creation.

Till the discovery of Sanskrit, Classical European mythology was a fragment of metaphors and dreams, pages torn form the book of Cleo, *The Muse of History*. With the rise of Comparative Philology and Comparative Mythology, it became possible to sift and interpret the several strands that wove the magnificent fabric of Classical myths, the artistic and ethical parameters that gave rise to creative symbolization in a galaxy of mythologies. The omnipresent Pan-hellenic god *Zeus* was Vedic *Dyaus* "sky", Latin Ju-piter = Sanskrit *Dyauṣ-pitar*. What at first was only an appellative of the sky became the supreme ruler of gods and men, whose will was law. Europe had to wait for 2,300 years to know the origins of Zeus, when Sanskrit was discovered in the eighteenth century, though Zeus was the mythical deep of European time. The word "Europe" itself was born out of the myth of the young princess Europa who was carried away by Zeus disguised. Today Europe awaits elopement by Sanskrti *Dyauṣ*. Modern civilization again needs the aroma of Sanskrit. Sanskrit is the eternal and the evolving in a fruitful unity. In it the endless past and the fleeting present live together for a thrust in the future sans end.

6

A Preliminary Search for the Common "Deoxyribonucleic Acid" of Indo-European Civilizations

(*The Slavonic Perspective*)[1]

"Ogień sławię kapłana . . . " "Agnim iḷe purohitam . . . "[2]

M. Krzysztof Byrski

Is globalization a curse or a blessing? Our answer to this question has to depend on the answer to another one: is humanity able to develop the communication code, which will ensure comprehension of the value systems proper to different civilizations and thus their preservation and coexistence? The long history of wars that mankind loves to fight, crowned in recent times with the morbid chain of events heralded by the fateful destruction of the Twin Towers of the World Trade

---

1. While working on this paper, I availed myself of the priceless help of my late colleague, an expert Sanskrit teacher and consummate linguist **Andrzej Lugowski**, to whom I am deeply indebted for his expertise and timely help.

2. The Polish word *ogien,* which means "fire" and which is the cognate word of the Sanskrit term *agni,* I select as a kind of the opening *mantra* for the present essay. Also because fire is the foremost manifestation of the perceptive reality possessing a dual character: creative and destructive.

Centre in New York, seems to augur ill for the future. It is precisely because of the threat of total misunderstanding among the representatives of different civilizations that our bounden duty is to look for all such elements of human experience, which could be of help in the task of forging a proper communication code. In the global village, where we are bound to brush against each other with increasing frequency thanks to the unprecedented development of technology, such a code would make us understand each other better.

"To what is One, sages give many a title: they call it Agni, Yama, Mātariśvan," runs the oft and on quoted passage of one of the hymns of the *Ṛgveda*.[3] These words, to my mind, belong to the not-so-long list of the most important thoughts ever couched in words for men. Let me suggest a following gloss, which these words seem to justify. First of all the Being is One. When the individual realizes this truth and experiences it, we call such an individual a *jīvanmukta*. What happens when such a perspective dawns upon the growing number of individuals and in effect the entire humanity? What happens when this process begins to affect our different ways of life, so dear to us? If the Vedic *ṛṣi*s are right and if the Being indeed is one, then globalization seems to be "Its" inherent feature. While the understanding of the *ekatva* of Being slowly ripening in our minds — thanks to technological advancement — spreads, our only problem should be how to assure that it will not mean "macdonaldization" of our existence. We should thus only worry how to salvage our right to call that Being in many ways and how to make all these multifarious ways of

3. R.T.H. Griffith, *The Hymns of the Ṛgveda*, Delhi; Motilal Banarsidass, rpt. 1995, p. 113. *ekam sat viprā bahudhā vadanti* (*ṚV*, I. 164.46).

our calling it or giving to it many a title comprehensible to the representatives of each one of those ways?

Thus the verb $\sqrt{vad}$ becomes the focal point. One of the dictionary meanings of this word is NB "to communicate." So it is this aspect of languages that we shall try to tackle now. How peoples using different languages can really communicate? The entire endeavour of the legion of philologists since antiquity has been aimed at the achievement of this end. Yet, it seems that the task is far from being completed.

Let me give you one example, which will well demonstrate the way I look upon the problem. During my mission as the Ambassador of Poland to India in the 1990s, I once found upon my desk a letter in Hindi. Obviously it was sent to all embassies. In it the author gave vent to his exasperation over the idea of religionless conduct (*dharma nirapekṣatā*),[4] obviously prompted by the well-known election slogan of the Congress Party about separation of religion from politics. It will come as a surprise to the reader that the problem was not of ideological nature but of purely semantic one. The author insisted that if we accept such mode of conduct then nature also may start functioning likewise and series of catastrophic events such as earthquakes may occur. Since each and every aspect of perceptive reality has its proper *dharma,* how can one separate one's conduct from one's *dharma?* Certainly the author of the said letter, traditionally educated, must have understood the term *dharma* in the way the *Kārttikeyānuprekṣa,* a Jaina treatise, formulates its definition: *dharmaḥ*

---

4. . . . *jab samvidhān aur vicārdhārāen dharma nirapekṣa hone lagatī hain to prakr̥ti bhī apne dharma se nirapekṣa hokar vikarāl rūp dhāraṇ karne lagtī hain.* From a letter of Mukesh Suman of Nazibabad dated 17.10.1995.

vastusvabhāvaḥ.[5] It is interesting to note in this connection that the Sanskrit word in question etymologically is the cognate word of the Latin *forma*. Had there been a more common awareness of the fact, *dharma* should not have been used so light-heartedly as the simple Indian equivalent of the European term "religion."

Having thus indicated broadly the direction of our argumentation let me invoke a thought, which I would like to make the principal point of reference. There is to be found in the *Tāṇḍyamahābrāhmaṇa* a very meaningful statement. It roughly runs as follows: "Prajāpati was one and Speech [Vāk] was his and Speech was his second. He thought — let me emit Speech and She will make manifest all. And he emitted Speech and She made all manifest."[6] Looking for a similar such statement in the European tradition we come upon the opening verses of the Gospel of St. John. It runs as follows: "Before the world was created, the Word already existed, he was with God, and he was the same as God. From the very beginning the Word was with God. Through him God made all things; not one thing in all creation was made without him. The Word was the source of life and this life brought light to mankind."[7] Thus at least several hundred years later the vision of Śruti found its repeated expression. We may of course get involved in a lengthy argument whether Sanskrit *Vāk* and the Greek

5. Svāmi-Kumāra, *Kārttikeyānuprekṣa*, Agās: Śrī Parama-Śruta Prabhāvaka Mandal, 1997, p. 364, (XII.478).

6. S. Levi, *La doctrine du sacrifice dans les Brāhmaṇas*, Paris, Ernest Leroux, 1898, p. 23. *Prajāpatir vā idam eka āsīt tasya vāg eva svam āsīd vāg dvitīyā sa aikṣatemām eva vācam visṛjā iyam vā idam sarvam vibhavanty eṣyatīti sa vācam vyasṛjata sedam sarvam vibhavaty ait . . .* (Td. Mh.- bh. 20.14.2).

7. *Good News Bible, Deuterocanonical Books/Apocrypha*, Bangalore: The Bible Society of India, 1979, p. 118.

Logos can be identified? But what is really important for us here is the fact that the creative stir of absolute consciousness manifests itself first and foremost through speech. It is thus only and exclusively with the help of speech that men can try to understand better the mystery of Being, which is described as *Ekam*.

The fact that we remain within the precincts of one great Indo-European family of languages makes the task easier and very rewarding. Indo-European linguistic studies have a long history and it is impossible — if necessary at all on the present occasion — to summarize their huge scholarly achievement in a brief presentation. For the purpose of this presentation it is enough to say that I was not able to trace any comprehensive study of Slavonic languages comparing them directly with Sanskrit. I cannot be sure if my brief search for the relevant source material has been sufficiently exhaustive. Yet, if it is so, then the obvious reason of that is a prevalent opinion among the comparative linguists that Slavonic languages cannot be simply compared with Sanskrit. This is so because in between the two there is the Old Iranian language to which the Slavonic languages are more directly related and scholars have given these relations more attention.

In such circumstances it is evident that in order to challenge this viewpoint on purely linguistic grounds somebody better equipped than myself would be required. Meanwhile let us consider the fact that there most probably existed a Proto-Indo-European language. It was spoken by a tribe, which later on dispersed [maybe as a consequence of the Deluge, the memory of which has been preserved in many traditions and not only among Indo-Europeans]. We may be therefore justified to conduct two types of comparisons: the *rūpavāda* one and the *arthavāda* one. While the first category takes as a point of departure the highly probable common etymology, the second one concentrates on the meaning shared, while the terms used although not cognate, yet express the said meaning in a strikingly similar way. This type of analysis helps immensely in better understanding of many terms. Comprehension of that is indispensable for proper perception of the value systems of our civilizations.

Let us then review some of the most striking examples, which to my mind justify well the approach proposed. But before we come to grips with the problem, may I share with you the memory of a certain event, which may be treated symbolically. Several years back Professor Satyavrat Shastri visited us in Warsaw and I took him for a boat ride on the Vistula river. My wife and sons accompanied us and since for the two little boys it was their first such experience, so naturally they were very much excited and repeatedly asked questions while addressing me loudly with the endearing term used by children in Poland while addressing their father — *tato.* Our guest with great amazement noted that we are still using in our everyday life the ancient Sanskrit appellation for a father, not so often used even in the classical Sanskrit. Having thus invoked the blessings of our common distant forefathers we may now take up our proper task.

The term *dharma* has already been mentioned above. Although *forma,* which is its European cognate, is Latin and not Slavonic, yet this word in exactly the same form (NB!) is used in Polish and some other Slavonic languages. When I try to explain to my students in Poland the full semantic value of the word *dharma,* I draw their attention to the fact that *dharma* semantically speaking carries also the meaning of the word *forma.* The nature of anything naturally includes also the form proper of the given thing. Thus it should be looked at as an indispensable aspect of its nature. Consequently the meaning of the word *dharma* cannot be simply equated with that of religion and much less limited to it. Much better equivalents of the Polish term *religia* [Eng. religion] are *sampradāya* and *pantha*,[8] while semantically speaking *yoga* would be the best one.[9] Certainly religion comes within the purview of *dharma* but *dharma* itself means much more. Ever since my return from India after relinquishing the post of the Ambassador in 1996, I have been trying to promote a neologism *dzierżma* as the Polish equivalent of the Sanskrit *dharma*. I took the clue from the fact that the Polish √*dzierż*, which means to hold strongly, to sustain, and to wield might be most probably a cognate verbal root of the Sanskrit √*dhṛ*. I am tempted to understand *dharma* first and foremost as a principle sustaining all elements of perceptive reality in their definite separateness and their characteristic form. There can be no question as to the possibility of separating form and content of any subject or object of perceptive reality. Therefore the author of that letter in Hindi, which I mentioned above, was right — it is impossible to separate the nature of a thing from a thing itself.

While the above argumentation is an example of what I called *rūpavāda*, let me now present a case of the *arthavāda*, which seems not less striking. One of the Sanskrit terms

---

8. It will not be out of place here to remember that Jesus Christ speaks about himself: *I am the road.* Besides "road" in the biblical language signifies following in life certain ethical standards of mode of behaviour. In the New Testament it symbolizes the Church. *Pismo Święte Starego i Nowego Testamentu*, Pallotinum, Poznan, 1980, p. 1422.

9. See *Lexikon der Religionen*, ed. Hans Waldenfels, Breisgau 1987. The verb *religare* means according to this source "to rebound" or "to bound tightly" with God. The meaning of the verb √*yuj* has a similar purport.

denoting happy lot, destiny, good fortune, luck, prosperity, happiness and welfare is *bhāgya.* One of its cognate words of course is the name of the god Bhaga — Dispenser — "the name of one of the Ādityas bringing welfare and love" and meaning also good fortune, luck and happy lot. The noun *bhāga* in turn, means portion, share, allotment, part, fraction and also happy lot. Further on the word *bhagavat* means possessing a happy lot, fortunate, blessed, and so on. All three are derivatives of the verb $\sqrt{bhaj}$ — to deal out, to divide, to distribute, to allot, to apportion, to share with, and to give a share. Before I proceed with my main argument let it be noted that "the Iranian form of the name is *bagha,* god which occurs as an epithet of *Ahura Mazda.* The word is indeed Indo-European, since it occurs in Old Church Slavonic as 'bogŭ' in the sense of 'god.'

> There is no reason to suppose that it designated any individual god in the Indo-European period, for it cannot have attained a more specialized sense that "bountiful god," if indeed it meant more than merely 'bountiful giver.'[10]

I may add that the word for god, in Polish is *Bóg* (read: *bugh*) and *Boh* in Russian. It also appears to be a cognate term of *Bhaga* albeit interrelated — as Macdonell indicated — *via* the intermediary of the Old Iranian. Please bear with me, if I am going now to make a few remarks, which may appear common place to you here, but they are indispensable for the coherence of my argument. The monistic vision of ultimate reality, which emerges from the Śruti texts, juxtaposes the oneness of it with the manifold perceptive reality. Thus the "One-without-the-second" had divided "It-self" into many parts or may be better

---

10. A.A. Macdonell, *The Vedic Mythology,*Varanasi: Indological Book House, 1963, p. 45.

decided to share "It-self" with many. So in a way a person called *bhāgyavat,* which means "having good qualities or fortune, happy, prosperous,"[11] may also be understood as being a happy shareholder of perceptive reality. But not only perceptive reality alone. For as a depository of *ātman* such person shares also the absolute reality although through ignorance may not be aware of that. Exactly this pattern of thought is reflected in the Slavonic languages. The word for part or portion is in Polish *część* and in Russian *czast'.* Now the word for happiness respectively is *szczęście* and *sczast'e.* It is created with the help of preposition *z,* which here means "with" added to the noun *część.* Consequently the deepest meaning of happiness in Slavonic languages is perceived exactly as in Sanskrit. "Being with part" or being in state of participating expresses adequately the state of happiness. If we may use religious terminology we may say that for both Slavs and Indians happiness is a state of shareholdership in God's reality.

To the same category of language reality belongs another example of the *arthavāda* similarity when both the Polish language and Sanskrit use pairs of cognate words to denote world and light. The Sanskrit terms, which I keep in mind are: *loka* and *āloka.* Both terms seem to be derivatives of the verbal root $\sqrt{ruc}$ — to shine, to be resplendent, to be radiant. In case of *āloka* it may be through the intermediary of the secondary verbal root $\sqrt{loc}$ and while *loka* means world, *āloka* means light. Needless to add that the term for an eye — *locana,* thanks to which we can perceive both light and the world, is also related. Now the Polish terms implied are *świat* and *światło.* The first denotes world and the second light. It is rather certain

11. M. Monier-Williams, *A Sanskrit-English Dictionary,* Oxford: Clarendon Press, 1899.

that both may be the cognate words of the Sanskrit verbal root √*śvit* meaning to be bright or white and to shine down upon. Phonetically identical word in Polish *świt* means dawn, daybreak or sunrise. Thus again we share the pattern of linguistic behaviour identifying in our language usage of light and the world.

It is not surprising that both the *rūpavāda* and the *arthavāda* categories of similarities can be traced in some cases of rural terminology. The Polish word for a village is *wieś,* which is almost unchanged form of the Sanskrit *viś* meaning a settlement, homestead, house and dwelling. It is interesting to note that in Lithuanian, which does not belong to the Slavonic family of languages but is the most archaic Indo-European language in Europe, the word *Viešpat* means Lord God. It is reminiscent of the Sanskrit *Viśa*s *pati* meaning "lord of the house" and applied to Agni and Indra. Yet another term of the same provenance is the Polish *gromada* (the Czech *hromada*) meaning the smallest administrative unit or a group of people. This is the cognate word of the Sanskrit *grāma* — village and probably of the Latin *gremium* — meaning a gathering of all and also a womb. Both these categories apply yet to one more word. Neighbour in Polish is called *sąsiad* (read: *sonshyad*). This without doubt is a cognate word of the Sanskrit *saṁsad,* which means one who is sitting in a gathering. In both cases the basic meaning — sitting together — is the same and the phonetic form is almost the same.

Some of the archaic forms have preserved themselves as the so-called hydronimes. The names of at least three Polish rivers come to mind. One is *Drwęca* (read: *drventsa*), which is a cognate word of the Sanskrit *druvanti* — running, hastening, flowing and melting. Another is *Nur* and also *Ner,* which would be the cognate Polish term for the Sanskrit *nāra* meaning waters. Interestingly this term in this particular meaning is not very frequent in Sanskrit so that Sir Monier-Williams suspects that in the *Manusmṛti* it has been invented specially to explain the appellation Nārāyaṇa. In the light of this example his opinion may be questioned. Finally the name of the river *Odra* (German *Oder*), which is a frontier river between Poland and Germany, is most probably a cognate word of the Sanskrit *udra* meaning "an aquatic animal" and in neuter gender "water." Exactly such an animal in the Polish language is called *wydra* (read: *vedra*). In English it is "otter." There can be no doubt that both these terms as well as those other listed above date back to the times immemorial when all of us Indo-Europeans were one people.

Let me finally invoke yet one more *rūpavāda* type of similarity, which may account for a special feeling of kinsmenship between Indians and Slavs. While starting this presentation I have quoted the beginning of the Gospel of St. John referring to the Word, equating it and identifying with God Himself. The Slavonic word for it in Polish and in Russian is *słowo.* The cognate word in Sanskrit is *śravas,* which means sound, cry, loud praise, glory, fame and renown. Obviously it is a derivative of the verbal root √ *śru* — to hear and so closely related to the term *śruti,* the importance of which not only for the Indian civilization but for the entire humanity cannot be overestimated. Now, it is not altogether improbable, although not acknowledged yet by professional linguists, that the term *Słowianie* (Polish) and *Slavyanye* (Russian) could have been derived from the word — *słowo* or/and its cognate *sława* — fame. They might have considered themselves as the only ones who possessed comprehensible words in contradistinction to the incomprehensible words of the speech of Germans, whom our forefathers therefore called *Niemcy.* This term is derived from the word *niemy, nie-mowa* meaning mute person, someone who cannot speak. This is of course the relic of the times when people were unaware that German language also belongs to the same Indo-European family. Happily after the painful experience of the second World War this awareness, not only in the sphere of languages, is slowly beginning to dawn upon both nations.

Thus Speech (*vāk*) and its constitutive element Word (*słowo*) may become a bond of our ancient kinsmenship worthy to evoke today, when technology makes us interact at an unprecedented scale and with an unprecedented frequency. Maybe the awareness of the common Indo-European cultural *"deoxyribonucleic acid"* enshrined in our languages will warm even more our hearts towards each other.

7

Sanskrit and German
A Study in Mutual Relationship

G.C. Tripathi

GERMAN is one of the most important languages of culture and science. It has a wonderful literature — which is not so well known in India — and in the field of original philosophical writings, it ranks supreme with an unchallengeable place at the top. The Germans like to call themselves "the people of poets and philosophers" (*Volk der Dichter und Denker*), although their achievements in the fields of science and technology are by no means less remarkable.

German is also one of those four main European languages (English, French, German and Italian) in which the scientists prefer to publish their research findings in order to communicate with their subject-specialists and to reach a wider readership of their area. Till very recently, for example, the Dutch, Polish and Czech preferred to publish in German rather than English, a trend which is now tilting in favour of English due to increasing importance of the United States.

German is presently spoken as a native language in three European countries with 100 million speakers. Besides the Federal Republic of Germany, it is also the language of the whole of Austria and half of Switzerland, i.e. of its northern and north-eastern parts. It also used to be the administrative language of the three colonies of Germany in South-West Africa which Germany lost in the First World War, and it is often claimed that because of the large scale of migration of Germans to the eastern part of the United States, this language was once on the verge of becoming the National language of that country, but it lost by a very slender margin to English !

German has a history of nearly two thousand years. It is very closely related to the three Scandinavian languages: Swedish, Norwegian, Danish, as well as to the Icelandic and much more to the Dutch. The language of Netherlands is just a dialect of North German. It has separated itself from German only a few hundred years ago. In fact, "Deutsch," the word for German in the German language and German people, is so akin to the word "Dutch" that the bond of deep relationship between the two is too obvious to be overlooked. All these languages, mentioned above, and in addition to them, the English (Anglo-Saxon) as well as the languages of Greenland and Friesland belong to one single group, which is known in the comparative Philology as the "Proto-Germanic" group of languages. A comparative study of all the dialects belonging to this group leads us up to the second century BCE for their first appearance. Germans were originally inhabitants of the Northern Europe. Around the beginning of the Christian era, they moved southwards and pushed the Celts (Gaelic people) to the West (France) or assimilated them.

The Germanic group can be divided into three main branches: north, east and west. To the *Northern group* belong all the Scandinavian languages. *East German,* also called Ostrogothic, exists no more, but we possess a valuable written record of this language in the translation of the Bible in the Gothic language by Bishop Wulfila which is thought to have been done around CE 350. Wulfila belonged to the German tribe of Goths who had migrated from the south of Scandinavia to the region near the Baltic Sea and settled later around the Black Sea. For about one hundred years (fifth-sixth century), they also ruled over large parts of Italy. To the group of *West German* belong the Anglo-Saxon or English (with a heavy admixture of French vocabulary), Friesian, Flemish (of Belgium), the Dutch and the various dialects of German proper (like low German or the "Platt-deutsch" of North Germany, Saxon or Sächsish and Bayerish of South-East Germany, as well as the German of Austria, very much akin to Bayerish.

That particular form of German which is today the *lingua franca* of the whole of Germany, Austria and the major part of Switzerland and is also the standard literary form for all sorts of written word, is called "Hochdeutsch" or "high German" and has developed itself basically out of the dialect of the mediaeval saxony State (presently Sachsen, Niedersachsen, Sachsen-Anhalt) and its earliest monumental specimen is the German translation of the Bible by Martin Luther done in the first half of the sixteenth century although this dialect can be shown to exist in a much older form already in the eighth-ninth centuries since a number of small glosses on the Bible written during this period have come down to us. It is often claimed that the best German is spoken around the city of Hanover which is the capital of the Niedersachsen (lower Saxony) State.

Speaking very roughly, the Germanic dialects of north, of which Dutch is a good representative, are known as *Low German* and the German of Germany/Austria proper as *High German*. The terms low and high are not indicative of quality or any specific feature but came into vogue simply because of the geographical fact that the southern part of Germany, as well as Austria and Switzerland are full of mountains, hence lie much above the sea level whereas the northern part lies adjacent to the sea, is hence a low-lying area.

Along with other European languages, German belongs to the *Centum* (pronounced: *Kentum*) group of Indo-European languages in contrast to Sanskrit which belongs to *Śatam* group, which means that wherever a palatal *ś* is found in Sanskrit (= old Persian: dental *s*), we have to expect a *k* in these languages. This *k* sound appears as *h* in the Germanic group because it first gets aspirated into *kh,* then assumes a fricative character (corresponding to the Greek letter khi X = ख़्) and with the drop of the initial guttural sound assumes the character of *h,* much on the lines of the Prakrit languages which also treat the Sanskrit aspirated consonants, especially the *media aspirata* in the same way (already in the Vedic language we see the root *bhṛ* becoming *hṛ* !). Thus Sanskrit *śatam* corresponds to Latin *centum* and to the Germanic *hundred/hundert;* the Sanskrit *śvan* (dog) corresponds to Greek *kúon,* Lat. *can*[*is*] and German *hund.*

In spite of radical transformation of the phonetic value of the consonants inherited from the Indo-European period, the German has basically remained an archaic language, at least in comparison to English and French. It still has a structure which to understand a good knowledge of its grammar is required, like in the case of Sanskrit. It has also the capacity of building long compounds similar to Sanskrit, a capacity which is totally lacking in French, for example, which has to say "the machine for writing" (*la machine d'écrire*) for "typewriter" or "box for letters" (*boit à lettre*) for letterbox. In German one can have compounds comprising even four or five words put together (*Ueberdonauschiffahrtsaktiengesellschaft*: i.e. "a shareholders company for ferrying across the upper Danube river with ships") which gives the languages wonderful capacity to express concepts and objects not only concisely, but also precisely. In this trait it is very akin to Sanskrit in which *samāsas* play a very important rôle.

The German has also the wonderful capacity of coining new words with the help of prefixes and suffixes. In this case also it has a great similarity with Sanskrit. Many modern languages have become so analytical in their structure that they find it difficult to coin new words and technical terms from their own stock and take recourse to their mother languages, which are more synthetic in nature. Example of Hindi may be cited in this regard, which is dependent largely on Sanskrit and also of English, which often coins words from Latin bases, though to some extent it is also capable of creating new words of its own.

The scholars of Germanic studies divide the history of High German language into four major phases:

1. Old German: CE 800–1150.
2. Middle German: CE 1150–1450.
3. Early High German: CE 1450–1650.
4. Modern High German: CE 1650 onward.

The "High German" or the German proper sounds today much different from English, although closely related, which is due to the fact that it has undergone not less than *three* phases of phonetic shift or change in the character of its consonants due to various reasons *after* its separation from "Low German" (to which English belongs). The initial change, which formed the character of Proto-German and gave it a separate identity was the most crucial one, whereas the subsequent three changes took place within the High German itself. This change was first noticed in a rudimentary form by a Danish scholar R.K. Rask in CE 1818 and was developed further into a system by the German scholar J. Grimm in 1822 who had termed it as *die erste Lautverschiebung* ("the first phonetic shift"). The system, today known as "Grimm's law" is a part of every textbook of comparative philology and the students of philology in India are also conversant with it. It is also well known that the discrepancies in this law were explained and straightened out again by a Danish scholar Karl Verner who for the first time (in 1876) also truly explained the role of accent in the change of the character of the Germanic consonants. Since it is only the language of the Vedas, which has faithfully preserved the Indo-European accent, the testimony of the Vedic word became crucial in this respect and also underlined the importance of Vedic accent for philology.

According to philologists the proto Indo-European language possessed only three groups of consonants: gutturals (*ka-varga*), dentals (*ta-varga*), and labials (*pa-varga*), each consisting of three phonemes only, besides the corresponding nasal. (We ignore here the controversial existence of the surd aspirates (*tenues aspirata*), *kha, tha* and *pha* which is open to doubt.) The Sanskrit palatals have come into existence due to a special combination of gutturals with palatal vowel (*i* or *e*) and the cerebrals *ṭ, ḍ,* etc. are supposed to be of purely Indian origin. Thus we arrive at the following system of nine stops (mutes) (*sparśa vyañjana*) in the mother Indo-European:

k *g* *gh* (with variants: k^w g^w gh^w)

t *d* *dh*

p *b* *bh*

Besides these mutes and the nasals (*ṅ, n, m*) there is linguistic evidence of the existence of the liquids *r* and *l* (oft interchangeable), semi-vowels *y* and *w*, sibilant *s* and the aspirate *h*. The vowels available in the IE language were *a, i, u, e* and *o*.

k, t, p are called surds or *tenuis* (pl. tenues), *g, d, b* are sonants or *media* (pl. mediae) and *gh, dh, bh* are aspirated sonants or *media aspirata*. According to a simplified form of Grimms law, all these undergo change or shift in the Proto-Germanic language in the way that:

(1)	*k,*	*t,*	*p*	become *kh, th, ph*
(2)	*g,*	*d,*	*b*	become *k, t, p;* and
(3)	*gh,*	*dh,*	*bha*	become *g, d, b*

respectively. These last ones (*g, d, b*) have an earlier form too which is of fricative nature (ग़ द़ ब़ [व़]). The IE sounds *y, r, l* and *v* do not change their character regularly, so also the sibilant *s* and the nasals.

There are also the letters in which the effect of the Indo-European accent is visible very clearly. The Proto-Germanic <u>th</u> (spirant, either surd or sonant, थ़ or द़) shows two different types of development in the German language. English *father* has an equivalent in German *Vater,* but Eng. *brother* is German *Bruder*. Thus <u>th</u> appears to have once become *t* and once *d*. It was Verner who found out the reason for this anomaly by looking for the accent of these words in the Vedas. He noticed that the word *pitár* has an acute accent (udātta) immediately after the letter *t* whereas the word *bhrấtar* is accented on the previous syllable. If the accent is behind the letter *t,* it becomes first <u>dh</u> (द़) and later *d,* but if the accent follows it, the accented <u>th</u> (थ़) develops into a *t,* not becoming a sonant.

The surd aspirates *kh, th, ph* (ख, थ, फ) developing out of *IE* *k, t, p,* later turn into surd fricatives aspirates X θ F (ख़, थ़, फ़,)

or spirants (i.e. sounds which can be pronounced in a prolonged manner in contrast to the mutes). The examples are:

Sans. *naktam* German: *Nacht* (ch = ख़/or Greek X)

Sans. *tri* English: *three* (*th* = थ़/or Greek θ)

Sans. *pitar* Gothic: *vader* (in Proto-German, *Vater* later in High German, v = f फ़).

This does not happen however when *k, t, p,* are preceded by *s* (Sans: *spaś*, German: *spähen*, Eng. *spy;* Sans. *stṝ*, Eng. strew).

The examples of *g, d, b* becoming surds (*k, t, p*) are as follows:

Sans. *go* Eng. *cow*, German *Kuh*

Sans. *sed* Eng. *sit*

Sans. *ad* Eng. *eat*

Latin *labium* Eng. *lip*, German *Lippe*

The few examples for the sonant aspirates (*media aspirata*) becoming *g, d, b* are as follows —

Sans. *janghā* Gothic *gangan*

Sans. *dhūmas* Gothic *dauns*, Ger. *Dunst*

Sans. *bhar* (- *ati*) Gothic *bairan*, Eng. *bear*, *Ger. ge-bären*

In the next phase, German goes its own way (more than once!) by changing the phonetic value of some more consonants, which it has inherited from the common Germanic stock, into different sounds, which imparts it a character of its own. We may take English as representing the older phase and observe the changes in German proper:

Old *k* becomes X (fricative <u>kh</u> as in Urdu <u>*kh*</u>*abar*), e.g. Eng. *weak*, Ger. *Woche*. The Proto-Germanic *t* in the beginning is changed into *ts* (written *z*), e.g. Eng. *ten* corresponds to German *Zehn*. In the middle and the final position *t* becomes first *z* (*ts*) and then gives rise to *ss* through assimilation (*ts*>*ss*); that is why the German equivalent of Eng. *water* is *Wasser*. Same phenomenon takes places in the case of final *t* as well but after a while one *s* is dropped, e.g. Eng. *that* has German equivalent in *das*. The sound of *p* in the beginning becomes *pf* as in Eng. *pipe* = German: *Pfeiffe*, however it appears mostly as *f* or *ff* in the middle and the end, e.g. Eng. *ship* = Germ. *Shiff* developed, from *pf*). Old Germanic <u>gh</u> (ग़) preserved by English, is simplified into a *g*, e.g. Eng. *ghost* = Germ. *Geist*; IE *dh* developing first into a fricative <u>*dh*</u> (द़) in Proto-Germanic gives rise to a *d* in the first phase of development and then turns into a *t* in High German, cf. Sans. *vidhavā*, Eng. *widow*, Germ. *Witwe*. Otherwise also Eng. *d* corresponds to German *t*, e.g. *day* = *Tag*, *door* = *Tür*. The letter *b* becomes fricative *v* and is preserved in this very form in English whereas it again becomes *b* in German, threfore English *give* (*v* is a labio-dental fricative व़) appears as *geben* in German. *Th* of English is German *d*, which is why *thank* is *danke*, and *to think* is *denken*.

What is given above is a small sample of the change of the consonants in German language. Many more complex issues of phonetics are involved in the consonantal change of German for which the reader may consult special works.

It may also be mentioned *en passant* that in all the Germanic languages (including English) the tenues *k* (*ca-*, *co-*, *cu-*), *t*, *p* are pronounced in an aspirated form k^h, t^h, p^h and because of this the Germans and the English-speaking people find it difficult to differentiate between Sanskrit *ṭa* and *ṭha* or *pa* and *pha*, etc. Further the medial stops *g*, *d*, *b* in German lose their sonance if they appear in the final position and are pronounced as pure tenues *k, t, p* exactly as it happens in Sanskrit (*Tag* = *ṭhaak, und* = *unṭ, Sieb* = zeep; cf. Sans. *Pariṣad* > *Pariṣat, Vāg* > *Vāk* etc.).

Whereas Sanskrit has changed the Indo-European short vowels *e* and *o* into an *a,* the German has retained *e/o* and has even mostly changed the vowel *a* into *e.* Therefore, the impression that one gets after hearing a few sentences of German is quite different in contrast to the Sanskrit. *E* is the vowel used to the maximum in German both in its long and in short form. But, German orthography based on Roman alphabet has no means to distinguish between a long *ē* and a short *ĕ*. Both are used side by side: for example in *leben* (life) and *geben* (to give), the first *e* is long and the second short. However, German has evolved its own method of distinguishing long vowels from the short ones — which is sometimes of great help though not always absolutely foolproof. The method is to put an *h* after the vowel, which is to be lengthened (*stuhl* = shtool, *ihn* = een, *mehl* = mail) or to double the consonant following the vowel if it is intended to be pronounced short (*immer* = ĭmer, *sollen* = sŏlen, spinnen = *shpĭnen*. It may be noted that the German never pronounces the consonants as double even if they are geminated: *Zimmer* is त्सिमर् not त्सिम्मर्, Müller is म्युलर्. For a long *i,* the German uses the combination of *ie.,* whereas *ei* is pronounced as *ai.* However, the German short and long vowels *a, i, u* do not have the same quantity as they have in Sanskrit. Even in their short form, they are longer in quantity than the corresponding short ones in Sanskrit and their longer form is much longer than the long vowels of Sanskrit. *Ae, oe* and *ue* are written as *ä, ö* and *ü.*

The Roman letters *c* and *y* are hardly ever used in pure German words. They are mostly found in the words borrowed from French (*c, ch*), Latin (*c*) or Greek (*y*) and their pronunciation usually follows that of their original language. Whereas *c* has acquired the phonetic value of *ts* which is also the value of German *z* (= *ts*, centrum = Zentrum), the intervocalic sibilant *s* is pronounced as *z* (*lesen* = laizen); however combined with following *t* or *p*, it become *sh* (*stehen* = shteyen, *Spāten* = shpāten). German alphabet does not posses the sound of Sanskrit *ca* and Sanskrit *ja*. Wherever it needs these sounds, it builds them in a very cumbersome manner with four letters: *tsch* and *dsch*. The first combination is found in the word for German (*Deutsch*) itself and the borrowed word *jungle* (from Indian English) is written as *Dschungel*. The letter *j* in German has the value of *y* (i.e. Sanskrit *ya*) and the letter *g* the value of Sanskrit *ga;* never to be pronounced as *ja*, not even in combination with *i* or *e*. The letter *v* has mostly the value of *f* (*vorn* = forn) and the *z* is *ts*, as mentioned above. German also has an additional letter which it called *eszet* (*sz*), written more or less like the Greek β (beta) and pronounced like double *ss* with which it is now being often replaced.

German has three genders (m, f. and n.) and exactly like Sanskrit they are only grammatical genders having nothing to do with natural gender or reality. Both the definite and indefinite articles (*der, die, das/ein, eine*) used in the beginning of the substantives follow the gender of the substantive or the noun, not only in the Nominative but also in other cases. Thus we have in masculine Nom. *der Tisch* (the table), *den Tisch* (Accs.) *dem Tisch* (Dativ) and *des Tisches* (Genitive). In feminine *die Lampe* (the lamp, Nom.), *die Lampe* (Acc.), *der Lampe* (Dat.) and *der Lampe* (Gen.), Neuter has the same form for Nominative and Accusative cases, exactly like in Sanskrit (*das Buch, das Haus;* the book, the house; both in Nom. & Acc.).

In Sanskrit, the adjectives follow the gender and number of the substantive, the same phenomenon is seen in German too. German language has different forms of adjectives for different genders and different cases. It has four cases in contrast to seven in Sanskrit. The missing ones are Instrumental, Ablative and Locative, the sense of which is expressed through appropriate prepositions (*mit/durch, von, in/auf,* etc.). There are more than one way of forming a plural depending upon the nature and gender of the word and the most common of all endings added to the word are: *e, er, n/en.* The Dative of masculine and neuter genders has often an *e* in the end (e.g.: *im wald-e* in the forest) which is a remnant of IE *ai* (cf. Sans. *āya* in *devāya* or *ayai* in *ramāyai*). The Genitive in the masculine and neuter words is indicated with an added *s* (or *es*) to the word, very much like the addition of *s* for Genitive in English which nicely compares with the phenomenon of adding — *sya* in Sanskrit in masculine *a*-declination. Very often the word *von* (original meaning: *'from,' off, of*) is added to the word as a preposition which serves the purpose of Genitive (example: *Das Buch von Rāma* = Rāma's book).

To speak of the conjugation, the German has far less *tenses* and *modi* than Sanskrit, a feature shared by all modern languages. It has a *Present Indicative* — but no Present Continuous like English or Hindi, a regular Past or *Praeteritum,* a *Perfect* — very much similar to the structure of English or Hindi, a *Future* which is formed with the help of an auxiliary verb *werden* (to become), *Imperative, Optative* (rarely used) and a *Conjunctive* corresponding partially to Sanskrit Subjunctive (*hetumadbhūta* or *lṛṅ* of Pāṇini). There are a number of points of similarity in the conjugational system of Sanskrit and German to deal with which shall take us too far. But we may observe at least the following:

The ending of 3rd person singular of the Present Indicative is *t* in German (*er kommt, sie geht,* he comes, she goes), the ending for 3rd person pl. is *en,* both of these remind one of the Sanskrit endings *ti* (*bhava-ti*) and *anti* (*bhav-anti*). The 2nd person singular is formed in German with the addition of *st* (cf. Sans. *si*) and the plural with *t/et* which corresponds to Sanskrit *atha.* The 1st person singular in German has preserved the ending *e* (*ich komme,* I come) which is also the ending of the 1st person singular of the verbs of *ātmanepada* in Sanskrit (*ahaṁ seve/labhe*); the plural is again formed with *en,* i.e. has assimilated itself with the 3rd person pl. as the Hindi has done (*ve jāte hain/ham jāte hain*). Imperative 2nd person singular has no ending, exactly as in Sanskrit *parasmaipada* (e.g. German: *Geh* ! *Komm* ! Sanskrit: *gaccha, paṭha,* etc.) whereas the plural takes a *t* or *et* exactly as in Sanskrit (*kommt/arbeitet, gacch-ata, paṭh-ata*).

The *Perfect Participles* of the German verbs correspond exactly to the Participle-Perfects of Sanskrit formed with *ta/ ita* like *gata* (gone), *paṭhita* (learnt) with which can favourably be compared the German forms like *ge-lernt* (learnt), *ge-schickt* (sent), *ge-bracht* (brought), etc.; *ge* is here an additional prefix to mark the Perfect forms otherwise they shall get confounded with the forms of Present Indicative 3rd p.s. (e.g. *lernt*). These P.P. forms are used together with the forms of *haben* (=to have) or *sein* (to be, i.e. *ist, sind* — is/are, etc.) to build the Perfect. It reminds us of the formation of Present- or Past-Perfect forms built in Hindi with the auxiliary verb *honā* = to be (e.g. *gayā hai/gayā thā*) in Hindi. The most interesting point in this context is the preservation of a large number of n-perfect forms (i.e. forms of Participle Perfect which are not formed with a *t* (*ta* of Sanskrit) but by adding the suffix-ending *n (en)* to the verb whose internal vowel usually appears in a changed form, called

Ablaut in German, corresponding to the change of the character of Sanskrit vowel through *guṇa, vṛddhi* and *samprasāraṇa.* With the addition of the *kta*-suffix to Sanskrit roots, usually *samprasāraṇa* of the vowel takes place which has the reason in the *tá* being accented. However, in German the vowels can undergo much more variations in quality, like *i* becoming *a* and *u*: e.g. *singen, sang, gesungen;* (sing, sang, sung of English). In Sanskrit the n-perfect participle is rather uncommon and is found primarily in the roots ending with *d: bhid* > *bhinna, chid* > *chinna,* or in the verbs ending with long *ṝ*: *jṝ* > *jīrṇa, kṝ* > *kīrṇa,* also sporadically elsewhere: *lūna* (cut), *nir-vāṇa* (blown out), or *līna* (dissolved, submerged). In German there are nearly one hundred verbs which form their Past Participle with *n (en)* instead of with *t.* The former are called "strong" verbs and the latter "weak" verbs in German (as well as in English) grammar. Some examples are *gegangen, gekommen, geschrieben, gegeben, getrunken,* etc. meaning: gone, come, written, given and drunk in the same order.

The future tense in German is periphrasitc, i.e. it is formed by adding the conjugated forms of an auxiliary verb to the Infinitive (the basic form) of the main verb. This auxiliary verb is *werden* = to become, and if one wants to say "I shall go" or "I shall write," one has to say: "I become going" or "I become writing," i.e. *ich werde gehen* or *ich werde schreiben.* It immediately reminds us of the periphrastic future (*luṭ*) of Sanskrit with the forms like *gantāsmi* ('I am a goer' = I shall go), *kartāsi* ('thou art the doer'), where the *asmi* and *asi* forms of the root *as* (to be) are prominently visible, conjoined with an Agentive. In fact, the original Indo-European language did not have any future tense and it has been developed by each language separately. The regular *sya*-future *(lṛt)* of Sanskrit has its origin in the desiderative element *sa* (*s/sya*) added to the non-reduplicated form of the root (*kṛ* > *kariṣyati* = "he wants to do," i.e. he has the intention to do) which is conceptually the same as the English expression "I will do," because it simply means "I wish to do."

Since we are presently dealing with the verbs, a very important and a sort of unique feature of the German language needs to be highlighted here which has direct parallels in our Vedic Sanskrit.

It is known to the Vedic scholars that the all Prefixes (*upasargas*) of the Vedic languages (and their number is more than twenty which is the standard number of prefixes in the classical Sanskrit) are accented on any one of their syllables. Carrying an independent accent also means that they have an independent existence of their own. Now, strangely enough, the verb in the Principal or main clause of a sentence is totally unaccented in the Vedic language, which leads to the phenomenon that prefixes and verb-forms can remain separated and the verb can conveniently be put elsewhere, usually at the end of a sentence. Look, for example, at the following verse from a famous Rudrasūkta (*Ṛ**V*, II.33) of the *Ṛgveda*:

1. (a) *ā́ te pitarmarutāṃ sumnám etu* . . . ।
   (b) *abhí no vīró árvati kṣameta* . . . ।
2. *prá babhráve vṛṣabhā́ya śvitīcé*
   mahó mahī́m suṣṭutím īrayāmi ।

— *Ṛ**V* II.33.1 ac, 8 ab

In the first *pāda* of the first verse *ā* and *etu* are related together (= come !) but stand wide apart with another four words coming in between. Whereas the Prefix *ā́* is accented, the verb is not. Same phenomenon is observed in the second *pāda*. *Abhí* and *kṣameta* are separated by three words. The second verse delivers an extreme example where the sentence starts with an accented prefix but the verb, to which it belongs, is met with after travelling through six words at the end of the sentence (*prá* + *īrayami* = *prerayami*, I am directing) in an unaccented form.

The case is different in the subordinate clauses of a longer sentence where the prefix and the verb are joined together and the verb carries the main or *udātta* accent:

yá idáṁ dīrghám práyataṁ sadhástham
éko vimamé tribhír ít padébhiḥ ।
— *R̥V* I.154, 3

This is an adjective clause starting with *yaḥ* (who) the verb *mame* is joined with the prefix *vi* and carries the accent.

Now, compare it with a highly significant and, in a way, singular trait of German syntax which provides that whereas in the Principal clause the verb invariably occupies the *second place* in the sequence of the words (similar to English), in a Subordinate clause — whether a noun, an adjective or an adverb clause — it is always placed at the *end*. Note the following sentence:

Er schrieb mir einen langen Brief vor zwei Monaten, der aus unerklärlichen Gründen immer noch nicht angekommen ist.

He wrote me a long letter two months ago, which has not yet arrived due to inexplicable reasons.

In the Principal clause *Er . . . . . . Monaten,* the verb *schrieb* occupies the second place whereas in the following adjective clause the verb *angekommen ist* stands at the end and the order of the auxiliary verb *ist* is reversed with the Past Participle *angekommen* (i.e. instead of *ist angekommen, 'angekommen ist'*).

There is absolutely no doubt as to the fact that the key to this unique or at least unusual construction lies in the proper comprehension and explanation of the Indo-European sentence-accent which is preserved only in the syntax of the Vedic language, where the verb of the main clause remains unaccented but of the subordinate clause carries the accent.

German is very rich in prefixes. Their number must have been even more in ancient times because many of them have either developed themselves into pure prepositions (i.e. instead of becoming a part of the verb or verbal roots, they now govern nouns) or stand halfway carrying out the function of a verbal prefix as well as that of a preposition. Examples of this sort are *aus* (out), *durch* (through), *ab* (away, Sans. *apa*), *um* (around) *ueber* (over, above), *vor* (front/before), etc. In Sanskrit only a few suffixes have managed to partially function as prepositions. Some of the examples are *ā* (used with Ablative: *ā kailāsāt*), *adhi* (used with Locative, *adhi grāme,* much more frequent in this sense in the Vedic language: *yo deveṣu adhi deva ekaḥ, R̥V* X. 121.8; also builds indeclinable compounds: *adhikauśāmbi, adhivelam*) and *prati* (= against, towards; used with Accusative, *vr̥kṣaṁ vr̥kṣaṁ prati dyotate vidyut*).

Of the pure prefixes some are perpetually unaccented, hence always appear as conjoined with the verb, which carries the accent (German has only stress accent) and some receive accent when the emphasis lies on the meaning of the prefix and lose it to the verb when the verbal activity is to be emphasized. The suffixes *ver* and *er,* for example, are always found as parts of a verb or a verbal noun: *verbinden* (to join; Past. Part. *verbunden* = connected, joined), *verbieten* (to forbid, prohibit; Past Part. *verboten*) or *erfassen* (to grasp, comprehend; Past, Part. *erfasst*), *erfinden* (to invent; Past. Part. *erfunden*), *erledigen* (to carry out, finish a task; Past. Part. *erledigt*).

Note that all the forms of the Perfect are without the prefix *ge* which is added to the Perfect form when the verb is alone or the prefix is separable, but disappears when the prefix added to the Perfect form is inseparable.

The suffixes which are accented always remain separate from the verb and its conjugated form, such as *áb, án, áuf, zú,* and in a Principal clause they are put at the end of the sentence whereas the verbal form comes at the second place: Take, for example, the verb *áb-fliegen* (to fly off, take off), *Das Flugzeug flog nach langer Verspätung áb* ("the plane took off after a long delay"), *Das Flugzeug ist nach langer Verspätung ábgeflogen* ("the plane has taken off after a long delay"); *Ábflug* (departure, take-off). The examples for other accented prefixes are *án-schliessen* (to join), > *ángeschlossen* (p.p.), *Er schloss sich der Gruppe án* ("he joined the group"), *Ánschluss* (connection); *Zú-lassen* (to allow), *Das Gesetz laesst das nicht zú* (the law does not allow this), *Dies wurde mir nicht zúgelassen* ("it was not allowed to me").

I give two examples of suffixes which, when accented, are separable from the verb and, when unaccented, are joined to the verb without a *ge* inbetween which builds the Perfect forms:

Verb: *Ueber-führen (-fuehren* = to lead)

1. to ferry across a river, etc. (accent on Prefix)
2. to prove charges in a judicial proceeding (accent on verb)

1. (a) *Man fuehrte die Passagiere mit einem Boot úeber* (One/ Somebody ferried the passengers over in a boat to the other side.)

   (b) *Die Passagiere wurden úebergefuehrt* (The passengers were transported to the other side.)

2. *Der Angeklagte wurde seines Vergehens ueberfúehrt* (The court conclusively proved [convicted] the crime of the accused.)

The word *ueberfuehren* has thus two different meanings depending upon whether the prefix *ueber* (über) is accented or whether it is the verb, which is the carrier of the accent. When the prefix is accented, it has a separate existence and it is separable from the verb. In the second case, it is inseparably attached to the verb. We may take another example to illustrate this phenomenon:

Verb: *durch-setzen* (*durch* = through, setzen = to put)

1. to get something through, to put across something.
2. to be interspersed or infested with.

In the first case the prefix is to be accented and in the second the verb. In the first case, therefore, the prefix remains separable whereas in the second case it is inseparable from the verb. The examples are:

1. *Ich setzte in der Versammlung meinen Vorschlag dúrch* ("I put across my suggestion/opinion in the meeting, i.e. could get it accepted").
2. *Die Matratze ist mit Flöhen durchesétzt* (The mattress is thoroughly infested with fleas.)

Another example with the verb *weichen* (to become wet):

Die Wolldecke ist völlig durchwéicht (The blanket is totally drenched/soaked.)

It may thus be seen that the Indo-European accent, so nicely preserved in the Vedic language has definitely left some traces in the further development of its daughter languages. Many knotty problems of the grammatical structure and phonetics, etc. of the Indo-European languages can be solved — or at least better understood — through a comparative study of these languages with the ancient classical languages.

It may further be remarked that due to its rich vocabulary and a specific archaic character of its structure, German is very well suited for translation of Sanskrit texts and thanks to the untiring efforts of the German Indologists of the past 200 years (the first French translation of *Śākuntalam* by Chézy, based on the previous English translation of Sir Willione Jones, appeared towards the end of the eighteenth century which enchanted Goethe and inspired a whole new generation of German scholars to study Sanskrit!), many wonderful translations of Sanskrit texts, especially of Vedic works, are available in German which a Sanskrit scholar must see and use in order to become a solid Indologist.

8

Sanskrit-English Relations
Some Reflections

Makarand Paranjape

I

Introduction

THIS is not a learned paper but the edited transcript of my Valedictory Address at the conclusion of the Sanskrit Week celebrations at the Special Centre for Sanskrit Studies, Jawaharlal Nehru University. I have tried here to offer some thoughts and ideas on the relations between two languages — Sanskrit and English — that are so crucial to the shaping of modern India. Constraints of both time and resources, especially books and journal articles, have made it impossible for me to engage with some of the current thinking on the subject, though I do, in the passing, refer to some secondary material. My purpose here is rather more limited — to offer a few pointers to how this relationship might be investigated.

Let me start on a personal note. I am a Professor of English with very little knowledge of Sanskrit. So, it might seem rather odd that I have been asked to deliver the Valedictory Address in this week-long celebration of the Sanskrit Week, much of which has been a rich repast of lectures, talks, papers, and intellectual exchange. Unlike some of the other speakers, I come here not as an expert or even as a student, but as a supporter of Sanskrit, Saṁskṛti, and Sanskrit Studies. The three are, obviously related. Because, as we all know, Sanskrit is at once more *and* less than an ordinary language. It is less than an ordinary language because few use it as a mother tongue or language of communication today. But it would be a gross error to call it a "dead" language as some have tried to. It is not dead because it is the language of a living culture, a language which is the repository of a vast body of knowledge and wisdom, a language which is central to an understanding of who we are as Indians. Sanskrit is more than a language; it is a cultural system. As a carrier of culture, it is the fountainhead of our civilization or *saṁskṛti.* Sanskrit Studies includes the study of the language, literature, philosophy, and culture that are associated with the language. But in addition to all this Sanskrit Studies includes the study of India, Indian thought, and Indian civilization. To that extent, I feel that as a Professor of English in India I have both a stake and a responsibility in Sanskrit Studies. I shall try to define this interest a little more clearly later.

But both my presence and my purpose here should not be too hard to comprehend because as Dr Shashi Prabha Kumar has already told you, the very founder of this Centre, Professor Kapil Kapoor, is a Professor of English. To me, this is more eloquently symbolic of the relationship between English and Sanskrit than my presence here today. Yet, if Professor Kapoor is the founder, manager and coach of this team, I like to consider myself the twelfth man. Now, you know what the twelfth man does in a cricket team. He usually brings out the drinks. Or, if he is lucky, he gets to be the runner when some batsman is retired hurt. But the twelfth man never gets really to play, either to bowl or to bat. Here the funny thing is that against the rules of cricket, I have actually been called upon to bat today, something the twelfth man is unprepared for. As the literal tail ender, I hope you don't expect me actually to hit fours or sixes. It has happened before — this last minute substitution. I had to speak instead of Professor Kapoor himself in the inaugural session of another Sanskrit Studies seminar. And now I have to substitute for Professor Kutumba Shastry, again, at the eleventh hour, as the Valedictory Speaker. So you must pardon me if whatever I say is nonsense or more nonsense than sense. But I will try, in my own limited way, to say a few words on my topic, which is the relations between Sanskrit and English. And I shall also use my presence here to make a small point about this.

II

The Three Phases of the Sanskrit-English Encounter

At the outset of this section, which is the main part of my presentation, let me state what I will not do. I do not want to address this issue in purely linguistic terms as most of the previous speakers have done. For instance, to examine the lexical borrowings from Sanskrit to English, looking for common word origins, tracing English words to Sanskrit, and so on. Neither do I wish to examine the relations between Sanskrit and English in terms of phonology or syntax. Instead, I wish to examine the relationship between Sanskrit and English in terms of the two cultural systems they represent. I am more interested in the cultural, political, social, relationships between these two-language systems in India since roughly the nineteenth century. I believe this is possible, even useful, because we know that languages are not merely some systems of communication but they embody world-views, entire ways of understanding the universe.

To illustrate, consider the fact that this very discussion on Sanskrit, for Sanskrit, during the Sanskrit Week, is taking place mostly in English. As a student of English it is a matter of great interest that this continues even today, a fact that I shall revert to later. Of course, this can be traced back to that colonial encounter during which period the modern system of education was institutionalized in India. It is interesing to note in the passing that after the destruction of Indian universities, after the Islamic conquest of India, our new rulers did not invest greatly in higher education. True, there were madrasas and theological colleges, but no major universities were built by any of the powerful dynasties that ruled India from the twelfth to the nineteenth centuries CE. It took the British, after they had consolidated their rule in Bengal, to put some money into promoting learning. However, the amount spent on higher education during the Raj was rather limited so that from the founding of our first modern universities in 1857 to the end of the British empire in 1947, the total number of Indian universities did not exceed twenty. The real surge in higher education, research, and the spread of knowledge only occurred in independent India, which has today resulted in our getting closer to becoming the knowledge society we always were.

But let me go back to that first phase of the encounter between English and Sanskrit. We all know of the controversy that preceded Macaulay's infamous Minute of 1835, the Minute in which he declared that a single shelf of a good European library was worth all the literature of Arabia and India. The Minute influenced the legislation that institutionalized the study of English as a medium of higher education all over India. But there was debate for about fifteen or twenty years prior to that about what should be the language of higher education in India. We know that there was a division or battle between two factions which were called the Orientalists and the Anglicists. Of course, both these groups consisted of Englishmen, with some Indian supporters on the sidelines. But there was also a third, less visible, position of the Vernacularists, which was never properly articulated, let alone considered seriously. In this whole debate what we must remember is that several leading Indians in Calcutta supported the introduction of English. These included Raja Rammohun Roy. In his letter to Lord Amherst, Roy asks for modern European education with subjects such as anatomy and chemistry, not just English literature, which, according to Macaulay, was supposed to civilize us just as the Slavs were civilized by French or the Western Europeans were civilized by classical languages. Nowadays, some scholars are arguing that Macaulay, though an imperialist, had India's best interests at heart when he forced the issue by threatening to resign if English was not made the language of Indian higher education. Whatever be the case, English did triumph and Sanskrit and Persian lost the battle at that time.

The swiftness of the "demise" of Sanskrit knowledge would suggest that it was already weakened and enfeebled by centuries of suppression and starvation. Perhaps, there is also truth in the by now cliched criticism that Sanskritic education was the sole preserve of a certain class of people. Not being available to the rest of society, some of which had come into prominence with the advent of Islamic and British rule, Indian society as a whole was bound to suffer if higher learning was denied to all but the brāhmaṇas. Whatever the actual facts, some of which are no longer known or easily available, British policies created a new intelligentsia. The old order was eclipsed in a very short time. Sanskrit, the language of the Gods, was almost banished from Bhāratavarṣa. So the first phase of the relationship between English and Sanskrit was that of competition, even conflict. English won, Sanskrit lost. With the suppression of Sanskrit or the substitution of Sanskrit by English came the eclipse or demise of traditional Indian thought. The traditional Indian system of knowledge was completely different from modern knowledge system which we got from post-Enlightenment Europe. This was the first phase of the encounter.

There is a very interesting project called "Sanskrit Knowledge Systems on the Eve of Colonialism," which Professor Sheldon Pollock of the University of Chicago is leading (http://www.columbia.edu/itc/mealac/pollock/sks/papers/index.html). He wishes to understand the state of knowledge of traditional knowledge systems in India prior to the imposition of English. He believes that it is important to know what came before colonialism, not just what colonialism brought. The traditional Indian knowledge system had survived in different forms through the almost seven hundred years of Muslim rule in north India. Then how come under the British rule this system collapsed within a space of may be thirty or forty years? It was displaced so completely that only a few remnants here and there are still visible — the ancient *Pāṭhaśalā* system or the *Gurukula* system, for instance. So what happened? How did it happen? How did this collapse take place — this colossal collapse — and with it the possibilities of the loss of so much knowledge?

This is an ongoing problem because even if you want to study any discipline today including medicine, you will start with the Greeks, you will start with Hippocrates. There is no mention of Caraka or Suśruta. Why? We know that Greek medicine may actually be Indian medicine in another guise because many of the principles and practices are the same. Indian knowledge systems, so vibrant and fecund, have been completely wiped out from all so-called international or Western histories of knowledge. This is of course a different issue, a different problem, but surely the collapse of these systems in India under colonialism had something to do with this later marginalization. Without digressing too much let me just repeat that during the first phase of the encounter between Sanskrit and English, the latter ended up totally dominating the former. English education engendered an almost total reaction against all forms of Indian or Hindu traditions. In fact, there is a joke about how one of the members of Young Bengala, after waking up in the morning, when his father asked him to bow before the family deity, Kālī, he said, "Good morning, Madam," before going off to Hindu College. Michel Madhusudan Dutt, considered the "first" modern poet of Bengal, wrote in an early essay that the Hindu was like a rotten tree trunk that had to be cut off. (This essay in now available in the *Vintage Anthology of Indian Writing* edited by Amit Choudhury.)

Let us now come to the second phase of the relationship between Sanskrit and English.

I would like to call this the phase of contact. What happens now is that there is an immense influence of Sanskrit on English. There is an interesting book which details one aspect of this contact. Again, let me offer a very short, not necessarily accurate, glance upon this book whose title contains the interesting phrase "Guru English." The author, Srinivas Aravamudan, who teaches at Duke University, argues that in the nineteenth century a new form of English was created by and large by translations from Sanskrit into English. This was a language also fashioned by a number of spiritual teachers like Swami Vivekananda and Sri Aurobindo who used the English language to convey ideas, experiences, and thoughts which were traditionally Indian, even spiritual, therefore, not necessarily available or accessible to Europeans. He calls this language, "Guru English," a term he uses pejoratively. But there are other ways of describing this new kind of English, developed specifically to communicate the higher Hindu thought to the rest of the world. My teacher of Linguistics, Professor Braj Kachru characterizes it as the conferring of the *yajñopavīta,* the sacred thread, on English. And thus English become *dvija,* twice born, fit to express a vast array of experience of the spiritual kind. While English writers, including the so-called metaphysical poets, did write on religious themes, this contact of English with the Sanātana *paramparā* brought a new dimension to the language. Thus, enriched English, and through English many other traditions of the world, came into contact with the wisdom of India. Not just Yoga or Dharma, but so many words from Sanskrit are now a part of standard English. In this way, through Guru English, English become a carrier of not just Sanskrit but of *Saṁskṛti,* not just a competitor, supplanter and destroyer of Sanskrit.

That is why this phase of contact can also be called a phase of synergy or mutuality. English borrowed from Sanskrit and was able to access and express the especially rich cultural storehouse of knowledge which Sanskrit embodies. Perhaps, this, and similar such borrowing, helped English attain its present position of the unrivalled global language, the language not just of power and of commerce, but also of knowledge.

We must also not forget that in the second phase many of the Orientalists contributed immensely to the revival of Sanskrit. A new method of studying Sanskrit — good, bad is a different issue — was developed by these Europeans. Modern, philological methods began to be adopted for the first time to study oral traditions. Gradually, our own tradition of memorization gave way to a new kind of textualtiy. For better or worse, a lot of Indian texts began to be reconstructed in the nineteenth century. Take, for instance, the *Nāṭyaśāstra*. This text was almost lost. The full text, at any rate, was neither well known nor easily available. When Sir William Jones translated *Śākuntalam,* he probably heard of it. I think he mentions in his Preface that he has been told that there is such a work but he has not been able to find it. This was in 1783. Jones, apparently, could only find scraps of it. Actually it was only in the 1920s that the first full edition was brought out. The case of many other texts is similar. It was with the help of the European orientalists that these texts first began to be edited and published. This was one of the contributions of Western oriental scholarship. If we had never been colonized, it is conceivable that we would have done this ourselves, found our own modernity. But in actuality, because of, and during, the colonial encounter, India's great knowledge traditions began to be recast and retrieved. This work was then carried on by Indians also. So we have a debt to acknowledge to the Western orientalists. It is a fact that many of the knowledge texts were scattered. Of course, this is not the first time in our history when such a scattering took place. Our society, as Professor Kapoor reminds us, had a mechanism of re-gathering and reconstituting our scattered — knowledge systems. Professor Kapoor calls this mechanism the Vyāsa *paramparā.* The loss and recovery of texts and traditions happen periodically in India. There is a rupture, it can be an invasion, it can be a flood, as the mythical flood that is a part of our heritage too. Whatever the cause, texts are lost — but they are brought together again by a process that is nothing short of miraculous.

In this latest of recoveries, some Westerners helped us immensely. They were the agents of the reconstitution. Their contribution cannot be either dismissed or undermined. Take for instance the simple scholarly tool of a Sanskrit dictionary. Even today the most consulted dictionary is that of Monier-Williams'. I know that there is a project in Deccan College, Pune, to create the standard Sanskrit dictionary, but when will this work ever see the light of day? It may turn out to be the best dictionary in the world, but, at the rate they are progressing, they may not finish in the next two thousand years — of course, we have a millennial notion of time, so what do another couple of thousand years matter? Be that as it may. What I want to stress was that by the end of the second phase of the encounter, Indian scholars gradually begin to take control of Sanskrit Studies, with the help of Sanskritists and scholars in other disciplines in India and elsewhere.

But more relevant to our topic, I think it is in this third phase of contact. This may be said to start around Independence and is still ongoing. Now for the first time, we have the opportunity of English working in the service of Sanskrit rather than being a competitor. This can happen because English has already won, so there is no real tussle. At least some among us who earn their livelihood from English would like to consider ourselves as supporters or helpers of both Sanskrit and *saṁskṛti*. There are many ways in which we do this. Through translations, through other forms of study, through bringing out critical editions, scholars and teachers of English are helping Sanskrit.

But here we need to make a distinction between Sanskrit and *saṁskṛti*. English seems to be helping in the latter, but how is it supporting the former? The language itself can only spread when more and more people start using it. Here English is not going to be of great help. We need a conscious Sanskrit bilingualism, perhaps. So that Sanskrit is learned in addition to other languages such as English or Hindi, which are livelihood languages. This is because the Israeli model is not likely to work in India. There they reconstructed Hebrew and now everyone uses it. I have taken some classes in spoken Sanskrit — it's a lot of fun. I think it is possible to make this form of Sanskrit popular. Indeed, they do talk about spreading Sanskrit *gṛhe gṛhe*. We cannot rule out this actually happening, but unfortunately, this seems very unlikely. Mainly because the state would have to play an active role from which we are at present very, very far. In fact, in the inaugural session of this very Sanskrit Week, a distinguished Member of Parliament and member of our JNU court himself said that Sanskrit is associated with caste-oppression in India. I think it is time that we utterly rejected such accusations. As Professor Kapil Kapoor reminds us again and again, it is not languages which oppress, but people who use languages do. If some people who used Sanskrit were oppressors, we must not take that out on the language. By that token, we should stop using English, French, or Arabic or Persian, because people using these languages colonized and oppressed others. Much of the spread of Sanskrit and of *saṁskṛti* was through cultural osmosis, not by imperialism or conquest. This was a case of "pull" more than of "push," to use Rajiv Malhotra's metaphor. *Saṁskṛti* was demanded, "pulled" in by people in different parts of the world, not pushed down their throats. So, as long as we continue to harbour such ideas I don't think any real progress in favour of Sanskrit can be made. But, my hope is that we will blunder through and it seems to me that the Englishwallahs are more pro-active and more vociferous, more kṣatriya-like in the promotion of Sanskrit sometimes than the Sanskritwallahs themselves, who tend to be very feeble and very soft spoken. We English professors can tom-tom the drum of *saṁskṛti* with greater enthusiasm and alacrity. Today, we need both Sanskrit and *saṁskṛti.* In the latter, English can serve Sanskrit, but in order to promote the former, Sanskritists will themselves have to work harder, supported of course by enlightened legislation and state power.

III

I think I have said whatever I needed to say. I just want to end by acknowledging what a great pleasure it has been to be here, to thank the Centre for making the mistake of calling me again. With such warm and indulgent audiences, I don't mind being the twelfth man, even being asked to bowl or bat occasionally for the Sanskrit team. To listen to Professor Lokesh Chandra, who spoke before me, is always enlightening. Thinking of Sanskrit, I am reminded of what he once told me. Sanskrit is like the thread that holds the pearls of Indian culture together. If the thread is snapped, the pearls get scattered; in fact, the necklace itself ceases to exist. Without Sanskrit, then, there is no *saṁskṛti* or at any rate, a very diminished and impoverished *saṁskṛti* for us Indians. In order to serve the larger cause of global culture, Sanskrit and English need to work together, the former yielding some of its wisdom and ideas to the latter, which can then spread it far and wide, for the benefit of all humanity. The latter may also enrich the former with its resources and power, especially in its continuing quest for truth and knowledge.

References

Aravamudan, Srinivas, *Guru English: South Asian Religion in a Cosmopolitan Language.* Princeton, NJ: Princeton UP, 2005.

Chaudhuri, Amit, ed., *The Vintage Book of Modern Indian Literature.* New York: Vintage, 2004.

Kapoor, Kapil, "Loss, Recovery, and Renewal of Texts in Indian Traditions." *Evam: Forum on Indian Representations.* 3: 1 & 2 (2004).

Malhotra, Rajiv, "Geopolitcs and Sanskrit Phobia." 5 July 2005. http://www.sulekha.com/blogs/blogdisplay.aspx? cid=4798#

Pollock, Sheldon, *The Language of the Gods in the World of Men: Sanskrit, Culture, and Power in Pre-modern India.* Berkeley: University of California Press, 2006.

9

Sanskrit in Indonesia

J. Gonda

EVERY student of linguistic science who does not deliberately, or from an innate tendency to onesidedness, limit his activities to the small domain of what is sometimes called "pure linguistics" — which has then almost nothing to do with the history of human civilization — will readily agree that the study of the problems connected with the influence of one language on another is one of the most attractive divisions of his particular province of knowledge. The motives which cause foreign elements to find access to another speech community, the various ways in which such a community which has come under the influence of another idiom reacts by receiving some foreign elements and by rejecting others, by differentiating loans from equivalent indigenous terms, sometimes even by absorbing so many foreign speech-units that its vocabulary may justly be called "mixed" — these problems and others bearing upon the phenomena usually labelled by such terms as "cultural or intimate borrowing," "substratum," "language mixture," "substitution" are of outstanding interest for any linguist who realizes that the vicissitudes of our languages are indissolubly connected with human history in general.

These problems accordingly play a large role in books on general linguistics and in the discussions of linguistic experts.[1]

Every speech-community learns from its neighbours, whether they speak another dialect of the same language or use an entirely different language. Merchandise and other objects pass from one region to the other, and so do technical procedures, tales and traditions, fashions of conduct, knowledge and even institutions and religious beliefs and rites, in short, cultural achievements of any description. Together with these objects, traditions and practices, the words by which they are named often spread from community to community. As a rule the moment of borrowing cannot be ascertained; the less so as the first introduction into a new area seldom leads to permanent reception, and many repetitions by the same or other speakers through whom the spreading comes about are needed to effect that result — if it is effected at all.

---

1. See, e.g. H. Paul, *Prinzipien der Sprachgeschichte*[5], (A.S. Halle 1920), ch. 22; O. Jespersen, *Language* (London 1992, etc.), ch. 11; L.H. Gray, *Foundations of Language* (New York 1939), Index, p. 470; W.L. Graff, *Language and Languages* (New York-London 1932), Index, p. 474; L. Bloomfield, *Language* (1933, London edition), ch. 25ff; E. Sapir, *Language* (New York 1921), p. 205ff.; O. Jespersen, *Growth and Structure of the English Language* (Leipsic), see Index; C. Moller, *Zur Methodik der Fremdwortkunde* (Aarhus 1933); E. Haugen, *Problems* of *Bilingualism, Lingua* II, p. 271ff. Special studies are, for instance: K. Vollers, *Beiträge zur Kenntnis der lebenden arabischen Sprache in Aegypten*, II *Über Lehnwoerter, Zeitschrift d. deutschen morgenländischen Gesellschaft* 50 (1896), p. 607ff., and 51 (1897), p. 291ff.; J.J. Salverda de Grave, *De Franse woorden in het Nederlands*, Verhandelingen Kon. Akademiev. Wetenschappen, Amsterdam, afd. Letterkunde, NR. VII, (1906); B.H. Wind, *Les mots italiens introduits en Français au* XVIe *siècle* (Thesis Amsterdam 1928); A. Stene, *English Loanwords in Modern Norwegian, A Study of Linguistic Borrowing in the Process* (London-Oslo 1945); E. Hellquist, *Det svenska ordförrådets ålder och ursprung* (Lund 1920-30).

Who are the persons or groups of persons, by whose intermediary the process of borrowing is, as a rule, brought about? Merchants, colonizers, military or other occupants, emigrants and immigrants, missionaries, learned people and similar categories, be it as individuals or in groups are usually credited with this activity. And not without truth, for, to mention only one detail, the use of at least a few foreign words is no doubt stimulated by the need for transacting business with tradesmen of another tongue or by any attempt to exert influence on people who do not understand languages other than their own. But such forms of contact, be they military or commercial, religious or literary, only give, like all other historical events, occasion for borrowing, they do not explain why and how a particular word has become popular in its new environment, whereas others failed to take root.

There must be a considerable element of truth in the verdict given by Hermann Paul, that the existence of a (more of less) bilingual group (the mother-tongue of which is the borrowing language) serving as the vehicle of interlingual influence must be regarded as indispensable to any borrowing on a large scale.[2] Speaking quite generally, bilingual individuals or groups come into being under the influence of linguistic pressure, that is, that special type of social, economic, political, intellectual or other cultural pressure which urges these persons or groups to be in harmony with the linguistic behaviour of a more important or more influential community. When two languages come into contact the ways in which they exert influence one on the other are, as far as we know now and without referring to particulars, proportionate to the degree of linguistic pressure. The many immigrant languages in the United States of America have, to mention only one instance,

2. Paul, o.c. p. 391ff., Haugen, o.c. p. 279.

been intensively affected by English, but have, on the other hand, left only local and evanescent traces in that general language of the states.[3]

Bilingual persons, including those whose knowledge of the foreign tongue is far from perfect, are, for reasons which will be specified hereafter, easily tempted to use foreign words without intending, as a rule, to introduce them for good and all into their own mother-tongue. Many repetitions, however, and the prestige of the speakers — which may be attributable to their very knowledge of the language of the "higher" community — give their neologisms a chance of spreading. Thus foreign words find their way into their native tongue when they speak it among themselves, and into the speech of their monolingual relations and companions. What terms penetrate, in this way, into larger parts of the community, depends on circumstances, but such factors as social pressure or solidarity, careerism, tradition or national self-consciousness, and the needs of understanding usually regulate, check or further the infiltration of foreign elements.

The tendency to adopt words from other languages is due to a variety of causes. The main factors which generally help to bring about a permanent adoption, and which did not fail to contribute to that process also in the particular case of the Indo-Indonesian contact, may be described as follows:

First, many instances of borrowing are due to the fact that the adopting language had no terms of its own to denote the foreign objects or ideas which were introduced or imported by various ways of contact. As a rule the name and the thing or idea known by that name are imported at the same time. That does not mean that all mutual relations between two

3. See also Haugen, p. 279ff.

nations or communities, all wanderings of inventions and institutions have left their traces in the language of those who were less fertile in ideas and inferior to others in certian economical respects, for the resources of their own language to fill up gaps in its vocabulary, so that ideas and objects thus far nameless can be expressed and denoted, often enable the members of the "importing" community to do without any foreign speech-unit. But, also when it would have been possible to find an adequate indigenous idiom or to coin one, the habit of seeking first in the mother-tongue is not natural to all, and is often easily counteracted. In this way the English and other European peoples already early learnt such words as *wine* (Lat. *vinum*), *mint* (Lat. *moneta* "coin, money"), *pound* (Lat. *pondō* "by weight") from the Roman and Latin-speaking merchants, *fresco, miniature* (It. *miniatura*) and other terms of art and architecture from Italian, *tea, rice, camphor* and names of other such products from the peoples of the East.

In the second place a foreign word may help the person speaking to be understood in a more accurate and convincing way, in finding the most adequate and forcible expression, in making manifest slight differences and delicate distinctions which he is, or feels, not able to express by means of indigenous words. This does not necessarily imply that the lending vocabulary is richer and that it enables those who use it hereditarily to express all these subtle distinctions. The very fact that a word impresses us as foreign or borrowed is often sufficient to furnish it with a particular emotional or expressive value. Compare, in English, such words as *abstruse, poltroon, pusillanimity, courtesan, riparian, donah, boss, nabob* and many others. Other loans have, in the community which welcomed them, only a restricted and, hence, more concise meaning, which is not only useful to the specialized scientist, but often also to the man in the street: in Dutch the Latin *examen* only means "examination (in schools and universities)." In this way the borrowing idiom not rarely gains possession of a useful set of half-synonyms, which sometimes represent etymological variants of the same word in derivatives of the same base: cf., e.g. Eng. *hearty* and *cordial* (from Late Latin *cordialis*); Dutch *blauw* "blue" and *bleu* (from French) which do not different shades of colour; Eng. *land* and *country* (from Old French and Low Latin); *ground* and *soil* (from Old French); *folk, people* (from Old French *pople,* Lat. *populus*); *population* (from Late Latin *population(em), populace* (from French *populace* < Italian *popolaccio, popolazzo,* from *popolo* "the people" which is the Latin *populus*).

In the third place, instances are not rare of borrowed words meeting a tendency towards ease, brevity and efficiency. Not only in the abstract domain, but also in denoting concrete objects one term of foreign origin frequently proves equivalent to a phrase or periphrasis in hereditary terms. Is not the French *parachute* "an umbrella-like apparatus held by one leaping from a height" in English, and will its "name" not be much longer if we also avoid using the Italian word *umbrella* and the Latin *apparatus*? And have such words as *risk* (from Fr. *risque*) and *foreign* (from OFr. *forain*), which have become completely naturalized, not materially contributed to enriching the English language? But Jespersen[4] and other authors are no doubt right in contending that mental laziness and regard to their own momentary convenience often lead speakers (and writers!) to retain even technical or uncommon foreign words, lacking also the opportunity to draw from the source of natural inventiveness which lavishly supplies other, and often comparatively less educated, members of their community with a variety of new words.

4. Jespersen, *Growth and Structure,* §130 and 157.

It is, further, a well-known fact that foreign words are often regarded as more refined. This is only what might be expected, the lending idiom as a rule, and especially when this case presents itself, enjoying a certain prestige, and the culture it conveys being considered worthy of imitation. It is interesting to see that the use of unnaturalized loans sometimes enhances the self-consciousness of the person speaking, that foreign titles and other terms often essentially add to the dignity and superiority of the persons in connection with whom they are used. In Dutch and German many such French words as *coiffeur* "hairdresser," *restaurant* (which are also English) must be ranged in this category, which borders on the next that includes the not less well-known instances of loan-words replacing unpleasant terms, which as a rule means those denoting unpleasant situations, indecent or dreadful objects or ideas. Many peoples have availed themselves of this euphemistic function of loans: in Dutch the Fr. *déconfiture* is a very polite term for "bankruptcy," and young ladies use English swear-words: *good gracious*, etc. Moreover, foreign words often gratify the desires, nay the whims of many speakers who without any other cause than the charm of the exotic resort to uncommon, but sweet-sounding or learned imports.

In the history of this language and others there have been periods characterized by an extraordinarily frequent use of words derived from a then highly appreciated foreign vocabulary. In the seventeenth and eighteenth centuries it had become the vogue in the upper circles of Germany, Denmark and the Netherlands to use hosts of French words, many of which found their way also to the other classes; but not an insignificant part of them has now completely disappeared.[5]

5. See, e.g. S. Ferwerda, *Taalzuivering en taalzorg in Denemarken*, Utrecht University, 1950.

In consideration of these tendencies we arrive at the conclusion that the word itself and the object denoted by it in its original language do not so much contribute to its success as a loan-word as the way in which the borrowing community takes advantage of its being imported.[6]

As far as may be gathered from the incomplete research into this particular subject,[7] the elements borrowed by different, and even non-adjacent languages and dialects from a great and prominent speech-community, the influence of which they all underwent for a definite period, tend to be strikingly similar. Here the question arises whether peoples living under the same or nearly corresponding conditions, when coming under the influence of a higher civilization, likewise tend to adopt a fairly identical or similar part of the "superior" vocabulary. It might be an attractive task to compare, from this point of view, all the borrowings from Sanskrit in various languages. However, conditions are very different in the Buddhist countries upon which India has exerted a lasting spiritual effect, in Indonesia where the direct relations with Sanskrit have been broken off centuries ago, and in those countries which had only a superficial contact with India's great culture. Drawing a smaller circle, we must confess that the amount of loans in Old-Javanese which cover as good as all ranges of interest, knowledge and civilization, and the much more limited, Indian vocabulary of Malay do not admit of a fruitful comparison. Moreover, the Malay community has not entirely been excluded from Javanese civilization; its language has adopted Javanese elements. The conditions under which Sanskrit elements reached the other parts of the Archipelago (inclusive of the Philippine Islands)

6. See, e.g. o.c. Wind, p. 12.

7. I refer to Salverda, de Grave, o.c., p. 120f. and o.c. Wind, p. 14.

and the neighbouring countries of Further India have likewise greatly varied, their reception proceeded along entirely different lines and the results of the process of borrowing differ to such an extent that it would serve no useful purpose to compare the exact number of Indian elements and these elements themselves in all the idioms. Moreover, we shall have occasion in one of the chapters of this book to dwell upon the fact that many IN languages owe their small amount of Indian terms almost exclusively to Malay, which has passed on part of its Indian vocabulary — and it can be added at once: in many cases largely the same part — to other languages of the Archipelago. It might, then, be of interest to compare the Sanskrit words in the main languages of the Philippines, Malay and the continental language of Further India, Cam, which, while being nearly related to the idioms of Indonesia proper, has adopted many Indian elements. However, the route followed by these elements in reaching Tagalog and Bisaya has, — how could it have been otherwise? — led to the Philippines via Cambodia and Malaysia. Yet, it may be of some interest to dwell for a moment on the number and the character of the Indian loans in Tagalog, Cam and Malay, and to make some provisional and superficial remarks in connection with the problem under discussion. It may safely be said that the vast majority of the 175 Tagalog words collected by Kern in his list of Tagalog loans from Sanskrit[8] is also well known in Malay, the greater part of the remainder being represented in Old-Javanese. That the difference of environment produced many differences of semantic development can be left out of consideration here. A good many of the terms which both languages have in common have succeeded in naturalizing.

8. H. Kern, *V.G.*, X, p. 251ff. (first published in 1880). See also chapter II.

The shorter list of Sanskrit words (± 100 terms[9]) in another Philippine idiom, Bisaya, while having a large part of its elements in common with Tagalog, also comprises many terms which found way also into Malaysia, the Gayo and Achehnese communities of Sumatra, the Sundanese territory in the west of Java, etc. Such words as Tag. Bis. *balita* "tidings," *basa* "to read, recite," *budhi* in Bis. "teaching," in Tag. *buḍhí* "inclination, design, treachery": Mal. *budi* "character"; Bis. *halága*, Tag. *halagá* "price": Mal. *harga* "price"; Bis. *katya* "glass, crystal": Mal. *kaca* "glass"; Bis. *puasa* "to fast": Mal. idem (also Skt. *vṛtta* (वृत्त)"what has happened, news"; *vāca* (वाच)"reciting," *buddhi* (बुद्धि) "mind," *argha* (अर्घ) "price"; *kāca* (काच) "glass"; *upavāsa*-(उपवास) "fast" are amongst the most widely scattered splinters of the tree of the Indian language in the Archipelago. Among the much more frequent Indian elements in Cam — in the dictionary by Aymonier and Cabaton[10] they run to about 700 items — a large part of the well-known Malay loans from Sanskrit recur. Yet it is worth mentioning — but not always easy to explain — that a number of the commonest Sanskrit words have been welcomed by Cam and Old-Javanese, but rejected by Malay and modern Javanese: *aṅgula* (अंगुल) "finger, thumb, a thumb's breadth": in Cam "a span (the breadth of the hand, as a measure)"; *āyus* (आयुस्) "life, vital power": Cam *āyuḥ; tārā* (तारा) "star," *jala* (जल) "water": Cam *jal* "id.," which apparently could not survive in Java and Malaysia beside *jala* (<Skt. *jāla.* (जाल) "casting-net."

The so-called "external" or "cultural" borrowing, is, as a rule, an almost one-sided process, in that the "superior" community places its special terms of art and science, commerce and administration, technics and fashion at the disposal of

9. H. Kern, *V.G.*, X, p. 279ff. (first published in 1871).

10. E. Aymonier et A. Cabaton, *Dictionnaire Cam-Français,* Paris, 1906.

the "inferiors." Whereas Mediaeval English borrowed hosts of French words, it has exerted practically no influence on that continental language. When Italian arts, music, architecture and painting became known and highly esteemed in the countries of the West, such musical terms as *lento, piano,* etc. found admission to the vocabularies of the French, the Dutch, the English. On closer investigation, however, this borrowing turns out a mutual process: when the English lavishly spread their technical and economical terms over the Indian peoples, these gave them a smaller number in return, mainly denoting things, phenomena or patterns of acting (*yoga, puṇḍit, rajah, puttee, gunny, bungalow*) but also some others (e.g. *loot* "plunder"). In a similar way Sanskrit has, already very early, adopted a very limited number of Indonesian terms, and here it will be convenient to dwell for a moment on these "reverse" loans.

The Indonesian words imported into Ancient Indo-Aryan are far from being easy to discern, because their structure is nearly the same as that of the Austro-Asiatic languages, which not only comprise the Annamese and the so-called Mon-Khmer idioms in Further India, but also the Muṇḍa or Kol groups in India itself. It has even been assumed that this group may be part of a greater family of languages comprising also the Indonesian idioms.[11] It is a matter of common knowledge that the latter groups are generally held to have spread in earlier times over much greater parts of India, that scholars have, not rarely with good reason, tried to trace the origin of

11. I refer to my "Austrisch en Arisch" (Utrecht 1932 with copious bibliographical notes.); C. Régamey, *Bibliographie analytique des travaux relatifs aux éléments anaryens dans la civilisation et les langues de l'Inde, Bulletin de l'Ecole Française d'Extrême-Orient* XXXIV (1935), p. 429ff.; S.K. Chatterji, *Indo-Aryan and Hindi,* Ahmedabad, 1942, ch. II.

elements of the Sanskrit vocabulary to this Austro-Asiatic substratum.[12] It goes, however, without saying that we shall do well to consider Sanskrit words, the Austrian origin of which is probable, as loans from the Muṇḍa group whenever India's plants and products and all other objects and ideas to be found in India are concerned. Words like *campaka* (चम्पक) "the *campaka* flower" and *laṅgala, lāṅgula* (लंगल, लांगुल), "plough"[13] are, notwithstanding their Indonesian occurrence, of Muṇḍa rather than of Annamite, Malacca or Indonesian origin — if at least they are rightly considered Austrian. The name of a well-known commodity such as camphor, which was produced in Indonesian regions (Formosa, Sumatra), may on the other hand be derived directly from IN. sources: in Malay and cognate languages *kapūra* means "camphor, chalk, or lime," covering a variety of matter, from fine camphor (the best quality was of old gathered in the Sumatran Baros) to cement and slaked lime. The Arabs were already early acquainted with both the substance and its name: their *kāfūra* came as *camfre, camphor,* etc. to the Europeans. The usual etymology of the Arab word "from the Skt. *karpūra* (कर्पूर)" must, however, in my opinion, be rectified; the Arab word as well as the Sanskrit *karpūra* were, on account of the *r* in the word itself and the character of the ancient trade between Arabia and the Far East (which was conducted by means of intermediaries, or at least availed itself of the Indian seaports[14]) imported directly from the Far East. Another word which, together with the commodity it denotes, seems to have been brought to India directly from Indonesia or the adjacent regions of Further India, is the Skt.

12. See my paper "Campaka" in *BKI, CV,* 1949, p. 137ff.

13. See J. Przyluski, in *Mémoires de la Société de Linguistique de Paris,* XXII, p. 205ff. (see also P. Ch. Bagchi, *Pre-Aryan and Pre-Dravidian in India,* Calcutta, 1929, p. 3ff).

14. For particulars refer to my *Austrisch en Arisch*, p. 23.

aguru "the fragrant aloe wood," which, in part of the IN. tongues is called *garu*, whereas the Sanskrit form has, to complicate matters, found its way into ancient Java.[15] The ancient Indians knew very well that this *aguru* or agallochum was "a produce of the country of the "barbarians," because they called it also *anāryaja* (अनार्यज). The clove tree, to give a third instance, is indigenous in the Moluccas and its IN. name *lawaṅ* well known in Malay, Javanese and other idioms; should not the Skt. *lavaṅga* (लवंग) and the Tamil *lawaṇa* be considered as imported from Indonesia[16]? Now and then, however, we come upon etymological puzzles defying all attempts to solve them, when the meaning does not point to a particular region where the object denoted especially belonged, and at the same time the outward form of the word is ambiguous.

Matters become complicated when the lending and borrowing communities live in the same country or region within the boundaries of the same geographical or political territory. Though, as a result of conquest or colonization this so-called "intimate" borrowing is, as a rule, predominantly an infiltration from the language of the upper group to that of the lower, it cannot be regarded as exclusively one-sided.[17] It has, moreover, justly been observed that this type of borrowing — which, of course, cannot always be distinguished from the other which is sometimes styled "cultural" borrowing — very often extends to speech-forms

---

15. Ibidem., p. 17f.

16. See my remarks in *Acta Orientalia*, X, p. 326ff.).

17. Bloomfield, Language, p. 461 soon corrects his first statement ("Intimate borrowing is one-sided") which might be understood as too strongly worded. In really bilingual communities the substratum seems to exercise a more thorough influence than consists in providing names for exotic things and the like.

which are not connected with cultural novelties. Whereas, for instance, the influence of the indigenous "substratum" on South-American Spanish has greatly been exaggerated and modern scholars have become more guarded in their statements,[18] the impact of Spanish upon these American idioms has been tremendous. Not only a large Spanish vocabulary has been adopted for things unknown until the European invasion, but these have also come to be used as though they were true indigenous stems: in the Nahuatl *oqui formar-oque* "they transformed him," *formar* is Spanish. Among the loan-words we even find terms of relationship, words denoting animals, plants, clothing, food, social relations (even *amigo* "friend"), and, further, numerals, verbs, particles, and other elements which are comparatively seldom subject to borrowing (such as affixes), not to mention words bearing upon religion, political organization, weights and measures.[19] "Above all, Spanish has eclipsed the prestige of every aboriginal language and dialect, not one of which serves any more to express an elevated or commanding idea."[20] We can easily imagine that a considerable part of the large amount of Sanskrit words in some Indonesian languages must be put down to intimate borrowing. And this, apart from the scantiness of our historical information, no doubt essentially contributes to the complexity of the problem with which we are confronted when studying the influence of Sanskrit on, say, Javanese.

Sounds, word-forms, grammatical structure of the idioms whcih have come into contact either by way of "external" or

18. See B. Malmberg, *L'espagnol dans le Nouveau Monde: Problème de linguistique générale, Studia Linguistica,* I, p. 79ff., Lund, 1947 and 1948 and II, p. 1ff.

19. See F. Boas, "Spanish elements in modern Nahuatl," in Todd Memorial volumes, I, New York, 1930.

20. W.J. Entwistle, *The Spanish Language,* London, 1936, p. 238f.

by "intimate" borrowing or by the former and the latter one after the other, or in cooperation, differ considerably. The foreign elements not rarely violate the patterns of the adopting language. Therefore, adaptation of the morphologic structure and of the phonetic pattern is, as a rule, effectuated. And we may, generally speaking, say that the more popular loan-words become, the more they are treated as though they were natives. Who would, without being so taught, know that such common English words as *wine, press, priest, large, frail* have been introduced by foreigners? The adaptation and assimilation of foreign sounds and words presents many interesting problems, to which, when bearing upon the spread of Sanskrit in the Archipelago, attention will be drawn in one of the following chapters of this volume. In studying these we should not lose sight of the fact that loan-words are, like native speech-elements, subject to the phonetic and other changes which occur in the borrowing idiom after the adoption. But this stage of evolution cannot always be sufficiently distinguished from the adaptive changes which take place in connection with the adoption. These changes, however, especially affect the phonetic aspect of the loans, for grammatically they are subjected to the system of their new linguistic environment, though in a minority of cases a simultaneous reception of several foreign forms may prevent them from being completely adapted. Thus the Greek plural in *-a* has been kept in *data, phenomena,* etc. when used in English. And sometimes the original grammatical form is preserved beside the native ending or affix: compare, in English, *genii* and *geniuses* (from the same Latin singular *genius,* with a differentiated meaning).

From the point of view of the historian of human civilization the study of loan-words is of outstanding interest. They reflect the degree of intercourse between one people and the other and they render perceptible the direction and other aspects of cultural borrowing. A thorough research into the borrowed elements in English, for instance, shows us what other peoples have taught, and have brought to, the inhabitants of the British Islands: the Scandinavians could import a number of terms referring to war and more particularly to the navy, because the English were, at the time, inferior to them in ship-building,[21] the Italians numerous terms of music and other arts, whereas the French have, in recent times, lent many words in the sphere of women's clothes, cosmetics, and other luxuries and fancy articles. The hundreds of English words which, through the activity of native bilinguals in the last century, have spread over many European and non-European countries largely refer to the fields of sports (*team, fair play, golf*); travel, railroad and other engineering, motoring, shipping (*globetrotter, trawler, steward;* trade (*bestseller, boom, pool*); dress and fashions (*tweed, make-up*); food and drink (*cocktail, bar*); government, politics and society (*home rule, gangster, gang, gentleman, flirt*), etc. They have been summed up as "representative of the age of Industrial Revolution,"[22] but such a formulation would fail to emphasize the position as a language of education and administration, as a vehicle of higher thought, science and world-culture English has in large parts of the world.

Yet this spread of English words is a modern phenomenon. As compared with the age-long and lasting influence exercised by Greek and Latin to which the Western scientific world still resorts in giving names to new ideas, products, instruments and medicines, to the enormous spread of Arabic elements in the Near, of Chinese in the Far East, the few hundreds of

---

21. E. Björkman, *Scandinavian Loan-Words in Middle English,* Halle 1900-02, p. 5. See, in general, F. Seiler, Die Entwicklung der deutschen Kultur im Spiegel des deutschen Lehnwortes[2] (1921-25).

22. Stene, o.c. p. 204.

English words adopted by many "modern languages" do not amount to much,[23] the less so as English has not yet "succeeded in entering into the lexical heart of other languages"[24] as Arabic has permeated Persian and Turkish — or, let us add, as Sanskrit imprinted its mark on Old Javanese, as to this day Siamese, Burmese and Cambodian bear the unmistakable impression of Sanskrit and Pāli.

In discussing the interesting problem how far "psychological resistances" to the borrowing of foreign words may be distinguished — a problem which should be tackled urgently, and with as complete a documentation as possible — Sapir[25] drew attention to the fact that some languages do not object to adopting words which are from the point of view of the native speakers unanalysable (e.g. English, Japanese), while others (e.g. Icelandic, Chinese) find it easier to create new words (often compounds) out of their own sources. Cambodian and Tibetan, he observes, offer a highly instructive contrast in their reaction to the influence of Sanskrit from which they are structurally totally different: Cambodian welcomed immense numbers of Sanskrit words, many of which remained in common use, but Tibetan, though embracing Buddhism and translating its literature, objected to doing so "because Sanskrit words could not automatically fall into significant syllables," as they should in order to fit in with the

---

23. It has been calculated that nearly half the 240165 words ("bases") entered in the great *Oxford English Dictionary* are learned Latin or Greek terms or modern forms based upon the classics; the vast majority of them are purely technical terms, unknown to almost all groups and classes of the population. See K. Brunner, *Die englische Sprache* I (S. Halle, 1950), p. 186f.

24. To use Sapir's words: *Language* (first published 1921), p. 207.

25. Sapir, o.c. p. 209f.

Tibetan structural scheme. It rendered Sanskrit compounds by periphrastic combinations, in contradistinction to Old-Javanese which, though very poor in compounds itself, welcomed them body and bones, and to modern Indonesian idioms which, in a manner, are able to give part of them a place in their own system. Whereas many Indonesians are proud of the beautiful Sanskrit appellations they bear, the Tibetans had even to translate the proper names.

Yet, difference of environment and sometimes mere ignorance, in short the natural trend of linguistic evolution in autonomous territories in general often produced differences of semantic development. Not unlike the vicissitudes of many Chinese words welcomed by the Japanese, a considerable part of the Sanskrit now used in Indonesia would be entirely unintelligible to a Sanskrit-speaking Indian.

The semantic aspect of loan-words, especially the search for a solution of such problems as: why and how special words have been selected and what has become their function?, or, what are the vicissitudes of several loans or of loans and indigenous terms when they have to compete?, or the systematic examination of the entire history of definite words in all the languages into which they were introduced, are of no less importance for the historian than the inferences which the study of these elements of speech has enabled us to draw with regard to pre-historic interrelations or the connections between the way in which the objects were, during the ages, denoted, and the history of these objects themselves.[26]

There would be no use in indulging in all kinds of conjectures about the exact relation between the Indian and

---

26. See, e.g. H. Schuchardt, *Sachen und Wörter*, *Anthropos*, VII, p. 827ff.

the Indonesian element in Malay, Javanese, Balinese as it was spoken in olden times, and in asking ourselves how far ancient IN. linguistic conditions might be compared with those of mediaeval England after the Conquest, with definite periods in the history of Rumanian when a considerable part of the inherited Latin vocabulary was replaced by Slavic words, or rather, with France during the reign of the Merovingians and Carolingians, or with an idiom as the so-called Malay-Portuguese. For the general impression we obtain from surveying the instances of intimate borrowing best known to us is that various situations and various relations between the languages appear to have existed. It has, for instance, been supposed that "the true originators of that curious patchwork which is modern English"[27] were the servants of the Norman-French nobles, who at the time of the Norman dominance learned more or less bad French to converse with their masters, who after having been, for a time (about 1300), practically bilingual, eventually gave up speaking French and proceeded to use the English they had learnt in the nursery and elsewhere from their own servants. But then English, which had always been the language of the mass of the people, was mixed with many French elements in favour of which it had lost part of its own vocabulary.

Quite different a situation had developed in the Philippines where after three centuries of Spanish rule about 25 natives in 1000 were able to speak Spanish, and a "Kitchen-Spanish" (*Español de cocina*), a jargonized version of the upper language with a varying but considerable element of vernacular terms, serving as a medium between Europeans and Philippinos and among the latter between themselves, had come into

27. Haugen, o.c. p. 281.

existence.[28] The results of deliberate efforts to secure a population of the own tongue and nationality can clearly be shown by the history of the Portuguese: thanks to a multiplying class of Eurasians and to the conversion of many Asians to Christianity the use of this language has, in various regions of Asia, outlasted the Lusitan empire. Even nowadays a "mixed form" of Portuguese continues in use among certain classes of Indonesians. In the Island of Java the speakers of a creolized idiom based on this tongue were so numerous that till the year 1808 special clergymen preaching in Portuguese were appointed.[29]

Speculations concerning particular aspects of the linguistic situation of ancient Indonesia after the arrival of the Hindus would be utterly unfounded because we are ignorant of not a few of the determining causes in the process, the results of which we partly know in the form of the modern IN. languages and possess in the shape of a collection of ancient books and documents. We know, indeed, as good as nothing of the numerical relations between the Hindu and the Indonesian elements of the population and of the spread of the former; very little of the relation between the persons of Hindu birth and the more or less Hinduized Indonesians, of the extent to which these groups really exercised influence on the mass of the people; we are, in short, almost entirely ignorant of other social, economical and cultural factors which must have played an important role. Moreover, we have reasonable grounds

28. See H. Schuchardt, Kreolische Studien IV. Über Das Malaiospanische der Philippinen, Sitzungsberichte der Akad. d. Wiss, Wien (Vienna), CV, (1883), p. 111ff.

29. I refer to the important treatise by Schuchardt, Kreolische Studien, XII, Über das Malaioportugiesische von Batavia and Tugu. Sitzungsberichte Wien (Vienna Academy), CXXII (1890).

for believing that the local and regional conditions, even at the same time, must have been very different: Indian linguistic influence no doubt made itself felt in sea-ports, at courts, in monasteries, and indirectly in other places, but not in the same manner, and not to the same extent.

Yet, there is at the same time room for some negative remarks. There were, as far as we know, no Hindu garrisons, occupation troops or similar concentrations of common people in the Archipelago. Apart from the seaports, some coastal regions, great rivers and other attractive parts of the immense territories may have been rapidly occupied or at least traversed by Hindus or directly controlled by Hinduized Indonesians. The work of internal expansion must have been much slower and certainly remained unfinished. Overland communications were, in addition, restricted and far from rapid: even in modern times, the greater part of the indigenous population has no relations with persons of another district or village. The very diversity of the Indonesian languages — in many smaller Islands three, four or more languages or dialects can be distinguished, Celebes has about 35 different languages and Javanese has rightly been called a conglomerate of rather divergent dialects — corroborates the inferences drawn from other evidence with regard to the scarcity of population and political weakness of many ancient Indonesian kingdoms. We can be certain that outside the cultural and political centra, a powerful pressure of a social, economic, and political nature as exerted by the ruling class on other groups of the population was wanting. Of whatever consequence the religious propaganda and the educational activities of the monks and brāhmaṇas to which we have to revert, may have been, schools, newspapers, radio, and which have such an overwhelming influence in the spread of languages in the modern world, did not exist. And although folk-tales and literary works were orally transmitted, literacy was for centuries to come beyond the reach of the vast majority of the population, and the commercial channels which nowadays transport so many neologisms and foreign terms, were not yet opened.

These conditions may, to a considerable extent, account for the comparatively low number of Middle-Indian[30] words imported or, rather permanently received into the Archipelago. Though their quantity, has been underrated, and though it can in this or that case not be decided whether a Middle-Indo-Aryan or a New-Indo-Aryan word has been the prototype of a particular Indonesian imitation, they are far outnumbered by the Sanskrit elements adopted, and also less frequent as might be expected on the strength of the number of Dravidian and New-Indo-Aryan words borrowed in later centuries. The difficulties with which we are confronted in trying to establish the exact stage of Indo-Aryan from which one word or the other has been borrowed increase when we wake up to the fact that Sanskrit has always remained widely spread in India proper.

The influence of such historical factors as have been enumerated is, indeed, a matter of common knowledge: the numerous Roman garrisons which maintained uninterrupted relations with the metropolis, the settlements of military men and merchants on the trade routes have played an important role in the spread of Latin over various countries of Europe, and comparable conditions have been influential in the infiltration of Spanish in the Philippines, and, in a striking manner in Chile, where the prowess of the natives having led to a great influx of Spanish soldiers who married native

30. This term must be taken in its widest sense.

women, Spanish has come to be the only language.[31] That the character of the penetration of Indo-Aryan in Indonesia has, generally speaking, been peaceful, may also be concluded from the strikingly small number of Indian military terms surviving in Javanese: "war, weapon, sword, lance, armour, shield, helmet, banner, battle, siege, fortress, soldier, officer, enemy, spy, etc." are expressed by indigenous terms, one of the words for "rifle" forming, curiously enough, an exception.[32] This vocabulary cannot compare with the English, which adopted a host of French military words when, after the Norman Conquest, the French-speaking upper classes had taken into their hands the management of military matters.[33]

The scantiness of the elements belonging to the languages which were actually spoken in India during the centuries of intensive relations with Indoneisa should prevent us from comparing the linguistic situation in ancient Java, Sumatra and Malacca with the history of the impact of Indo-Aryan in Ceylon (Sri Lanka). The most ancient Indian colonization outside India, which has been very intensive, has resulted in an overthrow of the original linguistic situation of that Island. Although the language of the ancient indigenous population must have left many traces, although Dravidian influences are far from wanting and Pāli has played a normalizing role, Singhalese is essentially an Indo-Aryan language based on a Prākṛtic dialect. In the Island of Ceylon Indo-Aryan has

31. See. R. Lenz, *Zeitschrift für Romanische Philologie* XVII (1893), p. 188 and M.L. Wagner, ibidem XL (1921), pp. 286 and 385.

32. The word *sĕnjata* is discussed further on. A personal enemy is, however, a *satru* (Skt. *śatru* (शत्रु).

33. For further information on the semantic classes of words borrowed or wanting see ch. V and VI. of the author's book.

established itself. Unlike the Indonesian languages, Singhalese is an Indo-Aryan idiom.[34]

It can, further, be taken for granted that some reiterated verdicts in connection with the spread of linguistic superstrata (that is to say with the impact of the tongue of a ruling nation or class on a community in which they are foreigners) are capable of being rectified in particulars.[35] When a group of foreigners have settled down in a country the linguistic consequences of their acclimatization do not only depend on numerical relations. Soldiers in a conquering army or occupational troops do not everywhere permanently adopt the language of their native wives. The social conditions — this term to be taken in its widest sense — obtaining at the time and in the region in which the linguistic influence comes to pass, the manifold relations between the "superior" and "inferior" linguistic groups, i.e. their social or intellectual standard are factors of outstanding importance in the process of linguistic infiltration or penetration.[36]

In discussing the relations between Indian and Indonesian languages scholars have usually lost sight of the fact that, as far as we know, the journeying and emigration of Indonesians

34. The reader might be referred to W. Geiger, *Grammar of the Sinhalese Language*, 1938.

35. See W. von Wartburg, *Die Ausgliederung der romanischen Sprachräume* (S. Halle 1936). Also *Zeitschrift für Romanische Philologie* LVI (1936), p. 48, n. 1.

36. I also refer to A. Meillet, *Linguistique historique et linguistique générale*, Paris, 1921, p. 110, and especially p. 119, "Les conditions politiques, économiques, religieuses qui déterminent la généralisation d'une langu sont complexes et diverses; on n'a jamais eu occasion de les examiner en détail, car, pour les expansions qui ont eu lieu dans le passé, on n'a que des données insuffisantes sur le procès de l'extension . . ."

to India was, to say the least of it, very uncommon. Such linguistic arguments as have sometimes been adduced — we may remember Kern's attempt to derive a set of numerals used by merchants in the Tamil districts of south India[37] — are far from convincing.

Though we must be cautious in relying on negative evidence it may be observed that it tallies with the linguistic situation in Indonesia, for a sojourn of long duration of a considerable number of nationals belonging to a borrowing community is an important factor in the process of borrowing which in other periods and in other parts of the world has materially influenced the vocabulary of a particular language. Although the relations between the famous Nālandā monastery and the Archipelago, for instance, must for a long period have been continuous, and Indonesian pilgrims, like their Chinese brethren, visited the sacred sites in India,[38] this aspect of Indo-Indonesian intercourse has, as far as I see, left no traces in the languages concerned.

For all this it would not be difficult to find Celtic texts in which the amount of French or English loans or Slavonic texts

---

37. H. Kern, V.G. III, p. 23ff. (the paper first appeared in 1894) tried to show that the numerals, discussed by S.M. Natesa Sastri in a paper "Traders' Slang in Southern India," published in *Indian Antiquary* XXIII (1894), p. 49ff., are of Indonesian origin, introduced by the well-known trade route. Ph. S. van Ronkel was, however, totally right in having serious doubts about this supposition ("Sporen van Dravida-Bataksche betrekkingen?" in Verslag van het VIIe Congress van het Oostersch Genootschap in Nederland, Leyden 1933, p. 40ff.), producing also another series of special numerals in Tamil, published by J. T. Lewis (Slang of Tamil Castes, *Indian Antiquary*, XIX, p. 160).

38. For the sake of brevity I refer to A.J. Bernet Kempers, *The bronzes of Nālandā and Hindu-Javanese Art*, *BKI*, XC (1933), p. 5ff.

in which the number of German words is entirely comparable to the Sanskrit element in Old-Malay or Old-Javanese books and documents,[39] and we may suppose that the native tongue of many educated ancient Javanese people was interlarded with Indian words in a way similar to the English of those learned Englishmen who had had, in former centuries, their whole education in Latin, and when using their mother-tongue unremittingly inserted foreign words. It has, indeed, long since been recongized[40] that the vast majority of the Indian elements permanently received into Javanese and the languages nearly related to it are Sanskrit, and that this Sanskrit has been introduced by the channels of learning and education, inclusive of that learning which served the purposes of religion and administration. It has been scholars, authors, court-poets, religious theorists and other educated people who were in the first place instrumental in introducing so many Sanskrit words bearing upon all provinces of spiritual and intellectual culture into the Javanese and Balinese languages. It has been court-scholars and other poets, who helped part of these terms to obtain a permanent position in the literary style of these tongues, from which a smaller part found their way also in the literature of the adjacent countries. We do well to remember that the main concern of the ancient Indonesian court-poets was to glorify, in a dignified way, the ancestors of the ruling dynasties, and to entertain the educated or even Hinduized court-circles, that the curious idiom in which they

39. The reader might be referred to the instances given by E. Windisch, *Zur Theorie der Mischsprachen und Lehnwörter, Berichte über die Verhand lungen der Kgl. sächsischen Gesellschaft der Wissenschaften, Phil-hist. Classe*, XLIX (Leipsic, 1897), p. 108f.

40. The Dutch scholar H. Kern already used to say that the Sanskrit loan-words in Indonesia "came from the books."

expressed themselves was inteded to be a vehicle of civilized thought and endeavour, and that a large part of the other texts which have been handed down to us, were of a rather technical character and studded with terms lacking any indigenous equivalents. Granting the poets were, for centuries to come, to be fond of unusual foreign words, caring little for the convenience of the uninitiated (and for that of the unborn generations!), the authors on technical subjects have rendered their compatriots good services by making known to them a host of Indian terms together with the ideas and objects for which they stood.

We may, in this connection, also take for granted that, under such linguistic conditions, only a very small part of the population was ever able to express themselves in the, or in a, foreign tongue. There is perhaps also room for another remark to be made: it is in my opinion not beyond the bounds of possibility that some of the Middle-Indo-Aryan words which, like the Tamil and New-Indo-Aryan terms in the subsequent period, must, in the first millennium of Indo-Indonesian contact, have penetrated in one or other of the Archipelago idioms, was, by scholarly influence, remodelled into closer resemblance with their Sanskrit equivalents:[41] already in early Old-Javanese texts, in prose as well as in poetry the "mahout's goad" is called *aṅkuśa,* which is also Malay, while modern Javanese used the word to denote a poker or "fire-hook" beside this shorter form, however, OJav. and Malay have *aṅkuśa, aṅkusa* respectively, the clipped form *kusa* serving as a Malay word-base. Now, the shorter word is no doubt an early loan from New-Indo-Aryan: cf. Hindi *ākus,*

41. For a similar process in English, where French forms (e.g. *Avril, vittles*) gave way to the Latin (e.g. *April, victuals*) see Jespersen, *Growth and Structure* § 116.

aṅkus. The longer has probably been introduced by literary channels and succeeded in taking root.

Dialect geography, the study of local differentiations in a speech-area, has greatly deepened our knowledge of the processes conditioning the infiltration of foreign elements in a given community. Some of the most striking general results to which this branch of linguistic science has led may be summed up like this: there is no question of uniformity over an area; every word has, speaking quite generally, its own history; innovations (including foreign elements as a rule, spread from centres along rivers and other trade routes to smaller centres, remote places having the best chance to remain unaffected by them.[42] It has repeatedly been observed that a word imported from another language first spreads among the educated classes of the more important centres (capitals, great cities) and afterwards from these to their neighbourhood, but again in the first place, to the educated of the more important villages. These results of geographical linguistics can help to form an idea of the ways in which foreign elements were diffused over the Islands of the Archipelago. Though it is, for the time being and presumably for ever, entirely impossible to retrace the main wanderings of Sanskrit words in an ancient Indonesian area, the more so as the methods of dialect geography have unfortunately only recently, and tentatively, been applied in the Island of Lombok,[43] we are, on the other hand, in a position to make some remarks with regard to the wanderings of part of the Sanskrit elements.

42. Instances may be found in the books mentioned by Bloomfield, *Language*, p. 519 (ch. XIX); see, further, K. Jaberg, *Aspects géographiques du langage* (Paris, 1936); E. Gamillscheg, *Die Sprachgeographie* (Bielefeld und Leipsic 1928); esp. ch. IV.

43. See A. Teeuw, *Bingkisam Budi* (Festschrift Ph. S. van Ronkel, Leyden), p. 281ff.

For one IN. idiom has under favourable circumstances undergone a more or less intensive influence of the other, and, although — apart from occasional references in dictionaries and other books — the internal IN. borrowing of words in general has not yet been studied to such an extent that any tenable inference migth be drawn with regard to many details, the important role played by Malay in spreading words over the Archipelago and the influence exercised by Javanese literature on the tales and poems of the adjacent peoples — to mention only two striking trends of borrowing may be regarded as established facts.

Passing mention may, in this connection, be made of an important detail which at first sight might appear strange: the influence of Sanskrit has been of a more intensive and most permanent character in Java than in Malacca and the Malay regions of Sumatra which are nearer to India. This fact is not only due to the earlier and in some regards more thorough Islamization of the "Malay world," and in its being more generally open to commercial and other relations with other peoples which have superseded the use of older Indian words, as they have taken the place of Indian religious beliefs and practices, of Indian customs and institutions. It may in part be ascribed also to the firmer rooting of Hindu literature in Java, to the age-long activity of writers and adapters, poets and scholars of that island, to the influence exerted by its courts and other centres.[44]

No Indonesian language has ever given up its hereditary character under the influence of Sanskrit, notwithstanding the cultural prestige of the latter and the long duration of the

44. For similar "leaps" in Europe see e.g. E. Öhmann, *Zum sprachlichen Einfluss Italiens auf Deutschland, Neuphilologische Mitteilungen,* Helsinki, XLVI (1945), p. 2f.

contact. Their inner resisting-power, their wide distribution over vast and often remote areas, the comparatively low number of immigrants and Hinduized natives, the very character of the influx of Indian speech-elements, in addition to the other factors already mentioned has prevented anything like such an evolution and has preserved them from ending in a mixture or a creolized idiom.[45] We can, it is true, easily imagine that the first commercial contact between Indian navigators and merchants led to the establishment of a more or less conventionalized jargon, based upon the natives' unsuccessful attempt to make some progress in learning the language of the foreigners, the latter's imitation of this, the "baby-talk" to which they resort in the hope of being understood and in which they often insert foreign words without discrimination as to their sources, and, finally, the natives' attempts at reproducing, in their turn, this grammatically simplified and lexically mixed talk.[46] After the fifteenth century such jargons based upon Spanish, Portuguese, English, and French have repeatedly come into existence and linguistic conditions in the Pacific after the first contact of the inhabitants with English whalers — their "conversation" developed into a jargon in which, e.g. "I like wine" is expressed like this: *me like him grog,* and "I can go there": *me savey* (from Spanish "to know") *go*[47] — can give us an idea of what was, in all probability, spoken in the South-East Asiatic seaports during the first centuries of our era. We may even suppose a *lingua*

45. I cannot agree with the opposite view held by C.C. Berg, Inleiding tot de studie van het Oud-Javaansch, Surakarta 1928, p. 199ff.

46. Further information may be found in the books and papers mentioned by Bloomfield, *Language*, p. 523 (ch. XXVI. 5).

47. See Schuchardt, Kreolische Studien, v. *Über das Melaneso-englische, Sitzungsberichte Wien* (Vienna Academy) CIII (1883), 151ff.

franca to have existed there, that is: such a jargon passed into general commercial use between persons of various nationality. As we had already occasion to remark, a Creole idiom based on Portuguese has for several centuries existed in the Archipelago, but, of course, only in coastal districts among persons of Eurasian origin, who according to race and speech were eventually absorbed in some form of colloquial Malay.[48] Whether such a *lingua Franca* based on Indo-Aryan elements has ever been the only language of an Indonesian community, that is, whether it has become a creolized language, may be discussed in the realm of conjecture; that it should have been based on Sanskrit is, I venture to assert, beyond possibility.

It is the author's endeavour to describe the chief vicissitudes and peculiarities of the Sanskrit elements in the Indonesian languages and to illustrate their significance from the point of view of a linguist who takes an interest in all things human. Hence, not only a discussion of such phenomena of a purely linguistic character as fluctuation of form and adaptation, sound substitution and other phonetic processes, loan translations, the productiveness of the borrowed elements as word-bases, etc. will be included, but also an examination of the semantic categories of the loan-words, their role in social and religious life, in literature and daily parlance, and an attempt will be made to show the bearings of linguistic history upon the history of Indonesian civilization in general. The Indonesian tongues themselves will be considered only insofar as is necessary to illustrate the part played by the Sanskrit elements. The words borrowed from other Indian languages

48. This creolized Portuguese was also in common use between many Europeans and their children by non-European women, between slaves and free Asiatic Christians, and among people of Siamese, Bengalese, south Indian or Ceylonese origin, who did not speak and understand vulgar Malay.

which besides being too nearly related to Sanskrit to be neglected, cast some interesting sidelights on our subject, are however, more amply dealt with.

As the facts discussed cannot be understood without a somewhat orderly survey of those provinces of linguistic science which have a bearing on our subject, nor without a knowledge of the historical background, many pages have been devoted to explanations which may be passed over by the advanced linguist or historian. The book is intended for any reader who takes an interest in one aspect or the other of the phenomena and problems treated of, not in the last place however, for Indians and Indonesians, whom it may help to arrive at a fuller understanding of their linguistic and cultural relations. So, while trying to give something for everybody, the author is aware that Western linguists or Sanskrit scholars, not to mention others, will find him sometimes guilty of focusing too much attention on Indonesian details. The author can only apologize by saying that he has done his utmost to express himself as intelligibly as possible (not even avoiding repetitions, cross-references and elementary elucidations), and by inviting the categories of readers mentioned to disregard part of the notes, and even some of the instances given in the text. The author considers himself, on the other hand, responsible only for part of the omissions which will not fail to strike the specialist. Many facts are indeed not included firstly because it was not deemed necessary to aim at anything like completeness, any new edition of an Old-Javanese text providing us with new instances of Sanskrit loans, and almost all dictionaries and other sources of information being incomplete, and secondly because our knowledge of the Indo-Indonesian relations in former ages will only, for the most part, go a very little way towards answering all the questions which may arise.

10

Sanskrit and Arabic

Similarities

Khalid Bin Yusuf Khan

APPROXIMATELY there are 3,000 languages that exist in this world.[1] The division of languages in the earlier stage was on the basis of country, caste or religion. But this proved insufficient. It is the age of science today. Hence, language cannot remain away from expansion.

The language explorers are of the opinion that the language could have been created at a place inhabited by large population together. Further, due to historical and geographical reasons and requirements, the language could have adopted various dialects and sub-dialects, though the original language must have remained intact. The world will recognize the number of language families on the basis of the basic languages that exist. For example, our language was Indo-European. But today it is recognized as Indo-Hittie which had two branches — the Indo-European and Hittie.

Due to increase in population at that original inhabited place, there could have occurred large migrations. This geographical change could have given birth to new languages.

---

1. Karan Singh, *Bhāṣā Vigyāna*, p. 67, Sahitya Bhandar, Meerut, IV edition, 1980.

This could also mean that the initial original language transformed itself into various languages in course of time as shown below:

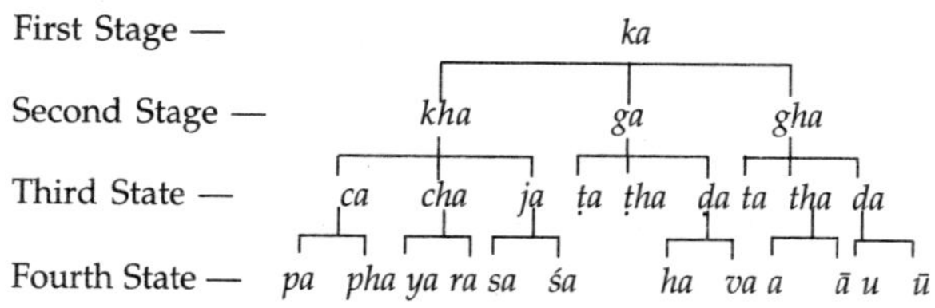

Various Forms of Languages

Various forms of languages have been derived in course of time from the original language. They are:

1. ***Literary Language***: Comparatively more developed and tougher than the common language.
2. ***Living Language***: The routine common language.
3. ***Dead Language***: Like the Hittite.
4. ***State Language***: Persian of the Mogul period.
5. ***Caste Language***: Languages in a village where brāhmaṇas and blacksmiths live and differ depending upon caste and living conditions.
6. ***Female Language***: The earlier form of Urdu, namely, Rekhtī spoken by females only.
7. ***Male Language***: The earlier form of Urdu, namely, Rekhtā spoken by males only.

Languages of the World

Today, the world languages have two popular categories:[2]

1. ***Morphological or Syntactical Classification*** — Here the shape and the form of the language are its base.

2. Ibid.

2. ***Genealogical or Historical Classification*** — Here the meaning and the form of the language are its base.

Shape of the Language and its Kinds

On the basis of the shape of the language, we could divide it into two categories:[3]

1. ***Isolating*** — Language category that **does not combine** the meaning content with the form content.
2. ***Agglutinating*** — Language category **that combines** the meaning content with the form content.

Making the common base for the meaning content and the form content (relations content), the languages are categorized. This is called the family classification. Under this classification we can assemble all the languages that were created from the main language. For example, all the languages spoken in India and Europe, can be categorized under the family of Indo-European language.[4]

Languages based on family classification can be divided into four categories. They are:

1. Geographical similarity
2. Words similarity
3. Grammatical similarity
4. Phonetical similarity.

Geographical proximity is no base for family classification because Marathi and Kannada, and Telugu and Oriya, though are geographically very close to each other, yet these languages do not fall under one family of language. Also, on the contrary, Hindi and English though do not have geographical nearness,

---

3. Ibid., p. 69.
4. Ibid., p. 78.

yet fall under one language family. On the basis of similarities of words, languages could be brought under one category and several languages could be classified under the family head. For this similarity, the words chosen should have similar phonetic sounds and also have the same meaning. For example, the word "Father" and "Seven" in various Indo-European languages would be as follows:

Sanskrit	**Persian**	**Greek**	**Latin**	**German**	**English**
pitṛ	*pidar*	*pater*	*pater*	*vater*	*father*
sapta	*haphta*	*hepta*	*septem*	*sieben*	*seven*

Grammatical similarity means similarity in the formation of word and syntax. Thus, grammatical similarity is more important than the similarity of sound. By mere give and take of sound and words the grammar of different languages may not be the same as word formation and sentence formation follow their own rules. Thus, grammar confirms the possibility or otherwise of a language joining a family.

If phonetics of any main language is not reflected in a sub-language, or if phonetics in any one language changes with the passage of time, then every phonetic group strongly protects the sound syllables of the main language. Even after adopting the words of other languages, this language does not lose its identity and does not accept the new words as its own. For example, the English word "Lantern" becomes *lālaṭena* in Hindi. Thus, languages having similar phonetic sounds should be considered to be of one family.[5]

On the basis of geographical divisions some scholars have divided all the languages into four zones.[6]

5. Ibid., p. 82.
6. Ibid., p. 84.

1. ***America Zone*** — American language families.
2. ***Africa Zone*** — Language families of Sudan, Bantu, Bushmaini, Hamitic, Semitic.
3. ***Eurasia Zone*** — Language families — Indo-European, Dravid, Bhurushaski, Ural-Altaic, Kakeshi, Chinese, Japanese-Korean, besides the great Hiperborie, Bosk and Sami-Hami (Semitic-Hamitic).
4. ***Pacific Ocean Zone*** — Language families of Malay group of Islands, Papua, Australia and South-East Asia.

Some scholars are of the view that the Semitic and Hamitic languages belong to African zone rather than to Eurasian zone and that they are related to different groups among themselves. "Akkādi" was the ancient language of the Sami sect. Armenian, Hebrew, and Arabic also belong to this sect. These languages are being spoken in Arab countries, Iraq, Palestine, Israel, Syria, and Egypt.

The languages that come under the "Hami" sect include the ancient Egyptian language and the "Barbar" language spoken in Northern Africa.[7] Islam and Christianity originated amongst these language people.

The languages of the Indo-European family are spoken in India (north), Afghanistan, Iran and in the whole of Europe. The ancient languages like Sanskrit, Greek and Latin and the modern languages like English, French, German, Hindi, Marathi, Gujarati, Punjabi, and Bangla are the popular languages belonging to this family.[8]

On the basis of the above classification, it can be seen that Sanskrit was the language of the Indo-Europeans while Arabic

---

7. Ibid., p. 85.
8. Ibid., p. 84.

belonged to the Sami language family sect. Apparently it may seem that both these languages had no common grammar, sound and meaning similarities. But the documents available prove that there are many similarities between these two languages on the basis of which the earlier theory could be rejected and it can be said that both these languages belong to one family.

It is a universal truth that the main Indo-European language did not have the clear phonetic sound of letters *cha* and *ṭa*. It had three genders, three persons and three numbers. The language had a tune and a flow.[9]

In Arabic language too, *cha* and *ṭa* (except *ja*) sections were not there. Further in Arabic too there were three genders — Muzakkar, Muannas and Mukhannas; and three numbers — Wahid, Tasniya and Jama; and three persons (Zamir) — Ghaib, Mukhatib and Mutakallim. Arabic language has a flow and special care is given to its tone. Moreover the word formation and its element are also used in Arabic language. Thus, from the grammatical point of view, Arabic language seems to be part of the Indo-European family.

For instance, on the ground of similarity in sound and meaning, words like *pitṛ* and *sapta* occurring in different languages were taken to determine the oneness of the family these languages belonged to. If this rule applies to Arabic, it proves to belong to the Indo-European group rather than to the African.

Sanskrit	Persian	Greek	Latin	German	English	Arabic
pitṛ	*pidar*	*pater*	*pater*	*vater*	*father*	*abbu or abbun*
sapta	*haphta*	*hepta*	*septem*	*sieben*	*seven*	*saba*

9. Ibid., p. 89.

In Arabic, the word *abbu* or *abbun* is used for father. The word originating from word *pitṛ* does not match in sound. The solution to this was found by Sri Aurobindo in Tamil. According to him, in Tamil we say *appā* for father which is derived by the combination of three Sanskrit words *apatyam, aptyam* and *apna* (progeny). Similarly, the Tamil word *appā* and the modern Arabic word *abbā*, have been derived from the three Sanskrit words *apatyam, aptyam* and *apna*. In the same way the word *sāta* is derived from *sapta* which is almost similar to the Arabic word *saba*. For word *mātā*, in Sanskrit we say *mātṛ*, and in Arabic it is *umma* which is not close to *mātṛ* but is quite similar when pronouncing the Sanskrit word *ambā*.

Here, along with the Sanskrit and Arabic, the example of Tamil is given because Tamil is considered to be the language of Draviḍians by experts. Whereas Sri Aurobindo is of the opinion that scholars of language divided the Indian castes into the northern Aryans and the southern Draviḍians, but on serious reviewing it is seen that from Kanyakumari to Afghanistan, minor differences prevail in India amongst these castes. Therefore, dividing the language is unscientific, in Sri Aurobindo's view.[10]

Sri Aurobindo again says that when Max Müller, after his in-depth study and investigation, gave the world the words like *pitā, pater, patair, fater, father*, and drummed his success on the closer relation between these words, he was in a way trying to debunk the new scientific theories. He was in fact taking us back from the existing as well as more authentic sources and in-depth and detailed facts. On the basis of this unfortunate source, many unique and extraordinary but, weak

---

10. Sri Aurobindo, *Ved Rahasya* (Part II).

and supportless edifices were built. Initially, the human race was divided into the Aryans, the Draviḍians, the Semitics and the Turānis, based on the categories of scripture and literature available in the ancient and modern languages.[11]

In Arabic and Sanskrit, divisions are made only because of words. Therefore, if we put these words anywhere in the sentence, its meaning does not change. For example:

In Sanskrit: 1. *zaidaḥ amaram ahanat*, meaning Zaid kills Amar.

2. *amaram zaidaḥ ahanat*, meaning Zaid kills Amar.

In Arabic: 1. *zarbao zaidun amran*, meaning Zaid kills Amar.

2. *zarbao amran zaidun*, meaning Zaid kills Amar.

Therefore, by changing the place of Zaid and Amar, the sentence form and its meaning remain the same. But this cannot be done in the case of an English sentence. For example:

In English: 1. Zaid kills Amar, meaning *zaid ne amar ko mārā.*

2. Amar kills Zaid, meaning *amar ne zaid ko mārā.*

In the above sentences, we will find that by changing the words' position, the meaning of the sentence changes.

From this angle too, we find that Arabic is more close to Sanskrit. The sound and meaning of the words of these two languages are quite similar and thus we can conclude that they belong to one family only.

---

11. Ibid.

Arabic	Sanskrit
1. *asra* = Time, specially dusk	*ahar* = Day
2. *ateeq* = Old	*atikrānta* = Old
3. *abtar* = Bad condition	*avatara* = *ava nīcai starah* with *tarap*-Suffix
4. *āyad* = Coming back	*āgata* = Came
5. *imam* = Leader	*amāmah* = *Amena jñānena saha amāti carati,* Root √*am* — to go, serve, *am* = strength, vigour
6. *īsā* = Powerful	*īśaḥ* = Capable, competent, master
7. *qari* = One who recites the religious book with accent	*kāru* = *stotā,* one who recites the religious book with accent, Panegyrist
8. *qamar* = Moon	*kamra* = Beautiful
9. *khāli* = Empty	*khālīnaḥ* = *khe śunye ālīnaḥ,* always empty
10. *ghaib* = Imperceptible, fate	*garbhyaḥ* = *garbhe rahasye bhavaḥ,* secret in the womb.
11. *zilzal* = Earthquake	*jayacāla* = Earthquake
12. *talāq* = Divorce	*tyāga* = Divorce (No "G" alphabet in Arabic)
13. *tariq* = Star	*tāraka* = Star
14. *najm* = Star	*nyagbhaḥ* = Star
15. *firaun* = Egotist, enjoyer	*priyayaunaḥ* = Enjoyer
16. *pheel* = Elephant	*pīluḥ* = Elephant
17. *bosā* = Kiss	*vosaḥ* = *vaktreṇa udgatya saṁyogaḥ,* union, face to face
18. *madina* = Sacred (city)	*madhīnaḥ* = *madāt doṣāt hīnaḥ* (without any defect, sacred)

	Arabic	Sanskrit
19.	*majeed* = Honourable, Prestigous	*manojit* = One who conquers heart
20.	*muāfi* = Pardon	*mamāviḥ* = *mama āviḥ rakṣeti, mahyam rakṣaṇam devīti*, pardon me
21.	*maulvī* = Scholar of Religion	*maulvit* = *maulam śāstram vettīti* (one who knows the religious books)
22.	*yagus* = Worship of a particular deity	*yajuṣ* = Worship or sacrifice
23.	*rasūl* = Messenger of God	*rasūlaḥ* = *rasena permānanden ullasatīti*
24.	*lāt* = Deity	*Lalitā* = Durgā, Deity
25.	*shams* = Sun	*haṁsaḥ* = Sun ("H" and "S" are interchangeable)
26.	*sahabah* = Friends	*sahāyaḥ* = Friends
27.	*hunain* = One who has beautiful eyes	*sūnayanaḥ* = One who has beautiful eyes
28.	*hutamah* = Fire	*hutamaḥ* = Fire
29.	*wahā* = Shine	*bhā* = Light, shine
30.	*tan* = Body	*tanu* = Body
31.	*ambaj* = Mango	*āmra* = Mango
32.	*aūj* = Higher	*ucca* = Higher
33.	*babar* = Lion	*vyāghra* = Lion
34.	*buhar* = Roving, frolic	*vihāra* = Roving, frolic
35.	*bhattā* = Rice	*bhakta* = Rice
36.	*istān* = Place	*sthāna* = Place
37.	*tutiya* = Blue vitriol	*tutha* = Blue vitriol
38.	*huba* = Pot	*kumbha* = Pitcher

	Arabic	Sanskrit
39.	*zanjbeel* = Ginger	*śṛṅgvera* = Ginger
40.	*saj* = Teak	*śāla* = Teak
41.	*shatranj* = Chess	*caturaṅga* = Chess
42.	sandal = Sandal	*candana* = Sandal
43.	*phuphal* = Betelnut	*pūgaphala* = Betel-nut
44.	*karanphul* = Earring	*karṇa puṣpa* = (ornament) Earring
45.	*kāfur* = Camphor	*karpūra* = Camphor
46.	*kirvās* = Cotton	*karpāsa* = Cotton
47.	*lakh* = Lac (Sealing wax)	*lākṣā* = Lac
48.	*mash* = Blackgram (kind of pulse)	*Māṣaka* = Pulse
49.	*neel* = Indigo	*nīlikā* = Indigo
50.	*neem* = Neem tree	*nimba* = Neem tree
51.	*itriphal* = Fruits of *Myrobalan*	*Triphala* = Said three fruits — *Terminalia chebula, Triminalia bellirica, Emblica officinalis*
52.	*baladak* = Anacardium tree	*bhallātakaḥ* = *Anacardium* tree
53.	*jazara* = Carrot	*gṛñjana* = Carrot
54.	*lemun* = Lemon	*nimbuka* = Lemon
55.	*ela* = Cardamon	*elā* = Cardamon
56.	*kot* = Fort	*koṭa* = Fort
57.	*tambula* = Betel	*tāmbūla* = Betel
58.	*beesha* = Poison	*viṣa* = Poison
59.	*kāsa* = Pot	*kalaśa* = Pitcher, pot
60.	*nārjeel* = Coconut	*nārikela* = Coconut
61.	*amlaja* = *Emblica myrobalan*	*āmalaka* = *Emblica myrobalan*

	Arabic	Sanskrit
62.	*mahtāra* = Great	*mahattara* = Great
63.	*saba* = Seven	*sapta* = Seven
64.	*dua* = Prayer	*duās* = To worship, to pray
65.	*shandala* = A low caste	*cāṇḍāla* = A low Hindu caste Hindu caste (It should be remembered that "C" and "T" category of alphabets are not found in Arabic except "J")
66.	*Ila* = Divine	*Ilā* = Deity, heaven
67.	*asvada* = Black	*aśveta* = Black
68.	*mukha* = Brain, essence	*mukha* = Face, essence
69.	*khafda* = To push, to move fast	*sapadi* = At once, immediately
70.	*umma* = Mother	*ambā* = Mother
71.	*hirā* = Place for hiding	*hirā* = *Śirā* (Blood vessel)
72.	*subha* = Morning	*śubha* = Shining, beautiful (*dyotate iti sataḥ dyu*)
73.	*maiyit/maitah* = Dead	*mr̥taka/Mr̥ta* = Dead
74.	*namāẓ* = To pray	√*nam* = *namati ajāya iti*= To pray before God
75.	*deenār* = Gold coin	*dīnāra* = Gold coin
76.	*bilā* = Without	*binā* = Without
77.	*taanni* = Late, lethargy	*tandrī* = Lethargy
78.	*ustuna* = Pillar	*sthūṇa* = Pillar
79.	*tibna* = Grass	*tr̥ṇa* = Grass
80.	*mā* = Not	*mā* = Not
81.	*kula* = All	*kula* = All
82.	*inteqāl* = Death	*antakāla* = Time of death

83. *nāri* = Hellish *nārakī* = Hellish

84. *sheikha* = Chief, main *śreṣṭha* = Chief

Looking at the above words, we can conclude that the division of language was unscientific and unnecessary and that Sanskrit and the Arabic are part of one language family only.

11

Sanskrit and Persian
A Comparative Study
With Special Reference to Yoga-Vāsiṣṭha

Lalita Kuppuswamy

NOT much work has been done on the comparative study of works in Persian and Sanskrit, the two rich literatures of ancient origin belonging to the same group of Indo-European languages having a close affinity.

Indian thoughts with all its mysteries and depth held an irresistible appeal to the Muslim intellectuals. All important works on Indian culture, religion and philosophy are preserved in this great Sanskrit language. So the Muslims came forward to learn Sanskrit with the help of enlightened Indian scholars who in turn improved their knowledge of Persian and consequently Muslim culture. The reciprocal learning paved the way for translations from Sanskrit into Persian and for the composition of Persian works on Indian culture. The intellectuals always yearned for a better understanding of each other's fundamental tenets and the best example of this intellectual exchange is Al-Beruni, the great scholar who discovered the glorious richness of Indian culture and philosophy and immortalized them in the eternal pages of *Indica*.

Translation played an important role in almost all encounters between cultures. Some translations had great value and came to be looked upon as classics in the translated language. Often translation was not just a tool for exchange of ideas. It was also an indispensible means of preservation. A notable case in this sense is the preservation and later dissemination of Greek science through Arabic translations in the eighth and ninth centuries CE under the Abbasids. This momentous enterprise in the history of ideas was well chronicled by De Lacy o Leary.[1]

In India also Muslim kings sponsored transfer of knowledge from Sanskrit before Jai Singh undertook similar work. Notable among these are Fīroz Shāh Tugluq (fourteenth century) and Jalāluddīn Akbar (1556–1605).

More details are available from the reign of Akbar on the nature of exchanges of ideas through translation. Akbar desired that the Muslim intelligentsia be made familiar with the classics of Hindu thought so that they have a better interaction with Hindus and therefore established the *Maktab Khānā* or Bureau of Translation.[2]

The procedure of translation is reported by two of the chief participants, viz. Abul Fazl and Abdul Qādir Badāyūnī.

According to these writers, translation was not performed by single scholars proficient in both source language and target language, in this case, Sanskrit and Persian. Rather the task was accomplished by teams of scholars, some proficient in Sanskrit and others in Persian. They did the work in three

1. *How Greek Science Passed to the Arabs*, 4th impression, London, 1944.
2. Saiyid Athar Abbas Rizvi, *Religious and Intellectual History of the Muslims in Akbar's Reign*, New Delhi, 1975, ch. 6, pp. 202-22.

stages. First, Hindu scholars prepared a paraphrase in Hindi of the Sanskrit text to be translated. In the second stage, this Hindi paraphrase was translated into Persian by one of the several Muslim courtiers. Finally, the Persian translation was polished and put into elegant prose and verse by one of the more accomplished scholars, often the emperor himself supplying the felicitous phrase. The Hindus who prepared the Hindi paraphrase were known as *ma'bar'an* (interpreters) and the Muslims who rendered the paraphrase into Persian were styled *motarajjimān* (translators).[3]

What resulted in this process cannot be termed an exact translation but rather a Persian paraphrase into which often the mediator's explanatory sentences crept in.

Among the various Sanskrit texts the *Yoga-Vāsiṣṭha* known also as *Mahā Rāmāyaṇa, Ārṣa Rāmāyaṇa, Jñāna-Vāsiṣṭha,* and *Vāsiṣṭha Rāmāyaṇa* is a popular monumental work at par with the Upaniṣads and the *Bhagavad-Gītā,* a source book for many schools of thoughts and seekers of self-knowledge and liberation. It is a highly honoured book for its philosophy and its hints on practical mysticism, as also for its literary beauty and poetry. Furthermore, the unique style of it is that the author has incorporated the technique of stories to make the great truths of philosophy homely and palatable. In the words of the author of the text "It is really a storehouse of wisdom and contains all that is best anywhere."[4]

The authorship of the text is attributed to sage Vālmīki, the author of the *Rāmāyaṇa*, who is said to have related the whole of *Yoga-Vāsiṣṭha* to sage Bhāradvāja as a dialogue between Rāma and the sage Vasiṣṭha.

---

3. C.H. Hodivala, *Studies in Indo-Muslim History*, Bombay, 1939, 1, pp. 564-66.
4. *Yoga-Vāsiṣṭha*, III.8.12.

The text holds that self in man is identical in essence with the ultimate reality. It denies duality and insists on the oneness of all beings. In this it finds affinity with the teachings of the Muslim mystics, for the Sufistic doctrine of *Wahadatul Wujud* (unity of being) is identical with the Vedāntic principle of *ekaṁ sat* (the reality is one), and the *Anal Haq* (I am the truth) of Sūfī is the exact equivalent of the great aphorism of the Vedāntin, *ahaṁ brahmāsmi*. The philosophy of *Yoga-Vāsiṣṭha*, so sublime and yet so practical, has a growing relevance in a world of narrow thoughts and material pursuits.

There are at present known to us two works by the name of *Yoga-Vāsiṣṭha*, the larger one going by the name of *Bṛhad-Yoga-Vāsiṣṭha* (bigger) containing 32,000 verses ascribed to Vālmīki and the smaller one *Laghu-Yoga-Vāsiṣṭha* containing 6,000 verses approximately. In the abridged text, the elaborate descriptions are clipped, retaining the quintessence of the bigger one. This work seems to have been written by Abhinanda in Kashmir in the ninth century. Still later, Vidyāraṇya (Madhvācārya) produced in the fourteenth century a shorter version known as the *Yoga-Vāsiṣṭha-Sāra-Saṁgraha* (the collection of the essence of *Yoga-Vāsiṣṭha*). There is, besides, an abridgement of 225 stanzas by the name of *Yoga-Vāsiṣṭha-Sāra* (the essence of *Yoga-Vāsiṣṭha*).

Naturally this celebrated work on Indian philosophy was selected for Persian translation more than once. It is said that all the Persian versions are the translations of *Laghu-Yoga-Vāsiṣṭha* written by Abhinanda.[5]

Under Akbar the Great, the work was translated into Persian by Naqib Khan, Abul Fazl and Mullā Shīrī. This

5. *Yoga-Vāsiṣṭha*, ed. Dr Tarachand and Dr S.A.H. Abidi, Aligarh: Aligarh Muslim University, 1968, p. 5.

manuscript has been noticed by Dr Ethe.[6]

Then the Persian rendering of *Laghu-Yoga-Vāsiṣṭha* was done by Niẓām Pānīpatī with the assistance of two *paṇḍits* at the instance of Jehangir. It caught the attention of Persian intellectuals, and Mir Abdul Qasim Findareski, an Iranian philosopher wrote marginal notes on it and prepared a glossary of difficult words and terms under the title *'Kashf-ul-Lughat-ī-Kulliyat-ī-Jog-Bhashisht.* Shaikh Sūfī or Sūfī Sharif Qubjahani made another translation of *Yoga-Vāsiṣṭha* and gave it the title of *Tuhfa-ī-Majlis* or *Kashful Kunuz* which is based on the *Yoga-Vāsistha-Sāra.*[7] A fragment of this work with the caption of *Atwar dar Hall-ī-Asrar* is preserved in the British Museum and was published from Lucknow in CE 1877 in a *majmua* (collection) along with works of similar nature.

The credit for the best rendering of *Yoga-Vāsiṣṭha* into Persian goes to Dārā Shukoh who under his supervision got it done in CE 1066 as he found the earlier versions were not true to the original source. It is believed by Dr Tarachand, the great historian of India, that the text was rendered into Persian by Babawali or Banwali Daswali, a *muṅśī* of Dārā Shukoh.[8]

Paṇḍit Sheo Narain[9] gives a detailed account of the translation made at the instance of Dārā Shukoh in his article on "Dārā Shikūh as an Author."

The translator in the Preface gives an account of the circumstances which led to the translation of the *Yoga-Vāsiṣṭha* into Persian:

6. Catalogue of Persian MSS, London: The India Office Library and Records, 1971.
7. *Yoga-Vāsiṣṭha,* ed. Dr Tarachand & Dr S.A.H. Abidi, Aligarh: Aligarh Muslim University, 1968, p. 11.
8. Ibid.
9. *Journal of the Punjab Historical Society*, vol. 11, no. 1, pp. 31-32.

> Let it be known to the noble souls that the scholars who have before this translated *Jog-Bashisht* into Persian and omitted some of the Sanskrit terms, have not been able to convey the subtleties and full sense of the text. It was for this reason that in one of the months of the year AH 1066 (CE 1656), the crown of the kings, the refuge of the world, the descendant of the glorious kings, God's best creature, the initiate in divine mysteries, the embodiment of what is grand and noble, the God-knowing king Dārā Shikūh, son of Shāh Jahān ordained as follows:
>
> Since the translations of this sacred book which are extant, have not proved of much use to the seekers of truth, it is my desire that a retranslation should be undertaken in conference with learned men of all sects who are conversant with the text. My chief reason for this noble command is that although I had profited by perusing a translation of it ascribed to Shaikh Sūfī, yet once two saintly persons appeared in my dreams; one of whom was tall, whose hair was grey, the other short and without any hair. The former was Vasiṣṭha and the latter Rāmacandra, and as I had read the translation already alluded to, I was naturally attracted towards them and paid my respects. Vasiṣṭha was very kind to me and patted me on the back and addressing Rāmacandra told him that I was brother to him because both he and I were seekers after truth. He asked Rāmacandra to embrace me which he did in exuberance of love. Thereupon Vasiṣṭha gave some sweets to Rāmacandra which I took and ate. After this version, a desire to cause the retranslation of the book intensified me.[10]

The most authentic and critical edition prepared on the basis of manuscripts by Dr Tarachand and Dr S.A.H. Abidi is taken

10. Bikramajit Hasrat, *Dārā Shikūh Life Works,* New Delhi: Munshiram Manoharlal Publishers, 1982, p. 236.

as a source book for Persian version for the comparative study in the present paper.[11] *Laghu-Yoga-Vāsiṣṭha* with the Sanskrit commentary *Vāsiṣṭha-Candrikā* edited by Vasudeva Sharma Paniskara is the source book for the Sanskrit version.[12] The Persian version is a prose rendering whereas the original Sanskrit is in verse form.

In the Persian version, *Yoga-Vāsiṣṭha* is written as *Jog-Bashisht*, sometimes Basiṣṭha for Vasiṣṭha.

The Technique of Translation — From Sanskrit to Persian

Problems and techniques of translation are interconnected. A good translation should contain four main qualities.

(i) Faithfulness to the original,

(ii) Readability,

(iii) Clarity, and

(iv) Achievement of purpose, i.e. the reader of the translation if he understands the original, then the purpose is achieved.

To remain faithful to the original is a difficult and responsible task of the translator. The majority feeling is that poetry is untranslatable especially in the rhyme and rhythm contained in the source language. In translation of poetry something is always lost in the process because affinity with the emotions and the mood in which the poet created the piece of poetry are not there while doing translation. But if a translator is geniune in appreciation for both, he can maintain it.

---

11. *Yoga-Vasiṣṭha*, ed. Dr Tarachand & Dr S.A.H. Abidi, Aligarh: Aligarh Muslim University, 1968.

12. *Laghu-Yoga-Vāsiṣṭha*, ed. Vasudeva Sharma Panasikara, Delhi: Motilal Banarsidass, reprint 1985.

When the philosophical texts are involved in translation, the translator needs the command on both the languages and the philosophy. Verse to verse translation is difficult. So from the points of clarity and readability, many a time prose rendering of the poetry is done as in the Persian versions of *Rājataraṅgiṇī* and *Yoga-Vāsiṣṭha* where the original Sanskrit texts are in verse form.

A language carries its culture and tradition in its vocabulary, and difficulty arises in finding equivalents in the target language, due to difference in culture. So many times a translator adds words to clarify the original. Sometimes, notes are added explaining the mythological allusions for clarity.

Sometimes the flow of the narrative is hindered if too many unfamiliar words from the original are retained in the text. Word to word exact translation may not convey the meaning properly. Those times, especially in Persian translations of Sanskrit works, many deviations in the translation from the original are seen because either they were done by a board of scholars, or they might not have been directly translated from the original texts, or they might have been translated as heard orally from others. Many a time the influence of the translator's time is reflected in the choice of words.

A gifted translator is an alchemist who changes a piece of gold into another piece of gold. Translations can only be metamorphic, not literal.

Literature in any language takes birth and lives within one's linguistic area and cannot live of its own beyond the specific language or locale. It is only the translators who enable literary creations to be reborn again and again, thrive from one province to the other, from one country to the other. In the field of literature, the role of a translator is not only immensely constructive but also indispensable.

In modern world where communication is playing a vital role in information dissemination, the translation can serve as the best means for preserving and enriching the cultural treasures of the world. The translation gives strength and dignity to the original.

Judged from these angles, the Persian version of the Sanskrit *Yoga-Vāsiṣṭha* (*Laghu*) stands as a classic apart.

In portraying the philosophy of India before the Persian audience, the author of the Persian version remained totally faithful to the essence of the original text and not to its form. He did not retain the *śloka*s, instead his translation is in simple elegant prose. But the structure of subject into six chapters called *prakaraṇa*s are maintained as in the original. They are:

(i) *Birāg Prakaraṇ* (*Vairāgya Prakaraṇa,* chapter on renunciation).

(ii) *Mumukṣu Bivahār Prakaraṇ* (*Mumukṣu Vyavahāra Prakaraṇa,* discipline for aspirant longing for liberation).

(iii) *Utpatti Prakaraṇ* (*Utpatti Prakaraṇa,* chapter on creation).

(iv) *Istit Prakaraṇ* (*Sthithi Prakaraṇa,* chapter on preservation).

(v) *Upaśam Prakaraṇ* (*Upaśama Prakaraṇa,* chapter on quiescence of mind).

(vi) *Nirbān Prakaraṇ* (*Nirvāṇa Prakaraṇa,* chapter on liberation).

The beauty of the translation is that the proper names and technical terms and the sequence of the stories are maintained as in the original Sanskrit. Only phonetic variation is seen such as *ja* for *ya* and *ba* for *va* which is a natural linguistic phenomenon seen in modern Indian languages. Examples:

Birāg for *Vairāgya*, Bālmīki for Vālmīki, *Jog-Bashisht* for *Yoga-Vāsiṣṭha*, Bisvāmitra for Viśvāmitra, Dasarat for Daśaratha, Icvāk for Ikṣvāku, Byās for Vyās, *baḍvānal* for *vaḍavānala*, Bedānt for Vedānta, Sukdev for Śukadeva, *bāsna* for *vāsanā*, *bicār* for *vicāra*, *abidyā* for *avidyā*, *rkshir* for *ṛṣi*, *byāla* for *vyāla*, *bideh* for *videha*, *bilās* for *vilās*, Pralād for Prahlāda, Sikadwaj for Śikhidhvaja, *saraptyāg* for *sarvatyāg*, Bringīsa for Bhṛngīśa, and *curāla* for *cūḍālā*. Some terms are the same like *śāstra*, *jīvanmukta*, *vedāntins*, *paramātmā*, *prakāśasvarūp*, *cidākaśa*, *saṁkalp*, etc.

Another striking feature is retaining the terms as found in the original and adding a small explanation to it as a tag to make it more explicit to the target audience. For example, Bhāradvāja, disciple (*Shagerd*) of Bālmīk; Bālmīk, the author (mosan-nef) of *Rāmāyaṇa*; *ahaṅkār ya'nee* (namely) *khod beene* (self-conceit); *kāma ya'nee shahvat* (lust); *saṁsāra ya'nee ālam* (universe); *avidyā ya'nee madanee* (ignorance) and *pātāla ya'nee tabaghe payeen zameen* (strata below the earth).

Though the author of the Persian version is a close follower of the original Sanskrit, yet he had added some new dimension. He has added local colouring conducive to the mind of the people for whom this has been translated. Sometimes the corresponding Persian terms are substituted to make the text more homely and appealing. For example, *sheytān* for *rākṣasa*; *gule neeloofar* (water lily) for *kamala* (lotus); *derakhte tooba* (a tree in Paradise) for *kalpavṛkṣa*; and *ābe hayāt* (water of life) for *jñāna* (knowledge).

Sometimes the words in vogue in those times of translation get reflected. Rāmchandar for Rāma, Avadh for Ayodhyā, and Mahādev for Śiva show the popular influence of *Rāma-carita-mānasa* of Tulasīdāsa.

Similarly in the first chapter when Rāma goes on pilgrimage the Persian version brings in Bharat whereas the original Sanskrit text mentions only Lakṣmaṇa. This popularity of Bharat reflects the devotional period of Tulasīdāsa.

The order of the stories is maintained as in the original. Sometimes some are added for explanatory background. For example, a detailed note on the enmity between Viśvāmitra and Vasiṣṭha, and Viśvāmitra getting the title of *brahmarṣi* is given in the Persian version and this is not found in the Sanskrit as the Sanskrit readers already conversant with the stories are aware. Some stories are omitted; for example, the story of *vilva* fruit, black stone, and *vetāla* as they are too typical of Indian religion, and too technical and cryptic for the Persian audience.

In the Sanskrit *Laghu-Yoga-Vāsiṣṭha* the poet has extraordinary skill and has employed similes and metaphors which speak of his highly developed poetic imagination and keen insight into human nature and deep observation. By profuse use of similies, the philosophy becomes exquisite.

The Persian version is crisp and lucid. The author composed for a different audience who do not have a background of Sanskrit. So his poetic similes are limited. Intentionally he avoided Sanskritic pedantry and literary embellishment, as he wrote for the Persian audience. Though he used most unvarnished language, yet some poetic excellence can be traced here and there.

One more striking feature is one stanza in Persian is inserted in every chapter in tune with the subject matter. This gives an individualistic character to the translation.

Here it was a mission. It was important for the author's mission to impart the ideas of the sacred Sanskrit text he was translating by making use of interpretative translation rather than conforming to literal style of translation. Spiritual wisdom needs not only translation but also cultural transference. His translation was as literal as he could manage so that those reading the Persian translation could grasp the purport of the original. Here the author succeeds in that. It is faithful to the original and at the same time maintains an individualistic character. Thus it sets as a classic in itself.

12

Greek Logos and Vedic Vāc
Creative Power

Nicholaos Kazanas

1. Abstract

ALTHOUGH the power of Speech is the means whereby many phenomena are created in the Judaic *Genesis* (ch. 1), the Greek and Christian *logos* (in the Gospel of John) does not seem to signify speech but rather "wisdom, reason, law" and the like — except in some gnostic writings where speech is a divine creative power. Only the *vāc-brahman* (later *śabda-brahman*) doctrine in India denotes creation through both wisdom and speech, and forms the basis for a full philosophical and grammatical system: Vāc is herself a creative deity. Notions like Darwinian evolution, intelligent design and materialization through the power of divine speech are also examined.

2. Introduction

Much has been written about Vāc, the Indic deity of speech and language; just as much and more, perhaps, about Logos. Some scholars have even brought the two in close connection: a good recent example is Th. McEvilley who, following others like W. Guthrie (1962), thinks that both Greek and Indic "cultures may have been purveying a Late Bronze Age cult of language which can be seen in Egyptian, Persian and other

Near-Eastern traditions" (2002: 672). This is an over-inflated and erroneous statement because there is not the slightest hint in the Greek (including Mycenaean) civilization that *logos* "speech, language" was worshipped as a deity. Certainly, Hermes, Apollon (with his Muses), or Athena, have connections with speech and writing but there is no deity "Logos," a deity embodying language, as Vedic *vāc* was. Neither did the Egyptians or any other Near-Eastern culture promote even minimally a cult of speech or the worship of language, again like Vedic *vāc* or the later *śabda-brahman*.

The *śabda-brahman* of the (mainly but not exclusively later) Vedic tradition corresponds to what has come to be known in the West as the Logos Doctrine. This doctrine — to sum it up — states that the Creator-god created the universe and all its beings through utterance or the word (= speech). This notion is explicit or implicit in several ancient teachings. But it is by no means certain that in all cases the word *logos* denotes speech, utterance; on the contrary, in some cases the word most clearly does not denote speech. I shall, in this paper, concentrate on the Christian, Judaic, Greek, Egyptian and Vedic traditions. The "Logos Doctrine" itself comes from John's Gospel in the Christian *New Testament* where it is said "In the beginning was the *logos* . . . and the *logos* was God" (1.1): the Greek word *logos* here has over the centuries been translated as "word" (Latin *verbum*). The gospel statement is, of course, only an image, a figure of speech and not to be taken literally since any Creator-god is (in time, space and power) prior to any manifestation of form and matter and therefore could have no mouth and speech. This notion of godly "speech" refers most probably to vibrations within God's own unmanifest substance and intelligence which produce manifest forms at different levels of materiality, subtle and gross. We shall see variants of this idea in the cultures we shall examine.

3. We begin with **the Christian tradition** since the Logos Doctrine derives largely from it. Contrary to widespread belief, we don't really know much about Christ's teaching (see, e.g. Ehrman, 2004, 2003; Pagels, 2003; Bauer, 1934/71). We have much material from later centuries, and the Church Fathers (East and West) certainly made Christianity a complete and viable religion with its system of ethics, ritual and theology; but Christ's own actual teaching is by no means easy to determine. The primary sources, whether canonical gospels or gnostic and apocryphal ones, have been severely tampered with from the very beginning and require fresh detailed study and re-appraisal. For instance, there is no cosmogony in the four canonical gospels and this is highly problematic since it is most unlikely that in the context of man's salvation Jesus would not have referred to cosmogony and man's genesis and place in the cosmos, even if he should only have referred to the *Old Testament*. In any event, Christ himself never alludes to any Logos Doctrine anywhere in the early writings including the gnostic and apocryphal texts, though some gnostic texts do refer to it.

In some places in the canonical Gospels he is shown to have awareness of the great power of speech as in the incident with the Roman centurion who points out that Jesus need not walk to the centurion's house to cure his sick servant; Jesus need only "speak the word" there and then, and the cure would be effected — as indeed was done (Mth 8.5 ff; Lk 7.2 ff). Jesus connects this miraculous power of the Word with faith, in this case the faith of the centurion.[1] Faith and power of speech are connected again in other miraculous deeds: once,

1. This miraculous power is quite different from the Sceptics' doctrine that they could "cure by *logos* [= argument] the opinions of dogmatic thinkers" (Sextos Empirikos *Outlines of Purrhonism*, 3.280-1).

he tells the disciples that they cannot expel a demon because they have no faith and that if they had only as much as a grain of mustard-seed they would say to a mountain "move" and the mountain would move indeed (Mth 17.20); on another occasion, after he caused a fig tree to wither, he told the disciples the very same thing (Mth 21.21). Elsewhere, when the Devil challenges him to turn the stone into bread, he says "It is written that man shall not live by bread alone, but by every word of God" (Lk 4.4). Here the "word" is Greek *rhēma* "word, utterance, saying" and it may well mean "commandment, teaching" or something esoteric and/or spiritual like a finer vibration or energy bringing a message from a higher level than man's ordinary existence. Again, Jesus says that this generation (i.e. his contemporaries) will not pass until all things be done and that "heaven and earth shall pass away but my words [=*logos* plural] shall not pass away" (Mk 13.31; Lk 21.33): but here as in most other places *logoi* denotes the utterances constituting his teaching. Thus, we have some clear statements showing that Jesus knew of the power of the Word even though there is no mention of the Word's cosmogonic power; otherwise *logos/rhēma* means "ordinary word, formulation; injunction, ordinance, teaching."

However, it should be added that at least one gnostic text, *The Gospel of Truth*, alludes to a metaphysical/magical system of Language with "letters of the truth which they alone speak who know them. Each letter is a complete "thought" like a complete book, since they are letters written by the Unity . . . for the Aeons [=worlds] in order that by means of [these] letters they should know the Father" (23: 7-19: RNL 43).

4. The only mention of the Word's cosmogonic power is in the beginning of John's Gospel. In the English of the King

James authorized version —

> In the beginning was the word [=*logos*] and the word was with God and the word was God. The same [=*hautos*: this one] was in the beginning with God. All things were made by him [=*autou*: God or *logos*? Not really clear]; and without him [=*autou*] was not anything made that was made. In him [=*autōi*: God or *logos*? Not really clear] was life; and the life was the light of men. . . . That was the true light which lighteth every man that cometh into the world. . . . And the word was made flesh and dwelt among us."
>
> — John, 1.1-14

According to this, then, the word was God and life and light; through it all things were made and it is within every man in the world. Here however we have a problem — apart from the ambiguity of the Greek pronoun *autos* which could refer either to *logos* or God (all masculine) but which we take to refer to *logos*. Were the translators of the authorized version justified in rendering *logos* as "word" (and of course many centuries earlier the Latin *verbum*)?. . . Although much has been written and it is now generally taken for granted that *logos* means "word," there are grave doubts about this in people like me who do not agree with this. In this context *logos* need not mean "utterance, word." It could with better reasoning mean "wisdom, reason, (Latin *ratio*), proportion, plan, measure(-ment), law, computation," etc.: there are almost three full pages in GEL.[2] Thus, we could just as easily translate, "In the beginning was Reason (or Law, or Wisdom)." There is nothing else at all in the Gospels, canonical or apocryphal or, to be more precise, in Christ's reported own words, to indicate that God created the world through Word-Speech (except some gnostic texts). As one expert puts it "Scholars generally agree

---

2. Oxford, *Greek-English Lexicon*: see Bibliography.

that the Word in John performs functions more commonly attributed to Wisdom" (Perkins, 1993:118).

Be it noted that we don't know who exactly evangelist John was. It is widely held that he is the same as the one who wrote the *Apocalypse* on the island Patmos. Perhaps so, but the two texts are so very different and the *Apocalypse* is so full of the visions and prophecies common to much Judaic "apocalyptic" literature (unlike John's Gospel), that it can hardly be by the same writer. Many Fathers of the early Church did not include John's *Apocalypse* in the *New Testament* canon (Ehrman, 2004). Then, the evangelist is identified with John, the "beloved disciple" of Jesus. But even here we are entitled to entertain serious doubts: nowhere is it stated that John was the beloved disciple; this Gospel was in all probability written originally in Greek and there is no evidence to the contrary; moreover, where the other Gospels refer to "people" in general, John's Gospel says "Jews" (e.g. John, 19.40) as though the writer is not a Jew. Therefore, it is not unreasonable that here *logos* belongs to the Greek philosophical tradition and means "reason, wisdom" and not "word."

However, in a non-canonical gnostic text, the *Trimorphic Protennoia* (= The First-inner-meaning having-three-forms), composed *c.* CE 150, this supreme Creative Power declares her attributes: "I am the First Thought that dwells in light. . . . I am the invisible One within the All. . . . [I dwell] within the Silence. . . . It is through me that gnosis [=knowledge] comes forth. . . . I am the real Voice. . . . I am the Mother [of] the Voice speaking in many ways, completing the All. . . ." (Robinson, 1990: 513, 517). All this sounds remarkably like two hymns of Book 10 of the Indic earliest text, the *R̥gveda,* in which speech-knowledge similarly declares her powers. In the *Apocryphon of John* we read that "By the Word the Anointed

[=Christ/Christos] divine self-originate [*Autogenes*] made the entirety (or all things)" (Layton, 1995: 33). But, although in other gnostic and similar texts of the second century CE, we find phonetic exercises, i.e. sounding aloud vowels and syllables, (e.g.: Robinson, 210, 324, etc.) as are found in the much earlier Vedic documents, (e.g. *Chāndogya Upaniṣad,* 1.1. ff), no trace can be found of a language system as in the Vedic Tradition (§ 11-14).

5. Thus, in the early canonical Christian sources there is no explicit doctrine that the world and its phenomena were created through word/speech and that this is reflected in man's speech/utterances. We have only Christ's statement that speech (utterance, word) is a mighty force that can produce results out of the ordinary. And in some gnostic texts we find an awareness that speech-knowledge is a great creative force.

6. The GEL cites *Corpus Hermeticum I,* i.e. *Poimandres,* § 6, "the luminous *logos,* son of god, coming from Nous [= Intelligence, Mind]," which is very close to John's Gospel both in meaning ("the word was made flesh," i.e. Jesus Christ, son of God) and in time of composition — say *c.* CE 80–100. It cites also several statements of Philo (the hellenized Jew of Alexandria), to the effect that the *logos* is God's wisdom (=Greek *Sophia*) and that through this the world was made.

7. The Greek culture from which, it is often stated, the Logos Doctrine derives, gives much the same meaning. The Stoics certainly had this doctrine and much has been written about it. Diogenes Laertius, who is really our most voluminous, though not the sole source, writes that, according to them, god is the "seminal (=*spermatikos*) *logos* of the Cosmos" (7.136): when the world gets dissolved in its periodic cycle, this remains to start afresh the new cycle of the Cosmos. Here again, the experts tell us that the term means rather "reason, measure, law" and the like but not "word/utterance." To quote an expert on the Stoics:

> *Logos* has many implications . . . not only is it *language* "speech, expression," it is the *explanation* of a thing, which may be the account or formula of its constitution, and the statement of its *purpose* . . . a *rational* activity . . . correct reason. . . . Perhaps "plan" . . . [as] the plan of a house not only indicates its shape but implies the intentions of a rational being, its architect. And a plan of a campaign does not relate to something static like a house, but to a process of which the later stages are foreseen from the first.
>
> — Sandbach, 1975: 72[3]

Consider too the statement Diogenes Laertius attributes to Chrusippos, one of the early Stoic leaders, that "Life according to *logos* [=reason] rightly becomes natural living; for logos supervenes like a craftsman to shape impulse (=*hormē*)" (7.86).

A.A. Long connects the Stoic *logos* (and fire) as a creative, regulating element with the ideas of Herakleitos (1986: ch. 4.2.4). This Ephesian pre-Socratic philosopher wrote of *logos* as something that can be heard and comprehended (not unlike the Indic *śruti* of the ancient *ṛṣis?*) but not necessarily as divine utterance.

> *Fragment 1 :* Of this *logos* which exists, people always fail to understand it both before they hear of it and after they have heard. For although all things happen according to this *logos*, people seem not to have experience of it, even when they experience the words and deeds which I explain distinguishing each thing according to its nature [=*phusis*] and explaining how it is.

---

3. The Stoics had developed logic and grammar but had connected neither of the two to different levels and powers of speech, as the Indians had done (see § 12 below).

> *Fragment 50* : Listening not to me but to *logos* it is wise to agree that all things are one.[4]

The last phrases of *Fr 1* clearly distinguish between what Herakleitos is saying and *logos* itself which is an impersonal, universal principle of reason, measure and the like. *Fr 50* does the same with equal clarity. So neither here, in Herakleitos, can *logos* be taken to mean word/utterance/speech (by a Creator-god).

However, the sense of utterance appears in an extant statement attributed to Xenophanes, a somewhat earlier pre-Socratic (born *c.* 570). In one of his extant fragments (KRS, p. 169) it is said that God shakes or puts into motion (= *kradainei*) all things without effort, only with the thought (*phreni*) of his mind or intelligence (*noou*). Thought (or "mental energy" for *phren-*) implies words or, at least, a vibration in mind, a movement of intelligence, that then affects physical things purposefully and therefore has significance from the start. This instance is the nearest we come in early Greek philosophy to the idea that God creates or governs things by the power of thought and (by extension) word.

8. If there had been an explicit Logos Doctrine, (i.e. that God creates through utterance) in pre-Socratic thought, Plato would certainly have mentioned it somewhere in his *Dialogues* or *Epistles*; if not Plato, then Aristotle would have referred to it somewhere in his voluminous work, especially perhaps in his *Rhetoric* or *Poetics*. In the *Timaios* where Plato describes in full the act(s) of creation, he mentions nowhere the instrumentality of speech. The sense one gets is that of a Master-craftsman manipulating gross and finer kinds of matter; there is nothing subtle like speech.

---

4. For a good discussion see KRS, 1999: 186-88.

9. In **the Jewish Old Testament** we find several references to the power of the word and we touched on one, "the almighty *logos*" (possibly "reason, wisdom"), in § 5, above. Psalm 19 (or 18 in some editions) has another reference: "The heavens declare the glory of god. . . . Day unto day uttereth speech. . . . There is no speech or language, where their voice is not heard. Their line is gone out through all the earth and their words to the end of the world. In them hath he set a tabernacle for the sun" (1-4). The implication in these verses is that the celestial sound or utterance permeates every speech and language of man. In other words, human speech is constituted of this higher sound or whatever it is. But this is a poetic metaphor: God's laws are impressed in the celestial phenomena and thence run through all nature everywhere. It is not really a statement of the Logos Doctrine.

The crucial passage in the *Old Testament* is in *Genesis,* ch. 1. "And God said, Let there be light: and there was light." And so on with the firmament, the waters, the earth, etc. In every case God spoke and the utterance materialized. However, before this we read that "In the beginning God created the heaven and the earth" but we are not told how this creation was effected. Then in verse 27 — "God created man in his own image . . . male and female he created them" but, again we are not told by what process they were created. Later, in ch. 2, verse 7, "God formed man of the dust of the ground, and breathed into his nostrils the breath of life." Thus we have two versions of man's creation and neither involved the power of speech. In *Genesis* ch. 1, only after heaven and earth were created in an unstated mode was the power of speech used for the creation and differentiation of light, firmament and stars, waters, land and plants (3-15). This description assumes, of course, creation through the word, but the Doctrine itself is nowhere stated.

Nor is there any hint of supernatural creation/ materialization through the use of language anywhere else in the *Old Testament* or any other early Hebrew writings. We meet only miraculous transformations and other wondrous events: thus the rods of Moses, Aaron and the Egyptian sorcerers become serpents before the Pharaoh and later there is diffusion of frogs and dog-flies and fall of hail throughout Egypt, etc. (*Exodus,* 7.8-13); still later Moses makes the waters (of the Red Sea?) part so that the Jews could pass, and so on. These miraculous events certainly required some magical/ supernatural power and speech, but they are, strictly speaking, transformations of already existing materials in our world, not materializations.

In the *Kabbalah* the creation is closely connected with the sounds of the (Jewish) alphabet. In this, three of them, Aleph, Mem and Shin (with which correspond the elements air, water and fire) are the "mothers" of the other 19 sounds all together forming "the Foundation of all things" (Poncé, 1997: 39. ff). All this sounds very interesting and certainly merits consideration. But since the earliest *Kabbalah* literature is thought to appear between CE 300 and 600, this (mystical but unorthodox) aspect of Judaism is too late to concern us in this study.

10. In the Egyptian culture one mode of creating man is through clay. Ram-headed god Khnum creates men out of clay on his potter's wheel and breathes into them life. Whether this view and that of the Judaic *Genesis* are linked causally it is not certain. If the Jews borrowed this idea of man's creation it is more likely that the Mesopotamian tradition (creation, again with clay) is the source, since they originally moved out of Ur (*Genesis,* 11.28; 15.7).

There are other accounts of cosmogony and anthropogony in the ancient Egyptian texts (Allen, 1988) but the most important and relevant to our study here is the one where the worlds are created through speech. One spell in the *Coffin Texts,* IV, 321 (Faulkner, 1973), says that the High God devised "the utterance" whereby manifestation will come about. A much fuller statement comes with the Memphite Theology where Ptah assumes the position of Supreme God outranking all others, including Atum[5]: in fact in this tractate all gods are literally expressions of Ptah. The relevant passages follow:

> "Ptah-Nun, the father who made Atum . . . is the heart and tongue of the Nine [principal gods of Heliopolis]." Thus Ptah displaces Atum and becomes the life-giving force and speech of the Heliopolitan Ennead. "There took shape on the heart, there took shape on the tongue the form of Atum. For the very great one is Ptah who gave [life] to all the gods . . . through his heart and through his tongue." Here all cosmic gods are concepts in Ptah's heart/mind and come to exist as utterances of his tongue.
>
> "Thus heart and tongue rule over all the limbs in accordance with the teaching that it (the heart, or he, Ptah) is in every body." Here Ptah, or his powers, enter into all beings. In John's Gospel likewise the Logos is said to enter into all living beings. — 1.9

This Egyptian account is akin to the absolute monism of the Veda which has the creative principle engender all beings from its own substance and enter into them to be their Self. As, to my knowledge, no other ancient tradition has a similar doctrine, we turn now to the Indic culture.

5. The text is that of the Shabaka Stone which is now thought to derive from an original *c.* 1300–1250. The text used is primarily that in M. Lichtheim, 1980.

11. In the Vedic Tradition the idea of creating through the word (or subtle vibration) is very prominent and is expressed in many different ways. The *śabda-brahman* (= Divine Sound/ Word) doctrine is finally and firmly established in the *Vākyapadīya* of the grammarian-philosopher Bhartṛhari, who is generally thought to belong to the fifth century CE. But the connection of speech *vāc* with the Supreme is well attested even as early as the *ṚV* (*Ṛgveda*). A cursory, rather introductory study was done many years ago by T. Murti (1974). Other relevant studies, close to the view expressed in this paper, can be found in H.G. Coward and K.K. Raja (1990).

In the *Śatapatha Brāhmaṇa,* XI.1.6.3, when Lord Prajāpati emerged from the cosmic egg he spoke: the sound *bhūḥ* became the earth *pṛthvī/bhūmi;* the sound *bhuvaḥ* became the mid-space *antarikṣa;* the sound *svaḥ* became the sky. In the *Taittirīya Saṁhitā* (Black Yajurveda), III.1.1. Lord Prajāpati creates different classes of creatures through desire, penance and speech. Numerous are the statements in the Upaniṣads that the Supreme or the Creator-god speaks, desires, envisions or thinks, and then creation proceeds: thus *Bṛhadāraṇyaka Upaniṣad,* I.2.4 says "He desired (*kāma-*) 'Let a second self issue from me' and he united speech with mind"; the *Aitareya Upaniṣad,* I.1.1 says "The *ātman* alone was this in the beginning . . . he envisioned (*īkṣ-*)" "Let me generate (*sṛj-*) the worlds" and he generated the worlds; the *Chāndogya Upaniṣad,* VI.2.3 says of the Primal Being "It envisioned "May I be many, may I propagate' . . ."; and so on.

This aspect goes back to the *ṚV* where not only gods but also *ṛṣis* "seers, powerful sages, wise visionaries" (=prophets, saints), could produce transformations and materializations through *dhī-/dhīti-* "power of insight, vision" (3.11.3; 3.12.7; 4.10.10; etc.). J. Gonda explored this theme most thoroughly in his seminal study *Vision of the Vedic Poets* (1963: see especially, p. 98 ff).

12. This formulation is very similar to that of Xenophanes in § 6 end, above, where god sets things in motion by thought or mental energy. The envisioning (*īkṣ-*) is similar also to the projection of creation through vision (*theōmai* "observe, look") in Plotinus. This is especially clear in one passage in the *Enneads*. According to the Plotinian view there is the One, indescribable, beyond it all, just like the One Absolute (*Brahman*) of the Vedic Tradition; from that One issues forth Nous (=Intelligence/ Mind) which is the Being and Nature of all and everything, and from which are created souls (*psuchē*) or subtle entities and, at a lower level, material things. This creation is an emanation proceeding from *theōria* "viewing, vision, observing," and *Enneads*, III.8.3-4 says explicitly that creation (*poiēsis*) comes about as a result of *theōria* which does nothing else except envision/look on. This view is unknown in previous Greek philosophy — except, as was said, in Xenophanes.

Projection of this supremely subtle sort through *theōria* "envisioning" is just as much a fine vibration as speech. Obviously both are images of the Creative Principle's innate creative power since, naturally, in that primal state, it has neither eyes to see nor tongue to speak.

13. In the *Maitrī Upaniṣad* we find the *śabda-brahman* doctrine clearly stated. The passage 6.22 says *dve vāva brahmaṇī abhidhyeye śabdaścāśabdaśca* "two brahma-aspects are to be meditated upon, sound and non-sound." "By *śabda* alone is the silent one revealed," the passage continues and ends with *śabdabrahmaṇi niṣṇātaḥ param brahmādhigacchati* "whoever is well-versed in the sound-*Brahman* reaches the silent-*Brahman*." From other texts we know that *śabda-brahman* has four states. Bhartṛhari's *VP* describes the four as *vaikharī* "gross language/

sound," *madhyamā* "middle-one," *paśyantī* "one who looks on" and *parā* "highest, beyond it all."[6] This fourfold division goes back to the *Ṛgveda*, of course, and should not be confused with the four kinds of speech mentioned in *Śatapatha Brāhmaṇa*, IV, 1.3.16, that of men, of animals, of birds and of small creeping creatures.

Goddess Vāc is well attested in the hymns of the *ṚV* and two of them in the tenth *maṇḍala* are devoted to her: 10.71, ostensibly to *jñāna* "knowledge, wisdom," but extolling Vāc; also 10.125, where the goddess herself speaks and declares her attributes. According to scholiasts many other hymns refer to her, e.g. 3.53.15-6, 5.78.8, etc. The best-known, perhaps, is the reference in 1.164.45 *catvā́ri vā́k párimitā padāni* "Vāc has been measured out in four divisions/levels." These four are not named but the same stanza says *turī́yam vācó manuṣyà vadanti* "men speak the fourth level of Vāc" — while the other three lie hidden (*guhā*). Here obviously Speech/Logos starts at the highest level (corresponding to Bhartṛhari's *parā*) and ends up at the grossest which is not "hidden" since men speak it (corresponding to *vaikharī*). This is confirmed by stanza 35 which says *brahmā́yám vācáḥ paramam vyóma* "the *Brahman* is the highest heaven (abode) of Vāc." This is not a merely descriptive academic-like statement. It is linked with man's highest aspiration and effort — self-realization. For in stanza 45 it is said that all four levels are known by true brāhmaṇas who are wise: *tāni vidur brāhmaṇā́ yé manī́ṣíṇaḥ*.

---

6. Cf. for instance, Bhartṛhari in *VP* I, 14 the first *yoga* of sound is "the door leading to liberation." Then I, 134 gives the four divisions: *vaikharyā madhyamāyāśca paśyantyāścaetad bhūtam; anekatīrthabhedāyās trayyā vācaḥ paraṃ padam*. This, together with its commentary, which Bhartṛhari himself is thought to have written, explains their connection with Grammar.

Thus the Upaniṣadic teaching in *Maitrī Upaniṣad* about *śabda-brahman* and Bhartṛhari's grammatical doctrines continue, in fact, the tradition of a Ṛgvedic system concerning Vāc and *Brahman*. But before going further let us consider another aspect found in the Upaniṣads.

14. The *Bṛhadāraṇyaka Upaniṣad*, IV.1.2 says unequivocally *vāg vai brahma*: "speech indeed is *Brahman*, the Absolute" and the *Brahman*'s abode (*āyatana*), again, is speech. In the same passage it is said that Vāc/Brahman should be worshipped/approached as (*upāsita*) *prajnā/prajñatā* "intelligence, wisdom."[7] S. Radhakrishnan commenting on this passage says that "Vāc is Logos, wisdom" (1953: 247). But while the two, speech and wisdom, are closely related, and from one point of view may in some contexts be denoted by the same word *vāc*, and so be identical, nonetheless *vāc* is different from *prajñā, prajñāna,*[8] *vijñāna* or *vidyā* since it involves sound, speech, utterance. And this takes us back again to the *Ṛgveda* where *śabda* "sound/word" is not found and *vāc, vacana, vǎcas,* etc. are used for language, sound, utterance, voice, word. (The word *nǎda* "roar" is Ṛgvedic but has no apparent association with *Brahman* or *vāc*. The verb *dhvani-* "sound" is attested in the *ṚV* but the noun *dhvani* "sound, roar, crackle," etc. appears first in the *Atharvaveda* and acquires great linguistic significance only in later writings: so this too can be ignored for our purposes.)

Leaving aside some enigmatic references to *vāc* in *ṚV*, 1.164, let us examine the two hymns in Maṇḍala 10. Hymn 71 says in st. 1 that the foremost utterance sent forth gave names

---

7. Cf. Greek *prognōsis* (see GEL) which is not only philologically cognate but also quite close in meaning "foreknowledge, immediate knowledge [coming from a higher level]."

8. See *Aitareya Upaniṣad* 3.3 or, in some editions, 5.5: *prajñānam brahma* "*brahman* is consciousness/intelligence/wisdom."

(*nāmadheya*) and, through love (*preṇā*), manifested (*āviḥ*) what was best *śreṣṭha* and faultless *aripra*. So creation began, according to this hymn, with love and names that manifested and materialized perfect forms — an idea rather incomprehensible for most of us. Then stanzas 2 and 3 say that wise men (*dhīra*) created (*kṛ-*) with mind language in which lies *lakṣmī* "blessedness, fortune, splendour"; yet this language *vāc* is found residing (*praviṣṭā*) within realized visionaries (*ṛṣi-*). Some misuse this power (st. 9), and, since they are dull of mind and do not follow the path of good action (*sukṛta-*), they have no share of *vāc* (st. 5-6): they see and hear but *vāc* eludes them; she reveals herself only to true brāhmaṇas and *ṛṣi*s (st. 4, 8). Implied throughout the hymn is the idea that humans can realize within themselves the power of goddess Vāc and so rise to a higher level of knowledge and being. St. 11 indeed mentions the true brāhmaṇa who declares the system of knowledge concerning living beings *vádati jātavidyā́m*.

Hymn 10.125 confirms our interpretation of 10.71 in declaring through Vāc's own mouth Vāc's attributes. "The man I love (*kāmaye*) I make immensely mighty, a sage (*sumedha*), a *ṛṣi* and a [true] *brāhmaṇa*" (st. 5). This omnipotent goddess sustains (*bhṛ-*) all the gods, even Varuṇa, Indra and Agni (st. 1-2). With her omnipresence she pervades earth and heaven yet extends beyond, forming and holding (*ārabhamāṇā*) all worlds and creatures (*bhuvanāni*); thus again all phenomena become manifest through Logos/Speech (st. 7-8). It is not therefore surprising that, especially since this Power is within humans (10.71.2-3), whoever realizes it within himself becomes a mighty sage.

15. The hymns are not limited to generalities as in 10.71; they provide particular examples as well. One of them is the Atri hymn 5.40.6. We have seen the close affinity between *vāc* and

Brahman, the force that empowers prayer and ritual. It is a holy power and, like *vāc*, it too has four levels of operation. Thus in 5.40.6 it said that the great *ṛṣi* Atri rehabilitated the sun by means of the "fourth [level of] holy-power" *turī́yeṇa brāhmaṇa*. Then, the other great *ṛṣi* Vasiṣṭha helped king Sudās defeat the confederation of the ten hostile kings again through the holy-power *brāhmaṇa* (7.33.3). But the deities also resort to *Brahman* and through its mediation place the sperm-drop (*drapsa*) of gods Mitra-Varuṇa upon a lotus (*puṣkara;* or pitcher: *kumbha*) whereby then seer Vasiṣṭha is born (7.33.11)! Like *vāc*, *Brahman* too is within man: as another seer put it after he had lauded the weapons of war, *bráhma várma mámā́ntaram* (6.75.19) "my inmost armour is Brahma-power." It may be thought that this Supreme Power is only in *ṛṣi*s, sages and saints. In fact, it is in every man, say the texts, and awaits the proper time and proper effort to manifest. Anyone can, if they so wish and make the simple attempt, have a good glimpse of the four levels or states; plain observation shows that, indeed, all forms of spoken or written language (*vaikharī*) come from thoughts (*madhyamā*); these from some sort of unformed, perhaps emotional, knowledge (*paśyantī*) and that again from a deep silence full of potency (*parā*). (For a full discussion with evidence from the *Atharvaveda* too see Kazanas, 2005a.)

Yet another *ṛṣi*, Viśvāmitra, asked two rivers to stop flowing so that he and his Bharata companions with their carts could cross, and the rivers complied (*ṚV*, 3.33) — an incident reminiscent of Moses crossing the (Red) sea with his Jewish people. Here, in this hymn, the *ṛṣi* uses manifestly the power of speech.

This power is clearly evident in the Ṛbhus, the three brothers, who create all sorts of wonders "with effective prayers" through unusual force of mind (*ṚV*, 1.20.2; 4.32.2,

36.2). They are said to use various aspects of supernatural energy like *manas* "mental power," *dhī* and *dhīti-* "visionary power," *māyā* "power of knowledge/measure" and *śaci* "skill, speech": with these powers they create not only concrete objects like chalices (ladles?) and a chariot but also prosperity, vision, longevity, fame and rejuvenation (*R̥V*, 1.20.2, 4; 3.54.17, 60.1-2; 4.36.2, 4, 5, 7; etc.). The R̥bhus started as normal humans and only after exhibiting these miraculous powers were admitted into the mansion of the Sun god Savitr̥, where they were granted immortality and were raised to godhood.

16. We have also examples of **materialization** from a higher to a lower sphere. The birth of sage Vasiṣṭha was mentioned immediately above: the All-gods Viśvedevāḥ placed the semen of gods Mitra-Varuṇa upon a lotus and the great *r̥ṣi* was born thereby. This was accomplished through *brāhmaṇa* "the holy-power" (7.33.11) and it is clearly a case of materialization. The "gods" are the invisible forces of nature and the "lotus" is the sky or *antarikṣa* "mid-space, mid-air," or ether *ākāśa*; or "lotus" could be a woman's womb (especially since the next stanza says that Vasiṣṭha is born of the nymph Urvaśī, who is a non-human, semi-divine being). Whatever "lotus" represents, the act is one of immaterial invisible forces causing the materialization and generation of a human being: it is a higher energy/quality (godly sperm-drop) descending and being incarnated as a man. Because of this higher nature, presumably, it is possible for Vasiṣṭha later to travel in the boat of Lord Varuṇa, his "father," together with him. For the same reason, again, we must assume, the R̥bhus being of a higher origin (having descended from a higher plane), can after appropriate action return to their initial divine immortality. This I think holds for all human beings: R̥gvedic hymns and the whole Vedic tradition teach that any human being can, with appropriate knowledge and action, ascend from the lowly mortal condition to a supra-mundane, divine state (Kazanas, 2005a) which is the original one, anyway.

Then, Urvaśī herself, an aquatic/celestial nymph takes on human form and for four years lives among mortals as the mistress/wife of (king) Purūravas, son of Iḷā or Iḍā (10.95). Later legendary gives them a son and make Purūravas immortal. The name Urvaśī means "far-reaching, wide-extending" (*uru+aś-*) and this is borne out by her description in 10.95.2/10/17.

A curious incident is the materialization of Iḍā/Iḷā in a passage in *Śatapatha Brāhmaṇa.* Iḷā is a goddess in the *ṚV* and is often invoked with other goddesses (1.13.9; 2.3.8; 5.5.8; etc.); but she is also the libation in sacrifices. In the *Brāhmaṇa,* 1.8.1.1-10 (or *Kāṇva* text, 2.7.3.1-8) sage Manu is saved by a fish in the Flood, lands on a mountain top and, now the sole human survivor, he practises worship and asceticism to obtain offspring. He also performs a sacrifice offering butter, milk and the like to the waters. Thence, in a year, was born a **woman who "arose becoming solid as it seemed"** *pibdamānēvodayāya.* She was Iḷā, now said to be Manu's daughter. Practising worship and austerities with her he engendered through her this human race, the race of Manu. As there is no hint of coition here, it may well be implied that, however incredible it seems to us, other humans were produced by the same magical process as Iḷā herself! In any event, Manu is repeatedly said to be the first institutor of sacrifice and father of mankind (*ṚV,* 2.33.13; etc.). Be it noted that the root *man-* from which the name Manu derives, is cognate with Greek *man-tis*"prophet, visionary" and English "man" and "mind." The Germanic tribes believed (according to Tacitus' *Germania,* 2) that they themselves ultimately derive from the sons of Mannus who was begotten of earth-born god Twisto: here also Mannus is cognate with "Manu."

Examples of materialization become more numerous in the epics *Mahābhārata* and *Rāmāyaṇa* and the Purāṇas, but enough has been said to illustrate this aspect.

17. Two aspects of the *vāc/Logos* doctrine remain to be briefly considered. One is the possibility of cross-influence among Greek, Judaeo-Christian, Egyptian and Indic traditions. The other is the implication of this doctrine regarding the Darwinian materialistic view of the creation of man.

It is fashionable in our days to see diffusion and cross-influences everywhere, even where none exists. This fashion goes back to synthesisers like J. Campbell (1949), Sir J.G. Fraser (1922) and Sir G.W. Cox (1882). Now, where there are obvious similarities of ideas (motifs, mythologems, themes) in two or more cultures we must decide between three possibilities: (a) The idea belonged to an older unitary system of thought which somehow broke into separate fragments that became separate traditions (e.g. the Proto-Indo-European culture and its subsequent branches). (b) The idea was borrowed by one culture from another and there is sufficient evidence (apart from the similarity of the idea in the different traditions) to demonstrate or, at least, suggest this. (c) The idea developed independently thanks to native intelligence.

Despite McEvilley's extravagant generalities, and the sources he cites to this effect (§ 2, above), I find no evidence of cross-influences except the early Christian "In the beginning was the *Logos*" (John, 1.1), and the subsequent doctrines developed by early Fathers and theologians (all very much later) are indebted to the Greek concept of *Logos* (in the Stoics and Herakleitos). The Greeks themselves most probably developed this doctrine quite independently: although *logos* does mean also "word, utterance, speech," the philosophical term means invariably "wisdom, reason, proportion, logic" and so could not come from Egypt or India since the Greek term here does not designate "speech" and since there is no evidence of significant Greek-Indian contacts before Alexander in the late fourth century (Kazanas, 2003). However, it is possible that the idea of the Unity of Being (i.e. the Self of man, *ātman*, is not other than the Self of the universe, *Brahman*), appearing in Hermetic and Gnostic writings and the Neo-Platonism of Plotinus, may well derive from India in the first century CE (ibid.).

It is possible that the Jews borrowed their own version of the Logos Doctrine (i.e. that God created the world(s) by utterance) from the Egyptians. If Moses is assigned to *circa* the twelfth century BCE, as most modern scholars think, and the Ptah text to *c.* 1300/1200 BCE, then, since the Jews were in Egypt and despite the absence of any other evidence, we have a very real possibility of borrowing by the Jews. However, if we take the traditional Exodus date 1446 BCE, then this Ptah text comes a little too late unless it did exist from an earlier period but was not so well known. Otherwise, I have argued elsewhere (2005b) that the Jews may during their stay in Ur (*Genesis* 11) have taken monotheism and the Logos doctrine from Indo-Āryan resident merchants there or visiting traders *c.* 1800 BCE or before.

What of the Indic Vāc Doctrine? . . . Bhartṛhari's *śabda-brahman* is later and need not concern us since it is obviously a development of the Ṛgvedic *vāc-Brahman* teaching. What is the date of the *Ṛgveda*? Of this we have no exact knowledge, but the available evidence suggests a date before 3200 BCE for the bulk of it. I have discussed the evidence in several papers (e.g. 1999, 2001, 2003, 2005) and so have others: S. Levitt places the early part of it in the late fourth millennium BCE (2003) while D. Frawley, like me, places the bulk of it before 3200 BCE (2001). I have, moreover, examined the possibility of "Vedic and Egyptian Cross-influences" and concluded that if there was any borrowing then it would be the Egyptians that did it, or else, and perhaps just as probably, both cultures derive this and many other ideas from an earlier, and to us lost, civilization. (Kazanas in press; for the theme "Creation Through the Word," ibid., § 15).

18. Creation through the *Logos* is a most important doctrine because, apart from anything else, it contradicts very plainly modern "scientific," evolutionary and materialist, views. I put "scientific" within quotation marks, because it is a term thoroughly misused by scholars, even scientists, and no longer deserves the veneration generally given to it. The so-called "scientific method" is nothing other than passionate interest in a subject, accurate observation, often entailing experimentation, and bright reasoning (attributes required in all research); it is no more infallible than other methods as has been demonstrated amply by T.S. Kuhn (1970), J.B. Cohen (1985/2001), C.B. Pert (1997/2003) and several others. Here I shall examine only the appearance of man.

Nobody really knows when or how man appeared on earth, despite the theory of evolution and various palaeontological finds. In fact, because they continually find new evidence, palaeontologists have to push back the date of man's emergence: at one time it was 40,000 BP, then 80,000, 10,0000, 150,000 and now (Hancock, 2005: 27) *c.* 200,000 BP. By the same token the appearance of modern man, *homo sapiens sapiens*, may well be pushed even further back to 500,000 or 5ml years BP. Surprisingly, although this "scientific view" rejects the notion of God's existence as unnecessary, yet it adopts the rectilinear concept of Judaeo-Christian theology, or the similar Platonic concept in the *Timaios*, that the world appeared at one specific point in time and has been "evolving" ever since; also that man emerged by the accident-prone process of natural selection out of some ape-like creature (different kinds of *australopithecus*) "evolving" first as a hominid (i.e. *homo habilis* = "toolmaker"; *homo erectus* = "upright," fire-user, etc.) and then modern man. There is enormous irony in this because **no real evidence** supports such a view. It is no more than a belief based on the interpretation of very few fragments of fossils: it is not something "scientifically observable/demonstrable." Real proof or hard evidence would entail an actual, sufficiently gradual sequence of evolving plants or animals, and this, even by the admission of evolutionists, is missing from the fossil record. In fact, some physical anthropologists reject outright man's *australopithecus* ancestry (C.E. Oxnard, 1975, 1984). (Yes, to look at a larger picture, there may well have been a "Big-Bang" but this may well be one of many, and no scientist ever bothers to tell us what there was before the "bang"; how from nothing — or if there was something what this was — arose energy/matter and started "evolving" into all the observable phenomena around us; and finally what caused it all!)

19. The literature on the subject is increasing enormously year by year. Promoting the Darwinian evolution theory are the numberless mainstream academics in the biological sciences — like R. Dawkins (1996, 1987), J.M. Smith (2000, with E. Szathmary), M. Ruse (2003) and numerous others.

On the other side of the fence we find an ever-increasing number of scholars, academic and non-academic, who doubt, challenge and reject Darwinism and its comrade reductionism: they advocate mostly some form of "creationism" (by God) — as termed by Darwinists. Among these there has now emerged a group of Christianity-committed (of all denominations) academics (scientists, philosophers, lawyers, et al.) who vociferously reject Darwinism in favour of Intelligent Design (see Dembski, 2004).[9] One of the most important among them seems to me to be M. Behe, a biochemist, who, with his concept of *irreducible complexity* posed a serious and as yet unanswerable challenge to Darwinian evolution: a system (biological in this instance) is *irreducibly complex* if it consists of several inter-related parts and, if any one part is removed

9. "Aspiring to be a scientific research programme ID [=Intelligent Design] purports to study the effects of intelligent causes in biology and cosmology" (Menuge, 2004: 32 in Dembski, 2004). This aspiration seems rather misplaced. ID may well postulate an Intelligent Primal Cause (=God) but can hardly be a scientific research programme since it is very easy even for laymen to distinguish between products of ID and those of chance material forces. This hardly requires a research programme. Nor can anyone "scientifically," i.e. with lab experiments, prove the existence of Divine Intelligence which in Itself remains unmanifest. If we say there is ID in the formation of a galaxy, a planet, a species like man and so on, we reach a limit. The implications are enormous, certainly, but since Intelligence itself is not an object of immediate sensory perception and therefore not susceptible to scientific approaches, we need to move way out of "scientific research programmes" and use other methods to explore the implications properly. Proponents of ID have, so far as I know, said little about all this. In fact, M. Cremo (next §20) goes a lot further in opening out these implications admitting openly that he is a follower of the Hare Kṛṣṇa (=Krishna) movement. ID publications have so far shown only that Darwinism, materialism, naturalism, reductionism and the like, are wrong or inadequate scientific approaches, nothing else on the implications. I suspect that some ID adherents would like to replace their materialist mainstream opponents and make their own Christian (fundamentalist) viewpoint mainstream orthodoxy ousting and excluding any other view that differs. But there may be aspects of ID that I do not comprehend.

completely, the system can no longer function; so this could not have "evolved" from a simpler form but must have appeared by a different process (1996).[10] Be it noted that an equally serious challenge had been formulated in an excellent study by microbiologist-geneticist M. Denton ten years earlier (1986; see also cantankerous S. Løvtruph, 1987).

20. Equally important is non-academic M. Cremo's research. First, he (in collaboration with mathematician R.L. Thompson) produced *Forbidden Archaeology* (1993) presenting an enormous amount of suppressed evidence (and in this case much older evidence now forgotten) which shows that modern man *homo sapiens* is in fact much older than is credited and goes back several millions of years. The study was, as expected, highly ridiculed by many die-hard mainstreamers in anthropology, archaeology, palaeontology and kindred disciplines. One line of attack aimed at Cremo's affiliation to the Bhakti-Vedānta Institute which follows Hindu religious aspects with particular devotion to Shri Krishna. Then, in 2003, he published another work *Human Devolution*, with well-documented evidence that through the power of faith (by a process which ordinary people usually describe as "miraculous"), incurable diseases were cured while bones and limbs grew afresh in place of (irretrievably) lost ones. Reductionists will ignore Cremo's work contemptuously but only because their own "faith" is in

---

10. Behe's work has been attacked (the term "criticized" would be euphemestic here) by several evolutionists. The attacks I have seen amount to no more than beating about the bush with irrelevancies and slurs on Behe's academic ability (usual mainstream practices) but not at all meeting his arguments and evidence. Behe himself replied very decorously to them in a sober article (2004). The debate continues, as is usual in such matters.

materialism. If read dispassionately, the evidence Cremo furnishes does indicate that out of the finer, ordinarily unperceived elements that make up the fabric of our material world and by extraordinary, unseen and unknown processes, palpable objects and living tissue can materialize within our own observable world.[11] After all, the quantum jump is the complete disappearance of an electron, or other similar subatomic entity, from one place and its reappearance somewhere else — a rather mystifying affair (Stapp, 2003; Goswami, 1995; Wolf, 1989). Moreover, studies in Neurophysiology also show that many psychiatric (neurological) cures can be effected and new brain-cell connections established through meditational practices or prayer or simply memory- and will-exercises (Paquette, et al. 2003; Schwarz, 2002; Pert, 1997).

21. What is Language/Speech ultimately? How is it studied?

In the end the method of Linguistics, just as of any other discipline or science, entails collection and interpretation of data and the whole process is supported or coloured by assumptions, mostly taken for granted. One of the assumptions is that "my method" is right. But this "right method," which is right in a well-defined area, does not take into account a larger area containing the first and an even larger area

---

11. Cremo's, 2003, study certainly has some weaknesses. A very serious one is his reliance on the Purāṇas and especially *Śrīmad Bhāgavatam* (and the two epics). The Purāṇas do contain very old material but, in the form we have them, they are young (after CE 500) with much late stuff, many obscurities and many contradictions: they are thus unreliable as basic evidence in the serious discussion Cremo attempts. At best the Purāṇas and the Epics can supply secondary, supportive evidence. In our case the primary evidence is in the *Ṛgveda* and, as we have seen, it is more than adequate.

containing the second and so on: our method is coloured by our belief that we are dealing with the whole, when, in fact, we are not, and therefore cannot arrive at sound knowledge, since sound knowledge can only be knowledge of the whole. For example, the study of an ear separated from the whole organism of which it is a member will doubtless reveal much about the structure and composition of the ear but not much about its true nature which involves its function in the whole organism.

Another assumption is that the measurable and ever-changing material world is the only reality and that anything not amenable to measurement by our senses cannot be the subject of objective or "scientific" inquiry and therefore cannot be "real/true" or object of knowledge: this is nonsense, of course, as seen in the next paragraph.

A third assumption is that the so-called "scientific method" despite its severe limitations is the only correct one! Everybody, especially scholars in humanities, love to use the terms "science, scientific"; but what do they mean really? . . . Telepathy is a well established phenomenon frequently occurring between twins and sometimes between a mother and her child(ren) or, more seldom, between other persons. Yet, at present, there are no scientific means to verify it, other than ordinary observation and common sense or reason. A modern scientist, J.M. Schwartz, an American neuro-physiologist, wrote of "the cult of scientism" as "the fallacy of believing that the method of science must be used on all forms of experience and, given time, will settle every issue" (2002: 6). Five decades earlier another American scientist wrote: "expressions such as "scientific truth" should only be taken in a very limited sense. . . . There is no scientific truth in the absolute sense. The phrase *ad veritatem per scientiam* [= To truth by means of science] is an absurdity" (du Noüy, 1949: 23). Again: "Physicist Wolfgang Pauli once put it that scientists went too far in the seventeenth century when they attempted to make everything understandable strictly as objective science. By denuding the subjective view from any firm ground, much was lost": so said a contemporary physicist (Wolf, 2001: 6). In any case, the scientific method like every successful method in any human enterprise requires three ingredients: interest, observation and reasoning. Interest directs attention to the particular field and keeps it there against all difficulties. Observation collects data related to the subject under research from natural processes or controlled events in a laboratory. Reasoning discriminates between relevant and irrelevant, accurate and inaccurate premises and data and so arrives at (correct) conclusion(s) (Beveridge, 1968). This holds for every discipline in the sciences and arts. The fact that a science like molecular biology uses many and complex instruments does not alter the three basic aspects common to all human enquiry. Because of faulty reasoning or inadequate observations, scientists make as many and big mistakes and hatch paranoic theories despite their instruments (Cohen, 2001: 32-34) as investigators in other fields. Furthermore, insight or inspiration and luck, all of which are out of one's control, play important parts in sciences (Beveridge, 27 ff, 68 ff) no less than in the humanities.

But, in fact, the ultimate observer, the ultimate consciousness/awareness which observes or has cognizance of all bodily and mental movements, including the measuring, evaluating and concluding and all thinking, is itself not subject to scientific enquiry since it is the ultimate observer and is in no way observable or measurable by the senses or any of the most advanced instruments.

22. The study of Language cannot be divorced from that of the ultimate or essential nature of Man. The assumptions about the latter will inevitably colour the study of the former. The general view today, the "scientific view," is that Man, *homo sapiens sapiens*, as was said (see § 18 above), has "evolved" from some ape-like creature by the processes of natural selection and random mutations and that consciousness and language arose more or less accidentally. As was said, this is no more than a belief based on the interpretation of certain data consisting of very few fragments of fossils and bones: it is not something "scientifically observable/demonstrable." The molecular biology and biotechnology which were supposed to give "scientifically observable" data of man's descent from an ape-like creature are in fact just as insecure (Gibbons, 2001: 1052; also Brooks, 2001: 410-11). Another "belief" holds that Man issued from the substance of the Supreme Being (= God, Absolute) but lost his initial perfection descending gradually to a lower state (Cremo presents this, § 20, but also in their different way many deists): this is termed the "creationist view" (or one variety) by the adherents of the "scientific view" (see § 18 above). Following certain religious, mythological and philosophical traditions, the "creationist view," putting spirit above matter, says that this creation-process repeats itself in cycles. The "scientific view," again as was said earlier (§ 18), adopts the rectilinear view of Judaeo-Christian theology (but without the theology itself, i.e. without God) that the world appeared once and has been "evolving" ever since and that man emerged at one point in time. In this view Language itself "evolved" out of animal grunts and bird twitterings after the vocal machinery and brain structure became sufficiently and fittingly developed (Hawkins and Gell-Mann, 1992: 21-83).

This view is wholly conjectural. Yet so strong is the notion that the physical world is the only or the primary reality that scholars can't accept abstract thought in ancient people but must derive it from material, concrete entities: e.g. T. Burrow (1973:258), an eminent Sanskritist and comparativist, suggested that the number "four" (Sanskrit *catur-*, Greek *tettara-*, Latin *quattuor*) comes from the "angle" (four angles in a room, square or rectangle). S. Misra (1975:109), eminent in the same field, prefers the "square, cross-road" (*catvāra-*). For "five" (S. *pañca*, Gk. *pente*, L. *quinque*, Germanic *fimf*) both give the five fingers. And yet Vedic language, which with the *Ṛgveda* is now thought to belong to the early fourth millennium BCE, has very many abstractions like *anumati* "agreement, assent," *amṛtattva* "state of not-dead, immortality," *asuratva* "the state of lordship," *devatā* "divinity, godhood," *paṅkti* "fiveness, group of five," etc. A different example comes from archaeology. The eminent archaeologist, M. Gimbutas describes the entry of IE concepts into Old Europe (after 4500 BCE) and the gradual fusion of old concepts with the new ones, their assimilation and transformation. "In ancient Greece, assimilation into the Indo-European pantheon of gods resulted in the creation of *strange and even absurd images* . . . most strikingly visible in the conversion of Athena, the Old European Bird goddess, into a militarized figure carrying a shield and wearing an owl helmet. The belief in her birth from the forehead of Zeus, the ruling god of the Indo-Europeans in Greece, shows how far the transformation went — from a *parthenogenetic* goddess to her birth from a male god! And yet this is not surprising: Zeus was a bull — in Indo-European symbolism the Thunder God is a bull — and Athena's birth from the head of a bull could well have been influenced by the memory of birth from a bucranium, which . . . was a simulacrum of the uterus in Old European symbolism" (1991: 118-19; emphasis added). All this sounds superbly true, but why is parthenogenesis not as absurd as Athena's birth from Zeus's forehead/temple? . . . And why stop at the memory of the Old Europe symbolism and not go further or in other directions? . . . The very Bird goddess could well be merely a concrete symbol of a non-material entity (like the bird symbolizing the soul in Ancient Egypt), a divine presence, we today don't wish to envisage in our mind. Then, Athena's birth can be interpreted quite differently from "a militarized figure," since she was also goddess of wisdom and creative crafts: it can symbolize simply the manifestation of reason/wisdom from the mind of the Supreme to inspire creativity and fight off manifestations of ignorance and selfishness.

Beyond such examples is the linguistic unit called "root" *dhātu* in Sanskrit. The Vedic language (= older Sanskrit) is by and large, but not exclusively, based on roots which can easily be separated through analysis from accretionary elements (prefixes, affixes, suffixes); these contain a core meaning: e.g. √*dhā* "(the idea of) putting, holding in place, forming." This essential root idea is the basic or central meaning in all related lexical forms generated by various lawful processes from the *dhātu* itself. Thus √*dhā* > *da-dhā-ti* "he/she puts," *a-dhā-t* "he/she did/has put" (verbs, present and aorist); > *dhā-tu* "layer, element, constituent," *dhātṛ* "one who puts, creates, establishes," *dhāman* "abode, domain," etc. Consider also √*jan* "(the idea of) engendering" > *ja-jan-ti* "he/she begets," *a-jan*[*-t*] "he/she did beget"; > *jan-tu* "creature, offspring," *janitṛ* "one who begets," *jan-man* "birth"; etc. Roots are present in other languages like Ancient Egyptian but are not clearly separable in other ancient Indo-European languages. The clear presence of the *dhātu* in Vedic (Kazanas, 2004 passim; Burrow, 1973: 34, 123, 239; Whitney, 1888: 34) shows that the mind of those people was fully capable of abstraction, i.e. pure mental concepts (like "divinity, five-ness, lordship") **before the perception of concrete entities and gross action in the physical world**. It is extremely difficult to see words designating activity and its aspects (verbs, tenses, moods), attributes, functions, qualities, states (nouns, adjectives) and modes of action or degrees of quality (adverbs) starting off separately, and accidentally over a long period converging into specific roots. This could happen in one, two, ten cases but it is highly improbable for over 800 such roots in Sanskrit. The attrition of the *dhātu* and its loss in the other Indo-European languages (and in Egyptian) shows that some languages at least started with roots. **Therefore, the presence of roots, more than anything else, indicates that language did not start at the gross material level but at a higher, subtler plane, the mind; it also demonstrates beyond doubt Intelligent Design of the highest order** (see also § 25, end).

23. Personally, I know nothing of Man's origin — how and when he appeared on this planet; and I do not think palaeontologists and kindred scientists know either. I incline towards the Vedic tradition which holds that man is engendered from the Supreme Being and has for his real Self the substance or spirit of that very Being (*ayam ātmā brahma* "this personal self is the Absolute Self"); also that the process of creation and "evolution" ("devolution" I would say) is cyclical in very long periods called *yuga*s and *mahāyuga*s; and that human language reflects divine Speech by which all things come to be in the material world. This inclination is not a capricious blind belief. For, quite apart from the ancient mythological statements, in our brief embodiment in this world we can observe many small and large cyclical phenomena like the day and the year, the seasons with their accompanying flowering, fruition and fall, the succession of seed and plant and seed, the development and degeneration of nations and cultures and so on; consequently it is not unreasonable to assume recurrence on the larger scale of solar systems and galaxies — projected and withdrawn in the rhythmic breathing of the Primal Cause termed *tad-ekam* in *ṚV X*, 129. As for the immense power of language one has only to consider a common gross example: the president or prime minister of a country gives an order and, upon that, hundreds of thousands of people (vehicles, ships and airplanes) move here and there, killing and being killed, destroying and creating. There are also many sages like Plato and Plotinus, many mystics and saints (Meister Eckhart or Jacob Boehme and modern J. Krishnamurti) who clearly reached higher levels of being and understanding. Finally, since the world displays order at every level, since different types of creatures on our planet have different degrees of intelligence, with human beings at the top rung, and since something cannot come out of nothing, it is not unreasonable to assume that a Supreme Intelligence (= Being), which for us is inconceivable except that we merge with It or realize It as our own ultimate, true Self, has been at work from the very start and at all stages — just as a poet conceives and generates a finished poem.

24. Some theology. Putting aside for the moment matters of language, speech, science and evolutionism, let us look at an aspect of theology, Christian or whatever. God or the Vedāntic Absolute, or the simple comprehensive Being of Melissos (see KRS: 390-401), is supposed to be omnipresent, omnipotent and wholly uniform. Consequently all entities and processes in the universe arise by His will and omnipotence from His intelligence and very substance: they all unfold and remain present within His substance since there is no other substance different and separate from His own. We can only envisage the formation of different grades or levels of substance from the finest one becoming denser and denser down to the grossest matter in our visible world, but all are all the time within, and wholly composed from, the primal godly substance (= energy, intelligence, spirit, if you like), just as icebergs coagulate from and float within water which is their primal source and constitutes their icy solidity. Being thus omnipresent, God watches all continuously and is aware of every detail in the creation which is in no way separate from Him. Consequently He can at any time (as we think and experience this unknown entity; for there can be no time or space in God's substance) act by His intelligence, omnipotence and will and modify an existing old form (any creature or phenomenon) or annihilate it or create an entirely new one. It is of course possible that He may have set up (always within Himself) lower intelligent mechanism(s) whereby certain phenomena will unfold and cease automatically (in some kind of Darwinian evolution) but, even so, such a process is not separate from God's substance/intelligence/energy. Thus everything comes into existence, remains there and goes out of existence through God's incessant, unblinking attention (§§ 7, 12).

One often reads of God being likened to an architect and His creation to a building, or to a watchmaker and a watch. But surely these analogies are false. A building or a watch are things separate from their maker and are composed of materials other than the maker's own substance: once made, these artefacts, can be approached only by their external surfaces — as happens in the case of all three-dimensional things in the world we know. But God's creation differs in that He is within everything with all His intelligence, power and will, and everything is formed from within outward and from finest to grossest from His own substance, since initially there is nothing else. The Christian theological notion of Creation from nothing (Latin *ex nihilo*, Greek *ek mēdenos*) is a rather absurd idea. What is this *nothing*? If it is "something" apart from God, then God is neither omnipresent nor omnipotent and is limited by this. If it is part of God, then it is within God's own substance and like everything it is made up from that substance. Thus man is first the godly substance itself, then with an underwear of nature or spirit, then the dress of mind or soul and finally the overcoat of the gross physical body — to follow the four levels of being of Plotinus (§ 12), or the three bodies of early Christian writings,[12] or one of many similar formulations in other systems. The same holds for everything else, the difference being that some have more nature (or spirit) or more mind, than others. A stone obviously has little mind. Naturally, everything has its own nature with its qualities and limitations, its own special form and function(s) and its particular lifespan. There are automatic mechanisms like the heartbeat and blood-circulation or the production of electricity from a generator, but nothing can exist or happen apart from God's will, omnipotence and intelligence.

Many people refer to evil, pain and suffering and say that these and similar features indicate or prove that the Creator is a bungler or that the world is the result of blind forces stumbling into accident after accident. But what is evil, pain and suffering? Do we really know? Certainly, a shark eats other creatures and an earthquake levels a town and thereby kills thousands. Certainly, many apparently innocent people suffer deprivation, torture, mutilation, loss of property and of life in all kinds of circumstances. All this appears unjust and cruel and causes anguish, stress, suffering. Yet some people go through such experiences but feel quite differently: they

---

12. See Paul's 1 Corinthians 2: 14-15 and 1 Thessalonians 5: 23 (spirit, soul, body). Also Ignatius (of Antioch) *Epistle to Philadelphians,* 11, "they hope with body, mind [=soul] and spirit."

come out of them stronger and feel gratitude. Are we sure we see the Whole and can therefore pass judgment on events, on the creation and its Creator? So long as our minds operate under the assumption that this material world is the only reality, we shall be baffled. Mystics, saints, *yogīs* and the like, some of whom have been through very great suffering, see things quite differently and have left their testimony that there are other, subtler aspects of the world, other, subtler planes of being and knowledge; some of these men have even left clear instructions on the steps and practices to be followed so that we might have similar experiences. Most of us choose to ignore their testimonies and instructions.

People also refer to man's "free will" or its absence and the opposite — determinism or its absence. This issue has provoked repeated and long theoretical discussion in efforts to establish man's responsibility and concepts of "choice" and "sin." Such discussions seem pointless. It is obvious that in some respects man has free will and in others not. By way of an example let us take a gross analogy. A man on vacation travels on a ship crossing the Atlantic from east to west. During the journey he can choose to do or not do many things: eat, drink, sleep, talk, read, etc.; he can walk about and even move on the deck from west to east. But he has no choice whatever regarding the route and destination of the ship.

These themes could be greatly elaborated and analysed in detail but enough has been said on the subject for the purposes of this discussion. I am not a Christian apologist by a very long stretch (see § 3) and in fact can't stand theological discussions but it seems to me far more reasonable to postulate an eternal, ungenerated Supreme Intelligence and genesis by *vāc/Logos* than materialism and (Neo-) Darwinian evolution. Back to Language now.

25. The Vedic tradition regards speech as a divinity, *vāc,* from its very beginning, in that remarkable document, the *Ṛgveda.* When Sanskrit appeared in the hymns of the *ṚV,* it was already a fully developed and highly complex language — but one already suffering attritions and changes (i.e. devolving to simpler forms). Ancient Egyptian too appeared more or less suddenly *c.* 3,000 BCE as a fully developed language — it too having recognizable roots, productive of nominal and verbal forms (Gardiner, 1957; Watterson, 1993). In fact, all the earliest recorded languages were highly developed — Chinese, Mesopotamian, Greek, etc. But subsequently they all changed to simpler systems, streamlining and regularizing declensions and conjugations: they began to use auxiliary verbs instead of the older tenses (some reduplicated) and moods, and prepositions instead of the nominal cases. Sanskrit itself came in later periods to use more and more complex compounds and much less the inflexions leaving unused the rich verbal forms of the Ṛgvedic language — which had already suffered losses. English, again, started as an inflected language but, by about CE 1500, became uninflected and genderless.

R. Dixon expresses a similar view writing that language originated "like an explosion." The human mind would have been ready for language and thereupon would have invented it almost as a complete system, whereupon "Language would have burst forth" (Dixon, 1997: 63-65). This fits very well with the abstraction or pure mental concept, inherent in the Vedic *dhātu* roots (§ 22 end).

It is therefore difficult to see how or why languages started with animal hisses, grunts and warbles (§ 22), then became very complex media of thought and communication and then, despite literacy which should have preserved the older forms more easily, they devolved into much simpler (synthetic) forms (see also § 22, end).

26. The historical beginnings of Man and Language are unknown. However, taking the Vedic *yugas* as framework, I propose this hypothesis. In the *Sat-* or *Kṛta-yuga*, when human beings lived in (near) perfection being of one mind (as the ancient accounts tell us), they had no language such as we know. When that unity was lost in a subsequent age, the *Tretā-yuga*, then arose language in full panoply, as it were, much like goddess Athena springing out of the temple of her father Zeus. "And the whole earth was of one language and of one speech," as the Judaic *Old Testament* has it (*Genesis*, 11, 1): with the root always as its basis, generating verbs, nouns, adjectives and adverbs, with all three genders and many more verbal aspects than we know, that language could express every possible nuance of human knowledge and experience reflecting in gross form the perfection of the Speech used by god(s) to generate all the phenomena of this creation. In that tongue every phenomenon in the world(s) had its corresponding sound or word and this signified and was that phenomenon. Today, except for some grossly onomatopoeic words, the various lexical units bear little relation to the phenomena they are supposed to denote (e.g. abbot, acre, age, alien, amok, atoll, etc.). Subsequently, in the next age, the *Dvāpara-yuga*, that unitary language devolved into different dialects losing many of its subtle nuances. One of these branches was what we now term Proto-Indo-European, others being perhaps Semitic (or Afro-Asiatic), Austric, etc. Finally, as that age drew to its close for the fourth age, the dire *Kali-yuga*, these languages again devolved into more branches and so on, down to all modern vernaculars losing even more subtle aspects and their connection with the original Mother-tongue.

Today we have moved even further away: we have specialized "languages" (= idioms) or "jargons" within any one "official" language. When I read books on Genetics and Biology some time ago, I had to proceed very slowly reading and re-reading passages and consulting relevant dictionaries, almost as in learning a foreign language. The same holds for Linguistics, Law, Physics, etc. Each "discipline" or field of knowledge becomes more and more specialized and "foreign" to the common language. This presumably is inevitable, but one wonders at times if we are not living in a new Tower of Babel.

And here it may be apposite to recall Caliban, that monstrous creature on the magic island of Shakespeare's *Tempest,* whom Prospero, an exiled duke and a wise magician, tried to educate. The incorrigible creature said to the sage: "You taught me language and my profit on it is I know how to curse"! Fortunately there still are, even in this *Kali-yuga* (= Hesiod's Iron Age), people who can put language to good use — great poets like Shakespeare himself. We may even hope that some few can gain knowledge of, or rather find within themselves, the very language (or a vibrant echo of it) that produced so many miraculous events in the past. As far as I know only K. Klostermaier touched on this theme criticizing modern studies of Language in a paper titled "Man carries the power of all things in his mouth" (1977). For what it is worth, we have, in opposition to the modern, widespread materialist view, the testimony of those non-materialist people who displayed so much confidence in the power of speech.

27. Thus, in conclusion, the *vāc* doctrine is not merely an academic affair. I stay with *vāc* because it has much greater certitude, comprehension and width in its connotations than evangelist John's *logos* which denotes "reason, wisdom" rather than "speech" as it was in the Greek philosophical tradition. Here I repeat that we don't know what Christ actually taught in this respect (§ 3): he may have propounded a Logos Doctrine like that of *vāc* in the Vedic tradition, but if he did so there are only warped formulations of it in the extant (mainly gnostic) texts. The Judaic view (in *Genesis*, 1-2) is also truncated: God is not presented as consistently creating by power of speech (or thought or vision) and there is no statement to that effect; heaven, earth and waters are said to have been created but the mode of creation is not spelled out and man is definitely said to be fashioned out of clay (in imitation of the Mesopotamian tradition). In the Egyptian Ptah text (§ 9) creation does take place through thought and utterance, as in Vedic texts, but here speech is only a faculty of god Ptah who is too anthropomorphic to pass as the Absolute — and, in any case, the text is late and a rather obvious attempt to subordinate all other religious systems (some much older) under Memphite authority. So we are left with one complete system, the consistent four-level *vāc-Brahman* (and later *śabda-brahman*) doctrine in the Vedic tradition which refers both to reason and speech.

> O Lord of holiness, Bṛhaspati,[13] they have sent forth the very beginning of *vāc* assigning names: what was best and faultless in them, that which was hidden, became manifest through love. — *ṚV*, 10.71.1

> I [Vāc] blow like the wind forming and holding all worlds and creatures, extending beyond earth and sky — so great am I. — *ṚV*, 10.125.8

---

13. "Lord of holiness" translates more properly the allonym Brahmaṇaspati, not Bṛhaspati. In post-Ṛgvedic texts he is also called Vācaspati "Lord of Speech."

Bibliography

All ancient Indic texts except *Bhartṛhari* are in several editions and translations.

The *Ṛgveda* has to this day no good English translation and Geldner's German one or Renou's French one need considerable improvement. Purāṇas are gradually appearing in good translations, published by Motilal Banarsidass.

The *Śatapatha Brāhmaṇa* is found in the series *Sacred Books of the East* (now published by Motilal Banarsidass).

The Upaniṣads are translated by P. Olivelle in the Oxford World Classics and are published text and translated by OUP and Munshiram Manoharlal, Delhi, 1998.

Except for the Pre-Socratics and *Corpus Hermeticum* all other ancient Greek authors mentioned in the text are in the Loeb Classical series of Harvard (Camb. Mass.) and Heinemann (London). All papers by Kazanas N. can be consulted at <www.omilosmeleton.gr/english/en_index.html >.

Allen, J.P., 1988, *Genesis in Egypt. . .*, New Haven, Connecticut.

Bauer, W., 1934, *Orthodoxy and Heresy in Earliest Christianity,* Eng. transl. 1971, R.A. Kraft & G. Krodel, Philadelphia: Fortress.

Behe, M., 1996, *Darwin's Black Box . . .*, New York: Free Press.

———, 2004, "Irreducible Complexity . . .," in Dembski & Ruse, 2004, *Uncommon Dissent,* pp. 352-70.

Beveridge, W., 1968 (1954), *The Art of Scientific Investigation,* London: Heinemann.

Bhartṛhari, *Vākyapadīya, Kāṇḍa*s 1 & 2, ed. & transl. K.R. Pillai, 1975, Delhi: Motilal Banarsidass.

———, *Kaṇḍa*s 2&3 transl. by K.A.S. Iyer, 1977, Delhi: Motilal Banarsidass.

Brooks, R., 2001, "The Relationship between Matter and Life", *Nature* (January 18), pp. 409-11.

Burrow, T., 1973, *The Sanskrit Language,* London: Faber.

Campbell, J., 1949/1993, *The Hero with a Thousand Faces,* London, Fontana: Harper Collins.

———, 1974, *The Mythic Image,* NY: MJF Books.

Cohen, I.B., 1985/2001, *Revolution in Science,* Cambridge Mass: HUP.

Corpus Hermeticum, eds. A.D. Nock & A.J. Festugière, Paris "Les Belles Lettres" (French transl). English transl. B. B. Copenhaver *Hermetica,* Cambridge: CUP, 1992/94.

Cox, Sir, G.W., 1882/1963, *The Mythology of the Āryan Nations,* Benares: Chowkhamba Sanskrit Series.

Coward, H.G. & K., Raja 1990/2001, *The Philosophy of the Grammarians,* Delhi: Motilal Banarsidass.

Cremo, M., 2003, *Human Devolution,* Los Angeles/Badger CA: Torchlight Hill Publishing.

Cremo, M. & R. Thompson, 1993, *Forbidden Archaeology. . .,* San Diego: Govardhan Hill Publishing.

Dawkins, R., 1987, *The Blind Watchmaker. . .,* NY: Norton.

———, 1996, *Climbing Mount Improbable,* NY: Norton.

Dembski, W.A., 2004, ed., *Uncommon Dissent . . .,* Wilmington (Del.): 151 Books.

Dembski W.A. & M. Ruse, 2004, *Debating Design,* Cambridge: CUP.

Denton, M., 1985, *Evolution: A Theory in Crisis,* Bethesda: Adler & Adler.

Dixon, R., 1997, *The Rise and Fall of Languages,* Cambridge: CUP.

Ehrman, B.D., 2004, *The New Testament: A Historical Introduction . . .* (3rd edn.), NY/Oxford: OUP.

———, 2003, *Lost Christianities,* Oxford: OUP.

Faulkner, R.O., 1973-78, *The Ancient Egyptian Coffin Texts* (3 vols.), Warminster: Aris & Phillips.

Frazer, Sir J.G., 1992, *The Golden Bough* (one-volume ed.), London: Macmillan Co.

Frawley, D., 2001, *The Ṛgveda & the History of India,* Delhi: Aditya.

GEL = *Greek English Lexicon,* 1996, Liddel & Scott, Jones & McKenzie, Oxford: OUP.

Gibbons, A., 2001, "Modern Men Trace Ancestry to African Migrants," *Science* 202, pp. 1051-52.

Gimbutas, M., 1991, "Deities and Symbols of Old Europe" . . ., in S.M. Lamb. & E.D. Mitchell (eds.), *Sprung from Some Common Source*, Stanford: Stanford University.

Gonda, J., 1963, *The Vision of the Vedic Poets*, Hague: Mouton.

Gospels, see *New Testament*.

Goswami, A., 1995, *The Self-aware Universe*, Putnam: Penguin (J. P. Tarcher).

Guthrie, W., 1965-81, *History of Greek Philosophy*, 6 vols. (vols. 1-2), Cambridge: CUP.

Hancock, G., 2005, *Supernatural*, London: Century.

Hawkins, J., & M. Gel-Man, 1992, *The Evolution of Human Languages*, Santa Fe: Addison-Wesley.

Kazanas, N., in press "Vedic & Egyptian Cross-influences," 2007. (See <www.omilosmeleton.gr/english/en_index.html>.

———, 2006b, "The diffusion of Indo-European Theonyms" in *The Quarterly Journal of the Mythic Society* (Bangalore, India), Jan-March.

———, 2005a, "Philosophy & Self-realization in the *Ṛgveda*" in D.P. Chattopadhyaya, ed., *Self, Society and Science* . . ., Delhi: PHISPC, Centre for Studies in Civilizations.

———, 2005b, "Vedic and Mesopotamian Cross-influences," *Migration & Diffusion*, vol. 24 (Oct. issue). (Too many misprints: see: <www.omilosmeleton.gr/english/en_index.html>.)

———, 2004, "Sanskrit and Proto-Indo-European," in *Indian Linguistics*, 65, pp. 75-100.

———, 2003a, "Final Reply," in *Journal of Indo-European Studies*, vol. 31, pp. 187-240.

———, 2003b, "Advaita & Gnosticism," in *VVRI Research Bulletin*, Hoshiarpur, vol. 2, pp. 43-112.

———, 2001, "A New Date for the Ṛgveda," in G.C. Pande, ed., *JICPR*, special issue, *Chronology & Indian Philosophy*, pp. 79-108.

———, 1999, "The Ṛgveda & Indo-Europeans" *ABORI*, vol. 80, pp. 15-42.

Klostermaier, K., 1977, "Man carries the power of all things in his mouth," in *Revelation in Indian Thought*, eds. H. Coward & K. Sivaraman, Emeryville, Calif: Emery Press, pp. 3-16.

KRS = 1999, Kirk, G., J. Raven, M. Schofield, *The Presocratic Philosophers*, Cambridge: CUP.

Kuhn, Th., 1970, *The Structure of Scientific Revolutions*, 2nd edn., Chicago: Chicago Univ. Press.

Layton, B., 1987/95, *The Gnostic Scriptures*, NY: Doubleday.

Levitt, S., 2003, "The Dating of Indian Tradition," *Anthropos*, vol. 98, pp. 341-59.

Lichtheim, M., 1980, *Ancient Egyptian Literature*, 3 vols., Berkeley: California Univ. Press.

Long, A.A., 1986, *Hellenistic Philosophy*, London: Duckworth.

Løvetrup, S., 1987, *Darwinism: The Refutation of a Myth*, London: Croom Helm.

McEvilley, Th., 2002, *The Shape of Ancient Thought*, NY: Allworth Press.

Misra, S.S., 1975, *New Lights on Indo-European Comparative Grammar*, (1994), Delhi: Sharada.

Murti, T., 1974, "Some comments on the Philosophy of Language," *Journal of Indian Philosophy*, vol. 2, pp. 321-31.

New Testament, numerous editions in Greek and many more translations in English.

Old Testament, numerous editions in Hebrew; Greek transl. of 70 and many editions of English Authorized version of King James.

Oxnard, C.E., 1975, *Uniqueness & Diversity in Human Evolution*, Chicago: Univ. of Chicago Press.

———, 1984, *The Order of Man*, New Haven: Yale Univ. Press.

Pagels, E., 2003, *Beyond Belief*, NY: Random House.

Paquette V., J. Levesque, B. Mensour, J.M. Leroux, G. Beaudoin, P. Bourgouin, M. Beauregard, 2003, "Change the Mind and You Change the Brain," *Neuro-Image*, vol. 18, pp. 401-09.

Perkins, Pheme, 1993, *Gnosticism and the New Testament*, Minneapolis: Fortress Press.

Pert, C.B., 1997/2003, *Molecules of Emotion*, NY/London: Scribner.

Poncé, C., 1997, *Kabbalah*, Wheaton (USA)/Madras: Quest Books.

Radhakrishnan, S., 1953, *The Principal Upaniṣads*, London: Allen & Unwin.

RNL = Robinson J., below.

Robinson, J., (ed.), 1990, *The Nag Hammadi Library*, San Fransisco: Harper.

Ruse, M., 2003, *Darwin & Design: Does Evolution Have a Purpose?*, Camb. Mass: HUP.

Sandbach, F., 1975, *The Stoics*, London: Chatto & Windus.

Schwartz, J., & S. Begley, 2002, *The Mind & The Brain . . .*, NY: Harper Collins.

Smith, J., & E. Szathmary, 2000, *The Origins of Life . . .*, Oxford: OUP.

Stapp, H.P., 2003, *Mind, Matter & Quantum Mechanics*, NY: Spinger-Verlag.

VP = see Bhartṛhari.

Whitney, W.D, 1888/1962, *Sanskrit Grammar*, Delhi: Motilal Banarsidass.

Wolf, F.A., 1989, *Taking the Quantum Leap*, NY: Harper & Row (Perennial Library).

———, 2001, *Mind into Matter. . .*, Needham (MA): Moment Point Press.

The Contributors

Maria Krzysztof Byrski was born in Wilno (now Vilnius, the capital of Lithuania) in 1937. He took up Indian studies under Prof. E Sluszkiewicz in 1955. A year after completing studies in 1960, he left for India to join Banaras Hindu University. In 1966, he was awarded the PhD Degree for his thesis entitled "Concept of Ancient Indian Theatre" (published in 1974). In 1978, he received the Degree of *Doctor Habilitatus* (D. Litt.) for his thesis "*Methodology of the Analysis of Sanskrit Drama*" (published in 1997). During the Emergency declared in Warsaw, he and his friends, initiated a sobriety *satyagraha* inspired by the salt *satyagraha* of Mahatma Gandhi. In 1990, he joined the Embassy of Poland and soon became its first Ambassador. He has to his credit over one hundred publications in Polish, English and Hindi. [**address:** Smolna Street 8, Apt. 58, Warszawa – 00-375, Poland; **e-mail-** <m.k.byrski@uw.edu.pl>].

Lokesh Chandra is a renowned scholar of Tibetan, Mongolian and Sino-Japanese Buddhism. He has to his credit over 400 works and text editions. Among them are classics like his *Tibetan-Sanskrit Dictionary, Materials for a History of Tibetan Literature, Buddhist Iconography of Tibet* and the present *Dictionary of Buddhist Iconography* in 15 volumes. Dr Chandra was nominated by the President of India to the Parliament in 1974-80, and again in 1980-86. He had been the Vice-President of the Indian Council for Cultural Relations and Chairman of the Indian Council of Historical Research. Presently he is Director, International Academy of Indian Culture. [**address:** J-22 Hauz Khas Enclave, New Delhi – 110 016].

Saroj Kumar Chaudhuri taught Japanese in School of Foreign Languages, University of Delhi and Aichi Gakusen University, Japan. He was a visiting Professor in the Institute for the Study of Languages and Cultures of Asia and Africa, Tokyo. His two published books are *Siddhamj in China and Japan* and *Hindu Gods and Goddesses in Japan*. His latest book *Lives of Early Buddhist Monks*, a translation of the biographies of India and Central Asian monks written in China between AD. 412 and 518, will be published shortly. [**address:** J-1867, Chittaranjan Park, NEW DELHI - 110 019; **e-mail** <chaudhuri1967@hotmail.com>].

J. Gonda had been Professor of Sanskrit and Indonesian Studies at Royal University of Utrecht, Utrecht, The Netherlands.

Nicholaos Kazanas studied English Literature at University College, Economics and Philosophy at the School of Economic Science and Sanskrit at the School of Oriental and African studies — all in London; also post-graduate at Deccan College in Pune. He taught in London and Athens and since 1980 has been Director of Omilos Meleton Cultural Institute, Has many publications in the West and India and is on the Editorial Board of *Adyar Library Bulettin* (Chennai). [**address**: 50-52, Aetideoan Str. Holargos GR 15561 ATHENS (Greece) Email: <nk@omilosmeleton.gr>].

Khalid Bin Yusuf Khan M.A., M. Phil., PhD, is Reader, Department of Sanskrit, Aligarh Muslim University, Aligarh (Uttar Pradesh). His field of specialization is Vedic Studies and Comparative Religion and Philosophy. Dr Khan has written five books, besides 35 research papers. He has won several awards/prizes including the Maulana Abul Kalam Azad Prize of SAARC Countries; Vijay Rattan Award by India International Friendship Society, New Delhi; Vividha Puraskara from Uttar Pradesh Sanskṛit Sansthanam; and has been felicitated by Dr Zakir Hussain Foundation Aligarh. [**address:** Yusuf Villa, Syed Colony, New Sir Syed Nagar, Aligarh - 202 002; **e-mail**: <khalidbykhan@Rediffmail.com>].

5. Shashiprabha Kumar, former Chairperson of Special Centre for Sanskrit Studies, JNU, is an acclaimed Sanskrit scholar, well-versed in classical Indian philosophy. Before joining JNU, she taught at the department of philosophy, University of Delhi; department of Sanskrit at Maitreyi College, New Delhi and R.G. Post-Graduate College, Meerut. More than twenty research scholars have obtained

M.Phil/Ph.D. under her guidance. She has fourteen books to her credit and has contributed more than seventy research papers to reputed journals and edited several volumes. She has participated in many International Conferences and National Seminars besides lecturing in India and abroad. Recipient of **Sri Ramakrishna Sanskrit Award** (World Education Foundation, Canada, 2003) for her distinguished and outstanding contribution to Sanskrit research and teaching and **Shankar Puraskar** (K.K. Birla Foundation, New Delhi, 1998) for her first book entitled *Vaiśeṣika Darśana mein Padārtha-Nirūpaṇa*, she has won many other prestigious awards and fellowships. [**address**: *Abhyudaya*, 295/Sector - 15-A, Noida (U.P.) - 201 301, **E-mail**: <shashiprabhakumar@yahoo.co.in>].

LALITA KUPPUSWAMY is currently working as a Senior Reader, Dept. of Sanskrit, Daulat Ram College, University of Delhi. She is M.A. and PhD in Sanskrit, M.A. Persian, Diploma in Pāli, Certificate in German and Arabic, all from Delhi University. Besides, she has also done Acārya Jyotish (Bharatiya Vidya Bhavan, Delhi) and B.A.L. (Annamalai University). Dr Lalita is presently working towards a doctoral programme on "Yoga Vāsiṣṭha — A Critical and Comparative Study of Persian and its Original Sanskrit Source," from the Dept. of Persian, University of Delhi. She is the recipient of Gold Medal on "Amaru Śatakam"; Firdausi Gold Medal in Persian; and Lal Mani Mahesh Tiwari Gold Medal in Pāli, from the Delhi University. She has published one book and about 50 research articles in various journals and magazines. [**address**: A3/5, Janakpuri, New Delhi – 110 058; **e-mail**: <kylalita@yahoo.com>].

HEM CHANDRA PANDE (1943–) taught Russian for over 40 years and has published book as *Bhāṣā, Mastiṣka aura Cetanā*, 1990; *Hindī-Rūsī Vārtālāpa Puṣtikā*, 2006; Rūsī-*Hindī Laghu Śabdakośa*, 2004; *Bhāṣā: Swarūpa aura Sanracanā*, 2006. He has also translated *Soviet Studies on Harappan Script*, 1969; *Proto-Indica*, 1973; *Apnī Zaban Men Kucch Kaho*,1983; *Teen Rūsī Upanyāsa*, 1996; *Ādhunika Rūsī Kahānī*, 2004. He has also published articles on contrastive grammar, Russian Indology, neurolinguistics. [**address:** Y-81 Hauz Khas, New Delhi – 110 016; **e-mail:** <hcpande1@rediffmail.com>].

Makarand Paranjape is Professor of English at the Jawaharlal Nehru University, New Delhi. He is the author-editor of over twenty-five books including *Decolonization and Development: Hind Swaraj Revisioned; The Penguin Sri Aurobindo Reader*; and *English Studies: Indian Perspectives.* He is founding editor of a multi-disciplinary international journal — *Evam*: *Forum of Indian Representations,* and a trustee of the Saṁvād India Foundation, a non-profit trust that promotes cross-cultural dialogue.

Anubha Shukla has done M.A. in Sanskrit (1995) and Russian (1997) from University of Delhi. Thereafter she joined the PhD programme in the Centre of Russian Studies, Jawaharlal Nehru University, New Delhi. In 2002 she completed her PhD on the vocabulary of common Indo-European origin in Sanskrit and Rusian. She has been teaching Russian since 1999 to the students of part-time courses at various colleges of the University of Delhi. [**address:** B-203, Vigyan Vihar, GH-19, Gurgaon – 122 003 (Haryana); **e-mail** <anubhashukla@yahoo.co.uk>].

Shashibala is a research scientist and a specialist in art and culture of Asian countries. An alumnus of Himachal Pradesh University, she has been a researcher at the International Academy of Indian Culture, New Delhi for the last thirty years. She has to her credit eight research projects and sixty research papers and articles. There are two editions of her post Doctoral thesis — *Comparative Iconography of Vajradhātū-maṇḍala and the Tattva-saṅgraha.* Her other books published include the *Buddhist Art; Buddhism: A Path to Nirvāṇa; Divine Art;* and *Manifestations of Buddhas.* [**address**: 38 Naya Ganj, Ghaziabad 201 001; **e-mail**: <drshashibala@yahoo.com>].

Satya Vrat Shastri (1930-), had his early education under his father, the eminent Sanskrit grammarian Prof. Charu Deva Shastri. He did his B.A. (Hons.), M.A. and M.O.L. from the Panjab University and PhD from the Banaras Hindu University. He joined the University of Delhi in 1955 where during the 40 years of his teaching career he held the positions of the Head of the Department of Sanskrit and the Dean of the Faculty of Arts. He was also Vice-Chancellor, Shri Jagannath Sanskrit University, Puri, Orissa and Visiting

Professor in six universities on four continents. He has attended and chaired a large number of conferences and seminars and delivered more than a hundred lectures in universities and institutions of higher learning in Europe, North America, Southeast Asia and the Far East. Prof. Shastri is both a creative and a critical writer and subject matter of seventeen theses for PhD and D.Litt. in Indian universities. He has received 54 awards and honours, national and international, including Padma Shree and four Honorary Doctorates. [**address:** C-248, Defence colony, New Delhi - 110 024; **email**<ssarin@del3.net.in>].

L.M. Singhvi is eminent Jurist, Philosopher, Sanskritist, Indologist, Vedic Scholar, Poet, Litterateur and President of Veda Pratishthan. He has been the member, Permanent Court of Arbitration at the Hague. He was the Member of Parliament of Lok Sabha (1962-67); of Rajya Sabha (1998-2004); India's High Commissioner in UK (1991-98); and has been senior adocate, Supreme Court of India. [**address:** B-8, South Extension Part-II, New Delhi – 110 049; **e-mail**: <lsinghvi@sansad.nic.in>].

Gaya Charan Tripathi (1939–) did his M.A. in Sanskrit (Agra, 1959), PhD on Vedic Deities (Agra, 1962), D. Phil. on Purāṇic Studies (Freiburg, 1966), and D.Litt. on Vaiṣṇava Temple Rituals (Allahabad, 1986). He is presently Professor at the Indira Gandhi National Centre for the Arts and Head of its Kalakosh Division. He had earlier been a fellow of the German Academic Exchange Service at the University of Freiburg in 1962-66. He has won the President's Certificate of Honour as a Sanskrit Scholar of Modern Stream. Prof. Tripathi has specialisation in Vedic Studies, Purāṇic Literature, Āgama, Sāhitya, Manuscriptology as well as Comparative Philology and has taught at the Universities of Freiburg (twice), Tübingen (twice), Berlin, Leipzig and British Columbia (twice), besides at Aligarh and Udaipur. He had been Principal of G.N. Jha Research Institute (Kendriya Sanskrit Vidyapitha), Allahabad from 1977–2001. His publications include about 20 books and around 90 research articles in Hindi, Sanskrit, English and German. [**address**: 126, Madanlal Block, Asiad Village Complex, New Delhi-110 049; **e-mail:** <gctripathi235@yahoo.com>].

Index